Stratification and Inequality Series
The Center for the Study of Social Stratification and Inequality,
Tohoku University, Japan
Volume 7

Status and Stratification

Stratification and Inequality Series
The Center for the Study of Social Stratification and Inequality,
Tohoku University, Japan

Inequality amid Affluence: Social Stratification in Japan
Junsuke Hara and Kazuo Seiyama

Intentional Social Change: A Rational Choice Theory
Yoshimichi Sato

Constructing Civil Society in Japan: Voices of Environmental Movements
Koichi Hasegawa

Deciphering Stratification and Inequality: Japan and Beyond
Yoshimichi Sato

Social Justice in Japan: Concepts, Theories and Paradigms
Ken-ichi Ohbuchi

Gender and Career in Japan
Atsuko Suzuki

Status and Stratification:
Cultural Forms in East and Southeast Asia
Mutsuhiko Shima

Stratification and Inequality Series
The Center for the Study of Social Stratification and Inequality,
Tohoku University, Japan
Volume 7

Status and Stratification

Cultural Forms in East and Southeast Asia

Edited by

Mutsuhiko Shima

This English edition first published in 2008 by
Trans Pacific Press, PO Box 164, Balwyn North, Melbourne, Victoria 3104, Australia
Telephone: +61 3 9859 1112 Fax: +61 3 9859 4110
Email: tpp.mail@gmail.com
Web: http://www.transpacificpress.com

Copyright © Trans Pacific Press 2008

Designed and set by digital environs, Melbourne. http://www.digitalenvirons.com

Printed by BPA Print Group, Burwood, Victoria, Australia

Distributors

Australia and New Zealand
UNIREPS
University of New South Wales
Sydney, NSW 2052
Australia
Telephone: +61 2 9664 0999
Fax: +61 2 9664 5420
Email: info.press@unsw.edu.au
Web: http://www.unireps.com.au

USA and Canada
International Specialized Book Services (ISBS)
920 NE 58th Avenue, Suite 300
Portland, Oregon 97213-3786
USA
Telephone: (800) 944-6190
Fax: (503) 280-8832
Email: orders@isbs.com
Web: http://www.isbs.com

Asia and the Pacific
Kinokuniya Company Ltd.

Head office:
Shin-Mizonokuchi Bldg. 2F
5-7 Hisamoto 3-chome
Takatsu-ku, Kawasaki 213-8506
Japan
Telephone: +81 44 874 9642
Fax: +81 44 829 1025
Email: bkimp@kinokuniya.co.jp
Web: www.kinokuniya.co.jp

Asia-Pacific office:
Kinokuniya Book Stores of Singapore Pte., Ltd.
391B Orchard Road #13-06/07/08
Ngee Ann City Tower B
Singapore 238874
Telephone: +65-6276-5558
Fax: +65-6276-5570
Email: SSO@kinokuniya.co.jp

All rights reserved. No production of any part of this book may take place without the written permission of Trans Pacific Press.

ISBN 978-1-876843-91-5 (Hardback)
ISBN 978-1-876843-97-7 (Paperback)

Contents

Figures	vi
Photo	vi
Tables	vii
Preface *Mutsuhiko Shima*	ix
List of Contributors	xvii

Part I: Japan

1. Social Status of Doctors in the Edo Period: The Cases of Bakufu and Han Doctors *Gisun Jang* — 3
2. The Curse of the Fugitive Samurai: A Look at Social Stratification and Conflict in Rural Japan *D. K. Andrews* — 32
3. Sports Books and the Culture of Inequality in Contemporary Japan: Discourses Emphasizing Effort and their Reproduction *Ryosuke Morooka* — 47

Part II: China, Taiwan and Korea

4. Kinship Organizations and Social Stratification in Late Imperial China: A Study based on Lineage in the Pearl River Delta *Yukihiro Kawaguchi* — 63
5. Common-Surname Tong-ism in Contemporary Taiwanese Society *Hisahiko Kamizuru* — 95
6. Reproduction of Status Traditions and Social Prestige in the Provincial Society of Colonial and Post-colonial Korea: A Case Study of Namwŏn *Hiroshi Honda* — 115

Part III: Southeast Asia

7. Women's Community Activities in the Kampung of Jakarta and Social Stratification *Ayami Saito* — 151
8. Local Security in Post-Suharto Bali: From Inequality to Equality of Participation *Kōsuke Hishiyama* — 163
9. Employment Structure of the Urban Informal Sector: The Formation of Porter Commitment Relationships in Hanoi *Erika Obara* — 180

Notes	206
References	221
Index	238

Figures

4.1 Land formation of Panyu, based on /Panyu county gazetteer/ (Panyushi siganzhi banggongshi, 1995:279) with partial modifications 67
4.2 Genealogical chart of Chen lineage of S village 74
4.3 A picture of the shrine of Chen Yuande and the pine tree he allegedly planted 80
9.1 Porter employment structure 204

Photo

9.1 Porter and market customer carrying goods purchased 188

Tables

1.1	Bakufu doctors' positions in the palace seating order	8
1.2	Income distributions of Edo Bakufu retainers	11
1.3	Income distributions of Bakufu doctors in 1712	12
1.4	Income distributions of Bakufu doctors according to their status in 1712	12
1.5	Income of Bakufu doctors, 1804	12
1.6	Income distributions of Bakufu doctors and Hatamoto	13
1.7	Income distributions of Bakufu doctors according to status, 1804	14
1.8	Status positions of doctors in different Han, some holding the status of lower vassals	16
1.9	Distribution of Han doctors according to status, including some vassals of lower status	17
1.10	Status positions of doctors in Han, excluding the status of lower vassals	18
1.11	Status distribution of Han doctors, excluding the status of lower vassals	19
1.12	Income distributions of the vassals of Fuchu-Han in Late-Edo period	22
1.13	Income of various Han doctors	24
1.14	Incomes of Han doctors in Nagoya-Han	28
9.1	Population migration by region: 1994–1999 (%)	182
9.2	Attributes and basic employment characteristics of porters	186
9.3	Presence or absence of employers with whom the porters have a degree of acquaintanceship, by hometown	190
9.4	How commitment relationships are forged	194
9.5	Diagrams of the relationships between porters and their employers by type	197
9.6	Risks and costs for the employer when hiring a porter	198
9.7	Work costs borne by porters	199
9.8	Characteristics of porters in weak and no commitment relationships	202

Preface
Mutsuhiko Shima

This volume presents the research of the Division of the Study of East Asia, one of four divisions of the Center for the Study of Social Stratification and Inequality at Tohoku University. Social stratification and inequality as such are universal phenomena, but as they manifest in everyday life, they are inevitably enmeshed in particular circumstances and contexts.

The most significant factors surrounding stratification and inequality as they manifest in concrete contexts are the social and cultural meanings they carry which lead to different forms of expression in each society. Each of the papers in this volume deals with a specific society at a specific historical period and grapples with particular social structures and prevailing cultural meanings to analyze how statuses are defined and manipulated while focusing on the social and cultural capital that is available to the actors concerned. The resulting volume presents a wide kaleidoscope of values and structural constraints that manifest in the lived experiences of particular people within East and Southeast Asia.

Part I presents three papers that examine social status as well as equality and inequality in Japan.

Gisun Jang takes up the problem of the position of doctors within the social hierarchy and the changes in their position during the Edo period (1603–1867) when the social structure rested on a four-class division of samurai, peasants, artisans and merchants, the last two categories often being treated as one of *chōnin*, or townspeople. Since the paper is a pioneering work assessing the social position of technical specialists in medical skills, Jang confines his research to those doctors who were employed by the government, both of the central bakufu and of many feudal fiefs, leaving the question of doctors whose status was *chōnin* (because their clients were *chōnin*) for future investigation. The choice is largely determined by the availability of historical sources for analysis.

These doctors were formally included in the samurai category, but their roles as medical specialists set them apart from other samurai. Thus, Jang's question is where the doctors were located within the samurai hierarchy. Their income level clearly is an index of social standing. Noting, however, that the Edo period society was characterized by meticulous ranking, Jang also analyzes the formal ranking of each doctor in comparison to other samurai employed in the bakufu and feudal fiefs. The ranking of those employed by the bakufu is indicated by their location in the seating arrangements within the palace. His finding is that doctors employed by the bakufu, although differentiated among themselves, occupied a middle-rank status compared to other samurai, on the basis of income and ranking. The status of those doctors employed in the ninety-two fiefs examined, varied widely in both salary and ranking, but Jang suggests that they can be categorized according to five major patterns.

It has long been assumed that in pre-modern societies, in both the East and the West, medical specialists had rather lowly social status, but the details are yet to be clarified. Jang's paper, although obviously tentative, should be seen as opening a new perspective on the social positions of doctors during the Edo period in Japan.

D. K. Andrews chose a small-scale agricultural community in northern Japan for research into the continuing belief in supernatural curses. He finds this inveterate belief to be manifest among a circumscribed group of households whose ancestors are widely acknowledged by the locals to have been fugitive samurai. The original war over national political hegemony occurred in the twelfth century, and the story is a well-known one in which the survivors of the losing Heike clan sought refuge in many parts of the country. Inherent to this peculiar noble ancestry is a notion that these households, both in the past and the present, stand apart from their fellow villagers. It is not only their "outsider" status that draws special attention, but also the perception that they have an elevated socio-political identity that has traditionally invested them with local authority. As Andrews reveals, issues regarding status and stratification take dramatic forms. The supernatural retribution that allegedly afflicts these households has in its most extreme form led these "samurai" descendent families to be the discriminated targets of death and other misfortune.

The outwardly public forum of village gossip is the medium by which knowledge of a given household's curse generally circulates. And it is a rather direct means of voicing contentions over disparity issues. Despite the firmly entrenched opinion that the identity of the Japanese household is passed on or carried down through time, this study reveals that identities attached to households are likely to be recreated by each generation and that opposing identities are by-products of social tensions and conflicts within the community. Yet labeling a household as 'cursed' does not appear to invite or presuppose any radical change to the established social order.

Ryōsuke Morooka discusses a genre of publications with substantial circulation in Japan called *supōtsu-bon*, or 'sports-books'— biographies of sporting celebrities, that typically emphasize the importance of effort (*doryoku*) in their success. Morooka argues that this discourse on effort has a considerable influence on the values of the general public. He has analyzed the content of more than three hundred such books to highlight the social role that the discourses of leading athletes play in producing and popularizing these values.

That an emphasis on effort is characteristic of the values of modern Japan is nothing new. Morooka's point, however, is that this value should not be understood as essential to or universal in Japanese culture. It is, instead, repeatedly reproduced in concrete social processes by particular modes of representation and articulation. These discourses undoubtedly arouse some degree of sympathy among the general population, but they are by no means simple representations of a universal value system. These sports-books function as an influential medium to selectively reproduce and maintain a certain set of values that reinforce the prevailing work ethic in Japanese society.

Part II presents the work of three anthropologists who take up kinship or kinship-related institutions in China, Taiwan and Korea. These kinship institutions were originally inspired by Neo-Confucian philosophers, but have come to be used for various purposes with quite different cultural meanings, meanings that could not have been envisaged by those philosophers. Most significantly, these kinship institutions were closely tied to questions of social status and stratification in pre-modern societies, and continue to have significance in certain social spheres today.

Maurice Freedman introduced the African model of lineages to Chinese studies. He and his followers produced a structural analysis of Chinese lineages (*zongzu*) and proposed certain environmental explanations for their development. Yukihiro Kawaguchi attempts to go beyond Freedman, asking whether it is appropriate to simply apply this African model of lineages to the Chinese context. From this perspective, Kawaguchi critically evaluates the cultural meanings attached to genealogies in China and queries the extent to which genealogies actually did provide the organizing principles for developing the frontier regions. In the process he discusses the ways in which lineages were constructed, and the cultural practices and norms that the resulting lineages adopted to articulate a newly emerging social order: they also provided congenial channels of communication between local elites and the state.

More precisely, by employing Neo-Confucian discourse, genealogies were constructed to authenticate authoritative descent positions as Chinese, in contrast to other ethnic groups in the region. This practice suited the pioneers who actively opened the frontier region of the Pearl River Delta after the fourteenth century. At the same time, since the state was unable to extend direct control to the peripheries of the empire, the local elites served as agents who accepted and maintained the principles of conduct authorized by the State. Kawaguchi's contention, based on his analysis of the historical records combined with sustained anthropological fieldwork, that lineages during the late-Imperial period provided suitable routes of informal communication between the state and the local society and served to sustain the system, provides a convincing account of the Chinese cultural system of stratification during that period.

Hisahiko Kamizuru also examines kinship institutions among the Chinese, focusing on the concept of *tung*-ism. This concept was first proposed by Morton Fried (1962) to highlight a particularly Chinese principle that works to link people of different economic and social standings on the basis of sharing at least one common cultural attribute. Conducting his research in contemporary Taipei, where the population is highly mobile and the principles of the state and the market set the basic social framework, Kamizuru researches a 'common surname association' in the oldest part of the city.

In this particular association, one which anyone sharing the surname Liu is eligible to join, relationships among the members characterized by closeness and mutual assistance are stressed. Ancestral rituals and the accompanying feasts are marked by friendly sociability where differences in other social fields are consciously down-played. Many people therefore join such associations expecting mutual help among the members. However, being of the same surname does not necessarily lead to help or support when personal interests are involved. Quoting many case studies, Kamizuru argues that Han Chinese society in contemporary Taipei is not primarily structured on the principle of kinship. Nevertheless, he identifies three ways in which surname *tung*-ism does serve to unite persons of vastly different economic or political standings. First is the Chinese cultural definition of surname as showing descent from a common ancestor which turns complete strangers into kinsmen: in Taiwan, same-surname associations provide an arena where leaders make new acquaintances and foster potentially beneficial relationships. Second, 'same surname' sometimes serves as a simple idiom for interpersonal relationships and thereby helps to bypass complex explanations that may lie behind the scene. Finally, they create a social field where the regulating principle is neither one of ability or competition, but of kinship itself.

Korea has been significantly influenced by Chinese culture. Although the social forms of organization and stratification are often quite different, there is nevertheless a strong emphasis on kinship relations there, too. To date, most studies of status and stratification in Korea have centered on the dominant *yangban* class. Honda, instead, turns his attention to a class called *rijok*, local patrilineal kin groups that produced functionaries in charge of administrative duties in local bureaucratic offices during the latter half of the Chosŏn period. *Rijok* were clearly differentiated, and of lower social status than the local representatives of *yangban*, but they nevertheless wielded considerable power in local politics.

In contrast to the *yangban* population that were rooted in the countryside, *rijok* lineages resided in the seats of local administration during the Chosŏn period, which have been urbanized in the post-colonial period. Social status distinctions were legally abolished towards the end of the Chosŏn dynasty, and de-emphasized particularly during and after the period of Japanese colonial rule. Based on his fieldwork in the inland township Namwŏn in Southwestern Korea, Honda records the reactions of *rijok* to these changing historical conditions. On the one hand, some tried to maintain the traditions of their social group by continuing an association called *Nogyeso*. On the other hand, as Namwŏn urbanized, it also became increasingly heterogeneous, both socially and culturally. Some *rijok* members took up the new movement and contributed to the invention of new local cultural traditions, such as the festival commemorating Ch'unhyang in 1931. Honda's paper is a pioneering examination of how different status groups adapt to the processes of modernization

Three papers by sociologists dealing with Southeast Asia, including Indonesia and Vietnam, constitute Part III of this volume. Each examines contemporary social situations.

Ayami Saitō has been researching residential areas called *kampung* in the suburbs of Jakarta. Her paper explores two closely-related but distinct topics. First is the socio-economic status of the *kampung* residents. In contrast to the widely accepted view that *kampung* residents are generally poor, she demonstrates that they are of diverse social classes and strata. Second is to explore inter-class relationships by focusing on a health-care activity called *posyandu*. *Posyandu* involve two different types of participants; female volunteers—called *kader*—who provide the health-care services, and the recipients of the services—infants and their parents. There are two 'levels' of *kader*—RW and RT, where RT is a sub-unit of RW—depending on the levels of the neighborhoods from which they are "elected". Saitō's investigation was stimulated, first, by the expression *mampu*, meaning 'well-to-do' or 'wealthy'. One volunteer *kader* explained her involvement by saying that "I want to dedicate myself to the people while I am still *mampu*." The other source of stimulation was the work of Logsdon, who had emphasized the hierarchical nature of community activities, pointing to the stratification among RW leaders, RT leaders and the other residents in that descending order, and might be read as suggesting the same kind of stratification among RW *kader*, RT *kader* and the service recipients.

Her research shows that recipients of *posyandu* services include people of all social strata, since the position 'recipient' is determined by one's life stage—when they have children under five years of age who require the services, irrespective of their social standing. Where the majority of the recipients' husbands are of the lower-income strata, this is not because of their position as recipients, but because *kampung* residents include a high proportion of low-income workers. Some of the *kader* are admittedly in the wealthy strata, but many are only of medium economic standing. These are people with moderate but secure incomes who are willing to serve others, partly due to their husbands' socio-economic status, but many volunteer as part of a process of self-realization. Through this analysis, Saitō unravels the subtle meanings of the word *mampu*.

Kōsuke Hishiyama conducted research in a tourism-oriented precinct of Sanur on Bali, Indonesia, focusing on measures for the maintenance of local security and their relationship to characteristics of Balinese social organization. He draws insights from the theory of Dahl and Tufte (1972) who, focusing on the scale of social units for democratic processes, argue that the effectiveness of the citizen is greatest when units are small and homogeneous, but this conflicts with efforts to maximize the problem solving capacity of the systems concerned.

Hishiyama traces the historical changes that have occurred in local security organizations since the mid-twentieth century. Under the Suharto regime's emphasis on centralized control, the functions of traditional local organizations were restricted and their autonomy denied. After the downfall of the Suharto regime following the economic crisis of the late 1990s, and in the face of increasing insecurity, the tourist industry in Sanur urged the City of Denpasar to establish an agency for local security. But without any means of surveillance or enforcement, the agency turned to the police and army for support, which quickly led to the agency being subsumed by the centralized authorities, and thus defunct in local matters.

In contrast, the locally established Sanur Development Foundation (YPS) decided to open itself to various local organizations, both traditional and informal, in its activities for maintaining local security. Hishiyama suggests that the successful operation of this organization stems from its retaining a basic sense of the effectiveness of local participants, as was characteristic of traditional Balinese organizations, and discerns a potential basis for decentralization and democratization in the tourist areas of Bali. His analysis invites us to consider the importance of local social and cultural capital.

Erika Obara's paper is based on a preliminary survey of women workers who, using bamboo sticks, carry merchandise bought and sold in a market place in Hanoi, Vietnam. These workers are among the many immigrants from rural areas who seek work in cities, a common feature of most developing countries. Many suggestions have been proposed concerning the importance of kinship and other interpersonal connections in securing jobs for those rural-to-urban migrants who work in the informal sector. Obara finds, however, that these female workers who come to Hanoi from surrounding villages do not use personal ties to find jobs. They are on their own, and must compete for work, even with others from the same village. At the same time, however, they share several spots in the market place where they casually exchange information about prospective jobs and troubles to be avoided.

Obara refers to Kollock's theory of how people establish mutual commitment and trust in uncertain situations and questions whether the theory is applicable for analyzing the relationships between workers and their employers. She identifies three categories of relationship, depending on the degree of commitment between the parties, and in analyzing sample cases finds some correlation between the length of time the workers have spent in the market and the extent of mutual commitment with their employers. Since her research is still in a preliminary stage, however, it remains to be seen whether there are any particularly Vietnamese traits in their way of consolidating commitments.

Not only do the disciplinary backgrounds of the authors vary, their research topics also cover a wide variety of issues, some of which have research precedents to guide them, while others present explorations into virgin territory. In both cases, however, the papers in this volume make significant contributions to cross-cultural comparisons of the universal phenomena of stratification and inequality.

List of Contributors

Gisun Jang is a Ph.D. candidate in Japanese history in the Graduate School of Arts and Letters at Tōhoku University, and a graduate student of CSSI.

D. K. Andrews (Ph.D., Tōhoku University, 2007) is associate professor of religious studies in the Faculty of Letters at Kanazawa University.

Ryōsuke Morooka (Ph.D., Tōhoku University, 2007), specializing in religious studies, was formerly a graduate student of CSSI, and is currently a special researcher in the Graduate School of Arts and Letters, Tōhoku University.

Yukihiro Kawaguchi (Ph.D., Tōhoku University, 2007), was formerly a graduate student of CSSI, and is currently a fulltime research fellow at the National Museum of Ethnology, Osaka.

Hisahiko Kamizuru (Ph.D., Hiroshima University, 2001), a social anthropologist, is assistant professor in the Community Liaison Center at Hiroshima Prefectural University.

Hiroshi Honda is associate professor of cultural anthropology and Korean studies in the Graduate School of Humanities and Sociology at the University of Tokyo.

Ayami Saitō (Ph.D., Tōhoku University, 2006), a sociologist, was formerly a graduate student of CSSI, and is currently a Postdoctoral Fellow of the Japan Society for Promotion of Science, with affiliation at the Graduate School of Education, Tōhoku University.

Kōsuke Hishiyama (Ph.D., Tōhoku University, 2007), also a sociologist and former graduate student of CSSI, is currently assistant professor at the Institute for International Advanced Interdisciplinary Research, Tōhoku University.

Erika Obara is a Ph.D. candidate at Tsuda College and served as COE Fellow at CSSI, Tōhoku University for two years between 2005 and

2007. She is currently a special researcher in the Graduate School of Arts and Letters, Tōhoku University.

Editor
Mutsuhiko Shima (Ph.D., University of Toronto, 1979) is professor of cultural anthropology in the Graduate School of Arts & Letters, Tōhoku University.

Part I: Japan

1 Social Status of Doctors in the Edo Period: The Cases of *Bakufu* and *Han* Doctors

Gisun Jang

Introduction

Prior to the modern era, the social status of medical doctors was not high in either the Orient or the Occident. Medicine was regarded as a lowly occupation that involved the treatment of diseases and injuries. In Japan, the term *hōgi* was used to refer to medical skills or doctors until the Edo period (1603–1867). This term is suggestive of how doctors were treated in those days. The term was originally introduced from China and simply meant skills or fine arts. But when the Chinese social classes were established based on Confucianism during the Han dynasty period, *hōgi*, or doctors, were forcibly contained in the common classes. This resulted in their valuable skills, as well as their profession, being regarded as lowly. When the term was introduced to Japan, it retained this implication. In 1206, during the Kamakura period (1185–1333), the ex-Emperor Gotoba (1180–1239) reproved his warrior guards for visiting doctors' or *onmyōji's*[1] houses for fun, based on the undervaluation of *hōgi* as an occupation. The situation appears to have been similar in the Occident. In *The Wealth of Nations*, Adam Smith (1723–1790) argued that doctors and lawyers should be given compensation and social status that were suitable to their services (Fuse 1979: 4).

What, then, was the status of doctors during the Edo period in Japan? In this paper, I focus, on the various types of doctors that existed during the Edo period, on the social status of doctors who were employed by governments. Specifically, these doctors were *baku-i*, or medical specialists employed by the Tokugawa shogunate (*bakufu*) (hereafter referred to as *bakufu* doctor) and *han-i*, or medical specialists employed by the feudal lords (*daimyo*) (hereafter referred to as *han* doctor. '*Han*' means a feudal domain). I focus on their relative status positions as well as their economic status in the vassalage as a whole. Considering the paucity of studies on the social status of these two types of doctors, I also discuss the methodology by which I measured their status positions.

Social status of *bakufu* doctors

Bakufu and *bakufu* doctors

In 1603, the *bakufu* started in Japan with the appointment of Ieyasu Tokugawa as *shōgun*.[2] The *bakufu* controlled the entire country by establishing a master-servant relationship with each of over 260 feudal lords called *daimyō*.[3] The members of the *bakufu*'s direct vassalage were each granted a fief or stipend of up to 10,000 *koku* and comprised two classes: the *hatamoto* class, whose members were entitled to *omemie*,[4] and the *gokenin* class, whose members were not entitled to *omemie*. While most of the *hatamoto* members were granted fiefs, *gokenin* members were usually provided with stipends in the form of rice. According to a survey conducted in 1722, there were 5205 and 17,399 *hatamoto* and *gokenin* members, respectively. Meanwhile, rice production for the nation in the Edo period had reached approximately thirty million *koku* per year. Of these, domains under direct *bakufu* control amounted to four million *koku*. Combined with the fiefs of the *hatamoto* class (approximately three million *koku*) yielded no less than seven million *koku*.

Some of the doctors retained by the *bakufu* and *han* were called *oku-ishi* (literally: interior doctor). This term is closely related to the living space of the *shōgun* family and *daimyō* families. The living space of the *shōgun* family in the Edo Castle was divided into the *Honmaru* (Main Enceinte), which was used by the *shōgun*, and the *Nishi-no-maru* (West Quarter), which was used by his heir. The *Honmaru* was further divided into the *Omote* (Exterior), where the *shōgun* attended to government affairs, and the *Ōoku* (Great Interior), where he lived his private life. Access to the Great Interior was subject to permission. *Oku-ishi* was the designation of a doctor who was granted this permission. In the beginning of the Edo period there were about ten doctors among the *shōgun*'s personal staff members who belonged to the *bakufu*'s vassalage. These doctors were given no specific positions in the *bakufu*'s organization. Kushimoto observes that it later became difficult to ensure the provision of medical care in the *bakufu* based solely on the non-institutionalized personal relationships (Kushimoto 1974: 333). The *bakufu* doctor system was established during the reign of Tsunayoshi (1646–1709), the fifth Tokugawa *Shōgun*. By 1683, Tsunayoshi had appointed twelve *oku-ishi* and had created a system of medical care for the Great Interior provided by *oku-ishi*, with the senior doctor Yōan'in Masateru Manase appointed as *osaji*[5]

(Kushimoto 1974: 334). Fuse calculates that the number of *bakufu* doctors increased as follows: fourteen during 1624–1643; fifty-one in the middle of the 1640s; 112 in the late 1730s; 180 in 1790; 190 in 1827; and over 200 in the latter half of the 1850s (Fuse 1979: 127). But according to publications called *bukan*, which were privately published directories of *daimyō* and *bakufu* officers, the number of *bakufu* doctors reached ninety in 1675 and, with some fluctuations, remained between 100 and 200 until the end of the Edo period (Fujinami 1942: 62–5).

The main types of *bakufu* doctors included the following: *oku-ishi*, who went to the castle every day and provided medical care to the *shōgun* and his family members; *ohiroshiki-ryōji*, who were in charge of medical services for *oku-jochū*;[6] *oban-ishi*, who engaged in the treatment of emergency patients on alternate days; *yoriai-ishi*, who were from distinguished families of doctors but had been out of office or had retired from active service; *kobushin-ishi*, who were young doctors under training or had been out of office for some reason; and *omemie-ishi*, who were picked out from doctors with excellent work records regardless of social status or affiliation (Kushimoto 1974; Shinmura (ed.) 2006).[7]

Status positions of *bakufu* doctors

According to Kushimoto, most *bakufu* doctors were appointed from among *machi-i*[8] and, even though these doctors were granted the status of samurai, there was a great subconscious disparity from professional samurai (Kushimoto 1974: 340). Other differences between *bakufu* doctors and other *bakufu* vassals pointed out by Kushimoto include the fact that in principle, samurai lived in residences granted by their masters, whereas many *bakufu* doctors lived among commoners in ordinary residential areas. Futhermore, samurai were subject to very strict rules on inheritance by an adopted child, whereas in the case of *bakufu* doctors their skills were of primary significance and *machi-i*'s children were qualified for adoption, and when ranks were granted to *bakufu* doctors, they were of those granted to priests[9] (Kushimoto 1974: 340–1). In this section, I analyze the position of *bakufu* doctors in *denseki* (palace seating order), according to which the *bakufu* vassals stood by for service in rooms, hallways and other spaces in Edo Castle, in order to confirm their status positions.

In the class system, where various distinctions were maintained in all aspects of people's lives, the seat on which a person was allowed to sit during ceremonies or other occasions was an indicator of the social status of the person or his affiliation. A *bakufu* vassal who commenced service at Edo Castle was assigned to one of the minutely divided palace seats. Where he was assigned depended on his official position. An incident occurred on 8 April 1662, when Yazaemon Tsuzuki, a *kachigashira*,[10] left the castle to protest an order that his audience with the *shōgun* would be after the *bakufu* doctor Roan Naritada Nakarai. A punishment of *hara-kiri*[11] was imposed on Tsuzuki, but was reduced to *daimyō-azuke*[12] in consideration of his ancestors' distinguished services (Kushimoto 1974: 340; Fuse 1979: 44–5). The Nakarai family had been granted 1500 *koku* and had held high positions among *bakufu* doctors, as the family had provided doctors who served as the *bakufu*'s *ten'yaku-no-kami*[13] for generations (however, at the time of the incident, Roan was not the *ten'yaku-no-kami*, although he had already been granted a priestly rank). *Kachigashira*, in contrast, was a title with 1000 *koku* (Sasama 1972: 346) and was ranked lower than Roan. This incident indicates the meaning of rank in the Edo period, as well as with the average samurai's attitude towards doctors (Kushimoto 1974: 340).

The first written regulations on palace seating order appeared in September 1659. These regulations covered the *bakufu* vassals and did not contain provisions on *daimyō* in general. June 1744 saw the first regulations on palace seating order in general including seats for *daimyō* (Matsuo 1981: 303). With respect to the meaning of palace seating order, Matsuo argues that it did not necessarily define the ranks of *daimyō* and the various *bakufu* officers, and that superior-subordinate relationships among different seats were somewhat vague (1983: 305). Although this claim seems to have some merit, I argue that although they might have become somewhat vague, the palace seating order basically reflected superior-subordinate relationships. The regulations established in 1659 identify fifteen palace ranks of seats and titles assigned to the respective ranks. The m*achi-bugyō*[14] class was assigned to the second highest ranked seats and the *chōnin* class was assigned to the fourteenth-ranked seats. There was a superior-subordinate relationship between these two classes and it would be safe to guess that this relationship was defined by the palace seating order. In the following, I analyze the status of *bakufu* doctors based on the assumption that the palace seating order basically reflected superior-subordinate relationships.

To measure the position of a *bakufu* doctor in the palace seating order, a fraction was calculated with the seat number of the doctor being the numerator and the total number of palace seats being the denominator. After the numerical evaluation of the position of each *bakufu* doctor, the values for all doctors were added together and the mean values were calculated for the different types of *bakufu* doctors. This makes it easy to evaluate the positions of *bakufu* doctors in the palace seating order as well as allowing comparisons between different palace seating orders.

Table 1.1 shows the positions of doctors in the palace seating order regulations established in 1659, 1744 and 1787.[15] There are two versions of the 1659 seating order regulation: one contained in *Ofuregaki Kanpō shūsei* (A *Kanpō* collection of governmental notifications) (hereinafter referred to as Version 1659-1) and the other contained in *Tokugawa kinrei kō: zenshū dai-2* (A study of Tokugawa prohibitory decrees: Part I volume 2) (hereinafter referred to as Version 1659-2). There are some differences between the two versions in the names of palace seats and the titles assigned to palace seats.[16] In most respects, however, the two versions are the same: both contain fifteen palace seating ranks and show the same names for the palace seating rooms to which the *bakufu* doctors were assigned. While the two versions differ in the seating orders of some of the *bakufu* doctors, in general the positions of the *bakufu* doctors are roughly the same. For reference, Table 1.1 contains data from both versions. It is not known exactly why *oban-no-ishi* doctors are ranked in two different positions in this 1659 regulation. Roan and Dōsan, in the fifth position, represent the two families that provided *ten'yaku-no-kami*. They held quite high positions, as per the numerical indicator 0.33. The lowest-ranked *bakufu* doctors were *tozama-no-ishi*[17] in seat number ten and *oban-no-ishi* in seat number nine, according to Version 1659-1 and Version 1659-2, respectively. The numerical indicators of the positions of all *bakufu* doctors average 0.42 and 0.43 in Version 1659-1 and Version 1659-2, respectively, indicating that these doctors held medium positions in general.

In the next regulation established in 1744, the number of palace seating ranks increased to twenty-eight, an increase of thirteen ranks. As described above, this regulation covers seating orders for both *daimyō* and *bakufu* officers. The *bakufu* doctors' had been demoted in rank: *Hōin* and *Hōgen* doctors were ranked thirteen, *oban-no-ishi* doctors were ranked fifteen, and *yoriai-ishi* doctors were ranked twenty-three.[18] The numerical indicators of their positions are 0.46, 0.54 and 0.82, respectively, with the average for all doctors being 0.61. These figures show a considerable decline of their positions from the

Table 1.1: Bakufu doctors' positions in the palace seating order

Seat no.			Position of bakufu doctor	
1659-1				
	4	oban-no-ishi	4/15	(0.27)
	5	Roan, Dōsan, Hōin, Hōgen	5/15	(0.33)
	6	oban-no-ishi	6/15	(0.4)
	10	tozama-no-ishi	10/15	(0.67)
	Average		0.42	
1659-2				
	4	oban-no-ishi	4/15	(0.27)
	5	Roan, Dōsan, Hōin, Hōgen	5/15	(0.33)
	8	tozama-no-ishi	8/15	(0.53)
	9	oban-no-ishi	9/15	(0.6)
	Average		0.43	
1744				
	13	Hōin, Hōgen	13/28	(0.46)
	15	oban-no-ishi	15/28	(0.54)
	23	yoriai-ishi	23/28	(0.82)
	Average		0.61	
1787				
	14	Hōin, Hōgen	14/29	(0.48)
	16	oban-no-ishi	16/29	(0.55)
	24	yoriai-ishi	24/29	(0.83)
	Average		0.62	

Note: 1659 and 1744 are based on Takayanagi and Ishii (eds), 1934. 1784 is based on Takayanagi and Ishii (eds), 1936.

earlier regulation, because in the process of incorporating *daimyō* into the palace seating system, five new seating ranks were added above the existing ranks. In addition, the previous rank seven was divided, creating new ranks eight through ten. This, in turn, resulted in the titles that had been assigned to lower seating ranks being lowered by the number of the newly added ranks. Also of note is that starting from the 1744 regulation, the lowest seating rank, number twenty-eight, was assigned to some samurai classes including the *okachi* class. In the former regulation, seating rank numbers fourteen and fifteen were assigned to *chōnin* and *sarugaku*,[19] respectively. These classes were excluded and the classes covered by the palace seating system became more homogenous.

In the 1787 regulation on palace seating order, a new seating rank was inserted just below rank eleven, resulting in a total of twenty-nine seating ranks. However, this seems to have made no substantial difference from the preceding order, as the new rank twelve comprised the lower fourteen of the twenty-four titles that had formerly been assigned to rank eleven, with the addition of a new title, sentō-tsuki.[20] A chronological look at the average numerical indicator of the *bakufu* doctors' positions in the palace seating orders reveals a declining tendency, from 0.42 (0.43) to 0.61 and then 0.62. However, if the indicators for the 1744 and 1787 regulations are calculated by subtracting five from the numbers of ranks six and below, the indicators for these regulations would be 0.52 and 0.54, respectively. These figures are still higher than for the 1659 regulation, but they show that the *bakufu* doctors maintained positions around the middle in the *bakufu* vassalage. Furthermore, considering that these positions were determined after the exclusion of the *chōnin* and *sarugaku* classes, there seems to have been no substantial changes to the *bakufu* doctors' positions.

Economic status of *bakufu* doctors

Studies have revealed that the *bakufu* doctors' income was 200 *koku* for *oku-ishi*, plus another 100 *koku* for *yakuryō*[21] (Kushimoto 1974; Fuse 1979). As an exception, *oku-ishi* doctors of internal medicine were entitled to 200 koku as *yakuryō*. Nonetheless, according to *bukan* and other historical materials, many doctors received income of over 200 *koku*. Kushimoto (1974) comments that the average *bakufu* doctors' income (100–200 *koku*) was sufficient to make a living in the beginning of the Edo period. He points out, however, that this was a relatively low salary by the end of the seventeenth century, when commodity prices rose, making living on this level of income increasingly difficult (Kushimoto 1974: 337). It seems, however, that *bakufu* doctors were allowed to provide treatment to *daimyō*. A *bakufu* doctor who treated the *rōjū*[22] Masamori Hotta (in office 1635–1638) was paid 1000 *ryō* in reward for his services (Kushimoto 1974: 339). In his *Azuma-no-hanamuke*, the scholar Seiryō Kaibo (1755–1817) mentions a *bakufu* doctor named Gentai Shibata. Shibata became a *bakufu* doctor after serving as an *omemie* doctor. He reportedly received an income of 200 *koku* and lived on approximately 2000 *ryō* a year (Ishii 1984: 21). Although this cannot be considered to be a typical case, it is an interesting example showing that *bakufu* doctors with advanced skills must have been in a strong position to accumulate economic power.

In the following, I analyze the economic status of *bakufu* doctors in comparison with the *hatamoto* and *gokenin* classes. As of 1712, there were a total of 123 *bakufu* doctors, including seventy *yoriai-ishi*, twenty-three *oku-ishi*, twenty-two *gokinban-tsukamatsuri-ishi*, two *kengyō*,[23] and six other doctors (see Table 1.4). Table 1.2 presents a summary of incomes received by the *hatamoto* and *gokenin* classes and *bakufu* doctors in 1712. For ease of comparison, amounts of income provided in different forms were all converted to amounts of *koku*. The mean value for the *hatamoto* class is 635.1 *koku*, while that for the *gokenin* class is only 52.6 *koku*. The mean value for both classes is 190.2 *koku*. The mean value for the *bakufu* doctors is 399, which is smaller than that for *hatamoto* by a little over 240 *koku* but is larger than that for *gokenin* by over 300 *koku*. Table 1.3 reveals the distribution of income received by *bakufu* doctors in units of 100 *koku*. Four hundred *koku* or more was received by 32.5%, 300–399 *koku* by 23.6%, 200–299 *koku* by 32.5%, 100–199 *koku* by 10.6%, and less than 100 *koku* by 0.8% of the *bakufu* doctors. Considering that as many as 56.1% of the *bakufu* doctors received over 300 *koku* and that the average income of *bakufu* doctors was 399 *koku* as described above, these data reveal that not all *bakufu* doctors received a 'low salary.' Table 1.4 shows the incomes received by *bakufu* doctors in different ranks. The highest average income is that of the *yoriai-ishi* rank, which received 499.7 *koku*. This figure raises the average income for all *bakufu* doctors. This seems to indicate that considerable preferential treatment was given to *yoriai-ishi*, considering that no specific service was assigned to these doctors. The *oku-ishi* doctors, who played a pivotal role in providing medical services at Edo Castle, received 348.7 *koku* on average, a value close to the average for all *bakufu* doctors. An average *gokinban-tsukamatsuri-ishi* doctor received 222.5 *koku*, which seems low compared to an average *oku-ishi* doctor. However, considering that *gokinban-tsukamatsuri-ishi* doctors were in charge of providing emergency treatment to patients on alternate days, the above incomes were perhaps not too low. The total number of the three types of doctors outlined above was 115, accounting for 91% of all *bakufu* doctors. Taking into account both services assigned to and incomes paid to different *bakufu* doctors, the incomes paid to these doctors do not seem to have been too low.

Table 1.2: Income distributions of Edo Bakufu retainers

Class	Number	Total income	Average income
Hatamoto	5,332	3,386,298.7	635.1
Gokenin	17,237	905,928.2	52.6
Sub-total	22,569	4,292,226.9	190.2
Bakufu doctors	123	49,070.88	399

Note 1. Based on Table 3 in Suzuki (1971: 195). The number and income of *hatamoto* and *gokenin* are based on Suzuki (1971: 199). However, some figures are missing so that figures in Table 2 and Table 3 vary slightly. Data on bakufu doctors is based on Suzuki (ed.), 1984.

Note 2: The income of retainers takes five different forms, with varying units. For convenience of comparison, however, all of the other incomes have been converted in terms of koku. Those forms of payment other than koku-daka are chiefly for retainers on lower ranks.

① *Koku-daka* refers to agricultural yield in fiefed land to which a retainer is given right or taxation, actual amount of taxation being fixed at 35% of the declared *Koku-daka*. For instance, if the declared *Koku-daka* of a certain fief was 10 *koku*, then the retainer's share of taxation was 3.5 *koku*.

② *Tawara-daka* refers to the amount of rice as expressed in the number of *tawara* pronounced as pyo (sack of rice). Thus, 10 pyo of Tawara-daka is equivalent to 10 *koku* in koku-daka. In both cases, the actual income was 3.5 *koku*.

③ *Genmai-daka* also refers to the amount of rice, but in this case, the expressed amount corresponded to actually provided amount. For the purpose of comparison, it is converted to corresponding koku-daka: Genmai-daka 10-pyo has been converted to koku-daka 28.5 *koku*.

④ *Fuchi-daka* is presented in terms of the number of persons to be sustained such as 1 *ninbuchi* (sustainable of one person). 1 *ninbuchi* was equal to 1.8 *koku* per year.

⑤ *Kin-daka* was salary payed in cash. Since the amount provided in *kin-daka* was negligible, it is omitted from this table.

Next, I analyze the economic status of *bakufu* doctors in the latter half of the Edo period. Although a comparison like the one I have made above would require data for both *bakufu* doctors and other *bakufu* vassals from the same year, due to the unavailability of suitable historical materials I used data from 1804 for *bakufu* doctors and those from the 1790s[24] for other *bakufu* vassals. There are three different documents on the amounts of fiefs received by the *hatamoto* class during the 1790s. As they show slightly different figures, the total and average values were calculated and used in the analysis. The total amount was 3,276,333.36 *koku*, with the mean value calculated by dividing the total amount by the average number of *hatamoto* members for a figure of 632.5 *koku*. This is slightly lower

Table 1.3: Income distributions of Bakufu doctors in 1712

Amount in *koku*	Number	%
400 or more	40	32.5
300–399	29	23.6
200–299	40	32.5
100–199	13	10.6
100 or less	1	0.8
Total	123	100

Note: Based on Suzuki (ed.), 1985.

Table 1.4: Income distributions of Bakufu doctors according to their status in 1712

Status of doctors	Number	%	Average
Yoriai doctors	70	56.9	499.7
Oku doctors	23	18.7	348.7
Gokinbanzukae doctors	22	17.9	222.5
Kengyo doctors	2	1.6	201.4
Other doctors	6	4.9	128.6

Note: Based on Suzuki (ed.), 1984. Gokinbanzukae doctors may have been the same as oban-ishi doctors. (See Kushimoto 1974: 331).

Table 1.5: Income of Bakufu doctors, 1804

Number	*Koku-daka*	*Fuchi-daka*	*Yakuryo*	Total in *koku*	Average in *koku*
107	31,087	4,009.2	4,700	39,796.2	371.9

Note: Based on Ishii (ed.), 1981. The number excludes seven sons of *oishi* and eighteen *omemieishi*.

than the average of 1712 (635 *koku*). Conversely, as indicated in Table 1.5, the average income received by *bakufu* doctors was 371.9, down by nearly twenty *koku*. This seems to indicate a slight decline in the economic status of *bakufu* doctors, but was this really the case? Table 1.6 shows the distribution of income received by *bakufu* doctors and the *hatamoto* class. For *bakufu* doctors, those who received 400 *koku* or more and those who received 300–399 *koku* decreased by 1.7% and 5.8%, respectively, compared to the data for 1712, whereas those who received 200–299 *koku* and those who received 100–199 *koku* increased by 3.9% and 3.4%, respectively. As a whole, the distribution of income seems to have shifted to a lower level. However, a different picture emerges when incomes are categorized by the type of doctor (Table 1.7). The number of *yoriai-ishi* decreased from seventy doctors in 1712 to thirty-four doctors, with their income decreasing by more than thirty-five *koku*, from 499.7 *koku* to 462 *koku*. Conversely, the average income received by *oku-ishi* and *omoteoban-ishi* increased by more than seventy *koku* (to 421.8 *koku*) and nearly eighty *koku* (to 300.6 *koku*), respectively. While *bakufu* doctors' incomes decreased overall due to the decrease in the number of, and the average income received by, *yoriai-ishi* who were assigned to no specific service, and due to the increase in the incomes received by *oku-ishi* and *omoteoban-ishi* who were in charge of the practice of medicine, we can say that the distribution of resources in the medical division became more reasonable. Incidentally, the incomes received by *bakufu* doctors falling in the 'other' category increased considerably, but the figures for the two years cannot be compared directly because members of this category were different for the two years.

Finally, let us compare the distribution of income between the *hatamoto* class and *bakufu* doctors (Table 1.6). The proportion of *hatamoto* members who received 400 *koku* or more was larger than that of *bakufu* doctors by no less than 8%. In addition, as many as 831 *hatamoto* members[25] received more than 1000 *koku*, which seems to be a factor that raised the average amount of stipends for the entire *hatamoto* class. The proportion of *bakufu* doctors who received 200–299 *koku* was nearly double the proportion of *hatamoto* members who received equivalent levels of income, showing an economic gap between these doctors and *hatamoto* members. However, if we look at the group that received less than 200 *koku*, 24.2% of the *hatamoto*

Table 1.6: Income distributions of Bakufu doctors and Hatamoto

Income	Bakufu Doctors (1804)			Hatamoto (1789–1800)	
	Number	%	Note	Number	%
400 or more	33	30.8		2,019	38.8
300–399	19	17.8		842	16.2
200–299	39	36.4		1,081	20.8
100–199	15	14		882	16.9
100 or less	1	0.9	No salary	381	7.3
Total	107	99.9		5,205	100

Note: Data on Bakufu doctors based on Ishii (ed.), 1981. Data on Hatamoto based on Table 6, Suzuki (1971: 208–9). Original data in *Kokuji-bunbu-kagami*.

Table 1.7: Income distributions of Bakufu doctors according to status, 1804

Status	Number	%	Average
Yoriai doctors	34	31.8	462
Oku doctors	21	19.6	421.8
Omoteoban doctors	43	40.2	300.6
Other	9	8.4	256.5
Total	107	100	

Note: Based on Ishii (ed.), 1981.

class and 14.9% of the *bakufu* doctors belonged to this group, showing a nearly 10% difference. This indicates greater gaps in the *hatamoto* class between members with high incomes and those with low incomes. Considering that 7.3% of the *hatamoto* class received less than 100 *koku*, the distribution of *bakufu* doctors' income seems to indicate smaller economic gaps and a more balanced distribution of resources among these doctors.

Social status of *han* doctors

There is a paucity of studies on the social status of *han* doctors. While some have reported cases of *han* doctors who did not hold high positions in the ranking system of the vassals (Narita 1976; Umihara 2003), others have reported *han* doctors who were promoted to high positions (Iwashita 2000). The situation is similar for studies of their economic status. There has been a report on *hittō-ishi* (a chief doctor) who was granted a ten-man allotment of rice (*jūnin fuchi*). Some say *han* doctors' income was no good (Umihara 2003). Others say *han* doctors were given preferential treatment by *han*, which granted doctors increased amounts of *chigyō-tori* (salary provided in the form of land) to hire competent doctors (Iwashita 2000).[26] Umihara (2007) argues that *han* doctors and some other members of the *daimyō* vassalage who served their master *daimyō* with certain expertise or performed skills—such as academics and artists—were placed in similar situations in the periphery of the samurai classes.

Because these previous studies are mere descriptions of individual cases in different *han*, they can be criticized on the following grounds: failure to grasp the whole picture of the status of *han* doctors during the Edo period; failure to make full comparisons with other members of the vassalage in terms of status position and of economic status; and lack of definite standards for evaluating the positions of *han* doctors. In the following, I attempt to grasp the general situation of *han* doctors by collecting as much data as possible from limited historical materials. In evaluating the status positions of *han* doctors, I use the same method as used in the analysis of *bakufu* doctors described above.

Status positions of *han* doctors

To analyze the status positions of *han* doctors, I studied positions of doctors in the ranking systems of different *han* described in *Hanshi daijiten* (The encyclopedia of *han* history) (Kimura et al. (ed.), 1988–1990). In order to improve the reliability of data, I excluded all *han* with less than twenty ranks, resulting in eighty-five *han* remaining for analysis. For seven *han*, their ranking systems were identified for two different time points. I counted each of these *han* as two cases, resulting in ninety-two cases of *han* in total. Such cases are indicated in Tables 1.8 and 1.10 as ① and ②. For further analysis, I divided these ninety-two cases into two groups: thirty-eight cases in which the ranking systems included *ashigaru*, *chūgen*[27] and other low ranks; and fifty-four cases in which these low ranks were not included in the ranking systems.

Table 1.8 shows the status positions of doctors, arranged in chronological order, in different *han*, including low-ranking vassals. I divided the Edo period into three eras and identified the following numbers of *han* that had doctors in their vassalages for each era: the early era (1603–1691), five *han*; the middle era (1692–1780), eleven *han*; and the late era (1781–1868), eleven *han*. The eras for another eleven *han* are unknown. The early era has only a small number of cases, which may not be sufficiently representative of the treatment of *han* doctors in that era. These cases still, however, help us to read the general trends if analyzed in combination with the data for the middle and late eras. The average value of the numerical indicator of the positions of *han* doctors is 0.468 for the thirty-eight *han*. In chronological order, the average values are 0.262, 0.45 and 0.565 for the early, middle and late eras, respectively. In general, *han* doctors held middle positions, and their positions seem to have declined with time. The high positions held by doctors during the early era seem unusual, even in comparison with their positions in ranking systems without low-ranking vassals, which are described later. This seems

Table 1.8: Status positions of doctors in different Han, some holding the status of lower vassals

No.	Han	Koku-daka	Proportion (fraction)	Proportion (decimal)	Average	Year
1	Tateyama	120,000	27/43	0.630	0.63	1610
2	Takato	30,200	7/60	0.170	0.17	1689
3	Tanagura	50,000	3/54, 4/54	0.06, 0.07	0.065	1693
4	Hachiman ①	27,000	18/72, 19/72	0.25, 0.26	0.255	1600–1692
5	Amagasaki	48,000	9/51, 10/51	0.18, 0.20	0.19	1635–1711
6	Murakami	150,000	40/111, 41/111, 42/111, 43/111	0.36, 0.37, 0.38, 0.39	0.375	1688–1703
7	Okudono	16,000	19/36	0.530	0.53	1735
8	Iwamura	30,000	1/12/2023	0.520	0.52	1740
9	Tahara	12,000	18/44	0.410	0.41	1750
10	Kashibara	20,000	24/59	0.410	0.41	1750
11	Tannan	10,000	18/42	0.430	0.43	1772
12	Okazaki	50,000	43/116, 44/116, 45/116	0.37, 0.38, 0.39	0.38	1793
13	Hachiman ②	39,000	13/85, 14/85	0.15, 0.16	0.155	1697–1758
14	Koriyama	151,288	26/43	0.60.	0.6	1716–1735
15	Shirakawa	110,000	60/173	0.350	0.35	1741–1823
16	Shonai	140,000	38/56, 39/56, 56/56	0.68, 0.70, 1.0	0.793	1764–1771
17	Takatori	20,500	13/57	0.290	0.29	1781–1800
18	Hukue		24/25	0.960	0.96	1810
19	Saijo	33,000	33/126, 48/126	0.26, 0.38	0.32	1841
20	Mori	10,000	33/33	1.000	1	1854
21	Oshi	100,000	22/149, 32/149	0.15, 0.21	0.18	1856
22	Matsushiro	100,000	46/226, 76/226, 89/226	0.20, 0.34, 0.39	0.31	1859
23	Numazu	50,000	9/28, 12/28, 17/28, 18/28, 19/28, 20/28	0.32, 0.43, 0.61, 0.64, 0.68, 0.71	0.565	1867
24	Sabae	40,000	45/86, 49/86	0.52, 0.57	0.545	1868
25	Toba ①	30,000	50/53	0.940	0.94	1857
26	Toba ②	30,000	23/134, 128/134	0.17, 0.96	0.565	1868
27	Hamada	46,000	36/72, 37/72, 38/72, 39/72, 40/72, 41/72	0.5, 0.51, 0.53, 0.54, 0.56, 0.57	0.535	1839
28	Katsuyama	12,000	16/33	0.480	0.480	1668–
29	Moriyama	20,000	21/63, 22/63, 50/63	0.33, 0.35, 0.79	0.49	
30	Sonobe	26,711	9/24, 10/24, 13/24	0.38, 0.42, 0.54	0.447	
31	Kiyosue	10,000	1/10/2022	0.450	0.450	
32	Yoshida	30,000	12/37	0.320	0.320	
33	Kochi	202,600	22/54	0.410	0.410	
34	Yanagawa	109,600	52/85	0.610	0.610	
35	Hirado	61,700	34/69	0.490	0.490	
36	Kumamoto	541,169	35/93, 75/93	0.38, 0.81	0.595	
37	Ryukyu	94,230	44/86, 46/86	0.51, 0.53	0.52	
38	Shibata	50,000	19/91, 57/91, 63/91	0.21, 0.63, 0.69	0.51	
Average					0.468	

Table 1.9: Distribution of Han doctors according to status, including some vassals of lower status

Status category	Number of Han	%
Upper (above 0.33)	10	26.3
Middle (0.34–0.67)	24	63.2
Lower (below 0.68)	4	10.5
Total	38	100

to be a consequence of the positions of doctors retained by *daimyō* in the Warring States period. Although it is only a hypothesis and needs further analysis, I suggest that doctors retained by these warlords were held responsible for maintaining the lives of their masters during the war-torn times and were, as such, in a position of close personal aid to their masters, which placed them higher in the ranking order among the retainers.

As a result, it is likely that these doctors were granted relatively high positions in the vassalage. Conversely, in the middle and later eras the average status position of doctors shows a declining tendency, as more and more *han* created new low ranks in the ranking system of doctors, including the heirs of doctors and *memie-ishi*,[28] although we need further investigation into the reasons and backgrounds in which these arrangements were introduced. Table 1.9 shows the distribution of the average positions of *han* doctors in different *han*. The positions of doctors in respective *han* are divided into three ranks: high, middle and low. In the largest proportion of *han* (63.2%), their doctors belong to the middle rank, followed by the high rank (26.3%) and the low rank (10.4%). This shows that the status positions of *han* doctors were not low at all—in fact, while some *han* doctors did hold low positions in the ranking systems with low-rank vassals, most doctors held middle or high positions. We must note, however, that the ten cases categorized under high rank represent average values for respective *han*. There were a total of thirteen *han* which granted high positions to *han* doctors in their ranking systems, including four in the late era and three whose eras are unknown.

Next, let us analyze the other group of *han* whose ranking systems did not include low-ranking vassals. I identified six, seven and thirty-one *han* in the early, middle and late eras, respectively, with ten *han* whose eras are unknown (Table 1.11). The average value of the numerical indicator of *han* doctors' positions in all fifty-four *han* is

Table 1.10: Status positions of doctors in Han, excluding the status of lower vassals

No.	Han	Koku-daka	Proportion (fraction)	Proportion (decimal)	Average	Year
1	Yamazaki ①	30,000	17/22	0.77	0.77	1679
2	Iiyama	40,000	23/46	0.5	0.5	1639–1706
3	Himeji ①	180,000	24/43	0.56	0.56	1639–44
4	Mito	350,000	23/89	0.26	0.26	1661–72
5	Yamazaki ②	10,000	5/21.	0.24	0.24	1673–80
6	Katsuyama	22,777	16/26	0.62	0.62	1691
7	Kohu ①	350,804	63/71, 64/71, 65/71	0.89, 0.90, 0.92	0.903	1695
8	Kohu	130,609	51/75	0.68	0.68	1719
9	Himeji ②	150,000	40/51	0.78	0.78	1720
10	Odawara ①	95,000	36/46, 41/46	0.78, 0.89	0.835	1724
11	Akashi	60,000	31/54	0.57	0.57	1731
12	Ono	40,000	39/85, 40/85, 41/85	0.46, 0.47, 0.48	0.47	1748
13	Hachiman ①	48,000	10/34, 19/34	0.29, 0.56	0.425	1759
14	Hirose	30,000	28/32	0.86	0.86	1786
15	Takamatsu	120,000	20/68	0.29	0.29	1787
16	Obama	103,500	32/46	0.7	0.7	1794
17	Tatsuno	51,000	26/27	0.96	0.96	1781–88
18	Ueda	53,000	30/47, 31/47, 32/47, 33/47	0.64, 0.66, 0.68, 0.70	0.67	1814
19	Shimabara	65,900	36/37, 37/37	0.97, 1.0	0.985	1814
20	Amamatsu	60,000	40/52	0.77	0.77	1817
21	Nagoya	619,500	36/133, 43/133, 69/133	0.27, 0.32, 0.52	0.37	1820
22	Kameyama	50,000	20/67	0.3	0.3	1829
23	Karasuyama	30,000	23/32	0.72	0.72	1839
24	Tsuchiura	95,000	32/55, 33/55	0.58, 0.6	0.59	1843
25	Sanuki	16,000	50/69, 51/69	0.72, 0.74	0.73	1843
26	Takasaki	82,000	48/72, 49/72, 50/72, 67/72	0.67, 0.68, 0.69, 0.93	0.743	1844
27	Matsuoka	25,000	8/27, 22/27, 26/27	0.30, 0.81, 0.96	0.69	1847
28	Niimi	18,000	9/20, 12/20	0.45, 0.6	0.525	1851
29	Kitsuki	32,000	18/44, 30/44	0.41, 0.68	0.545	1852
30	Ojima	10,000	28/30, 29/30	0.93, 0.97	0.95	1856
31	Odawara ②	95,000	39/44	0.89	0.89	1858
32	Hachima ②	48,000	25/60	0.42	0.42	1859
33	Kurume	210,000	24/46, 25/46, 26/46, 27/46	0.52, 0.54, 0.57, 0.59	0.555	1862
34	Asada	10,000	13/23	0.57	0.57	1863
35	Naegi	10,021	23/53	0.43	0.43	1866
36	Okabe	20,250	6/24	0.25	0.25	1868
37	Kawagoe	80,442	27/41, 28/41	0.66, 0.68	0.67	1868
38	Nagashima	20,000	28/61	0.46	0.46	1868
39	Okada	10,300	10/20	0.5	0.5	1869
40	Amagasaki	40,000	16/52	0.31	0.31	1804–17
41	Yoshida	70,000	49/70, 69/70	0.7, 0.99	0.845	1830–43
42	Suzaka	10,053	19/30	0.63	0.63	1859

43	Inuyama	35,000	31/56, 32/56	0.55, 0.57	0.56	1865–67
44	Oka	70,440	27/44, 29/44, 30/44	0.61, 0.66, 0.68	0.65	1865–67
45	Kariya	23,000	10/42	0.24	0.24	1747–
46	Tatebayashi	61,000	34/55, 39/55	0.62, 0.71	0.665	1707–28, 1747–1836
47	Aizu	230,000	40/49, 44/49	0.82, 0.90	0.86	
48	Shinjo	68,200	41/69, 42/69, 50/69	0.59, 0.61, 0.72	0.64	
49	Iwatsuki	23,000	19/42, 22/42	0.45, 0.52	0.485	
50	Mariyama	10,000	18/35	0.51	0.51	
51	Takasu	22,777	7/42, 35/42, 37/42	0.17, 0.83, 0.88	0.627	
52	Yagyu	10,000	14/22	0.64	0.64	
53	Marugame	51,467	23/40	0.58	0.58	
54	Miike	10,000	50/63, 51/63	0.79, 0.81	0.8	
Average					0.607	

Table 1.11: Status distribution of Han doctors, excluding the status of lower vassals

Status category	Number of Han	%
Upper (above 0.33)	7	13
Middle (0.34–0.67)	28	51.9
Lower (below 0.68)	19	35.2
Total	54	100.1

0.607. In chronological order, the average values are 0.492, 0.666 and 0.617 for the early, middle and late eras, respectively. These average values are lower by more than 0.1 than those for *han* doctors' positions in the ranking systems with low-ranking vassals. This shows that status positions of *han* doctors in the vassalages treated as samurai were slightly lower than middle. The number of *han* categorized in the early era is larger by one than that for the group of *han* whose ranking systems included low-ranking vassals. The average numerical indicator for the early era is not considerably different from the figures for the middle and late eras. Still, as was the case with the group of *han* whose ranking systems included low-rank vassals, the positions of *han* doctors were higher in the early era than in the middle and late eras, suggesting that this is likely to have been a general trend. While the average value changed from 0.666 for the middle era to 0.617 for the late era, this should be reasonably interpreted as a consequence of the small number of samples for the middle era, not as an improvement of the positions of *han* doctors towards the late era. Table 1.11 shows the distribution of the average positions of *han* doctors in different *han*. The positions are divided into three ranks. In 51.9%, 35.2% and 13% of the *han*, their doctors belonged to the middle, low and high ranks, respectively. The number of *han* categorized as high rank is the smallest (seven *han*), but this figure represents an average value, while the actual number of *han* that granted their doctors high positions was eleven.

In the above, I have painted a general picture of the status positions of *han* doctors in the vassalages to which they belonged. In the following, I discuss some of the characteristics of their status positions. First, the number of *han* doctors who held high positions in the ranking systems was not small. The number of *han* in which *han* doctors were granted high positions was fourteen (36.8%) and thirteen (20.4%) in Table 1.8 and Table 1.10, respectively. Previous studies have not recognized this point and have taken the view that *han* doctors did not hold high positions. It is certainly true that *han* doctors generally held middle positions and, in a few *han*, even held the lowest position. However, we need to recognize the fact that the situation was different in different *han*, including the fact that some *han* doctors did hold high positions. While it was not common that *han* doctors held high positions, it was not completely uncommon either.

The next point relates to the first characteristic mentioned above. I could point out that, unlike other occupations, *han* doctors were given a wide range of different positions, from high to low, in different *han*. It is also noteworthy that this tendency was maintained throughout the Edo period. While *karō*, *metsuke* and other executive officers common to the different *han* were generally granted similar positions, *han* doctors were given extremely different positions in different *han*. For instance, in Tanagura *han* (Table 1.8, line 3), physicians and surgeons were located in the third and fourth, respectively, of the fifty-four ranks. In terms of the numerical indicator, their ranks can be expressed as 0.06 and 0.07, respectively, showing that they held very high positions. In contrast, in Mori *han* (Table 1.8, line 20), doctors were in the lowest rank—the thirty-third of thirty-three ranks, or a numerical indicator of one. Why were doctors given such starkly opposed ratings? One possible factor that may have led to the low positions of some *han* doctors is the concept of *hōgi* mentioned above, which regarded medicine as a lowly occupation. This idea might have remained deeply entrenched in the Edo period. Despite the existence of this concept, however, the positions of doctors had begun to change little by little since the middle ages.[29] During the

Warring States period, some doctors attained high positions due to the peculiarity of their occupational skills. Here, I propose a hypothesis that this later led to the high positions of some *han* doctors in the Edo period. The various positions held by *han* doctors during the Edo period are evidence of these conflicting ideas. In the period when the individuality of different *han* domain systems was maintained, different views taken by different *han* must have shown up clearly.

Economic status of *han* doctors

Let us take another look at the previous studies on the economic status of *han* doctors. Umihara has reported that in Fuchū *han*, *hittō-ishi* (the chief doctor) was granted 51.4 *koku* (a ten-man allotment of rice) and commented that this does not represent a very high income (2003: 59). Umihara also mentions other doctors who received 15.42 to 41.12 *koku*. It is true that doctors of Fuchū *han* received relatively low incomes compared to those of some other *han*. Aside from the fact that this was a matter of a single *han*, we must first consider the meaning of income received by *han* doctors in the context of the amounts of income received by all vassals employed by Fuchū *han*. Table 1.12 is a modification of Umihara's table of the ranks and incomes of the vassals of Fuchū *han*. The numbers in the first column represent ranks, with the corresponding incomes shown in the second column. According to the table, the highest income paid in Fuchū *han* was 200 *koku*, which was paid to the third-ranked officers. The total fief granted to the *han* was 20 thousand *koku*, which means it was quite a small *han*. We can infer that the *han* held down the incomes of its vassals. In the case of Sendai *han*, whose total fief was 620 thousand *koku*, at least eight vassals received incomes of more than 10 thousand *koku*. There is a clear disparity between these two *han*. The table shows that in Fuchū *han*, some of the vassals in the sixth rank, which is higher than the eleventh rank in which the chief doctor was placed, received incomes between 24.28 and 51.4 *koku*. Of the 224 vassals shown in Table 1.12, the number whose incomes were higher than the chief doctors (51.4 *koku*) was only thirty-four at most. The chief doctor's income does not seem to have been low, if not high. Thus, in order to evaluate the economic status of *han* doctors, we must take into consideration the fiefs granted to other *han* vassalages.

Below I discuss the general trends in *han* doctors' income by analyzing data on their incomes inform the *Hanshi daijiten* (Table

Table 1.12: Income distributions of the vassals of Fuchū Han in Late-Edo period

No.	Income (*koku*)	Number	Note
1	125–155	2	karo
2	130	1	
3	100–200	2	
	100–150	7	
	70	1	
4	70–120	5	
5	70–100	3	
6	50–51.4	2	
	24.28–80	3	
	51.4–70	4	
	51.4	1	
	51.4	1	
7	51.4–70	5	
8	51.4	1	
9	50–80	5	
10	8–51.4	13	
11	51.4	2	Hitto Ishi and one other doctor
12	24.28	5	
13	8–10	13	
	(no record)	1	successor-to-be of the Hitto Ishi
14	< 24.28	42	
	41.12	1	Han doctor
	25.7	5	Han doctor
	15.42	5	Han doctor
15	< 21.28	26	
16	< 20.28	17	
17	(no record)	7	
18	25.7	3	
19	(no record)	1	
20	(no record)	1	
21	< 30.56	12	
22	25.7	3	
23	25.7	1	
24	10.28–30.84	9	
25	25.7	2	
26		8	
27		4	
Total		224	

Note: Based on Umihara, Table 1 (2003: 60), with minor corrections. Original Data in *Eppu kyucho*, 1856–1963.

1.13). I classified twenty-six cases of *han* into five types based on income distribution. For five han, we have records for more than two periods. These cases are indicated in Table 1.13 as ①, ② and ③. Considering that the average income of the *bakufu*'s *gokenin* class was 52.6 *koku*, a low income was defined as fifty *koku* (or a ten-man allotment of rice) or less and a high income as 100 *koku* or more. The first type is the 'bipolar type,' in which some doctors received over 100 *koku* while other doctors received less than fifty *koku*. There was only one *han* that can be classified as this type. A second type is the 'balanced type.' In this type, the distribution of doctors' incomes was either not concentrated in any particular range or it did not fall under any of the other four types. The largest number, or twelve, of the *han* were of this type. A third type is the 'high income type,' in which doctors invariably received an income of 100 *koku* or more. Four *han* belong to this type. A fourth group is the 'average type,' in which doctors' income distributed between fifty and 100 *koku*. Two *han* belong to this type. The last category is the 'low income type,' in which all doctors received income of fifty *koku* or less. Seven *han* come under this heading, constituting the second largest group after the average type.

One characteristic of *han* doctors' incomes evident from Table 1.13 is that there were significant differences both between different *han* and within each *han*. Let us take a look at some of the differences between different *han*. The *han* doctors of Ojima *han* (line 19) received income of a two-man allotment of rice which, if converted to *koku*, is only a little more than ten *koku*. On the other hand, Himeji *han* (line 13) and Odawara *han* (line 14) paid each of their doctors more than 100 *koku*. In particular, Himeji *han* paid no less than 200 *koku* to each doctor. This reflects substantial differences between different *han* in economic treatment of their doctors, similarly to the considerable differences between different *han* in status positions given to *han* doctors described above. It is not easy to find similarities among the seven cases of *han* belonging to the 'low income type.' Of note is the fact that no less than four of these seven *han* had fiefs worth about 20 thousand *koku* or less. *Han* doctors with low incomes were commonly seen, however, even in *han* which do not fit the 'low income type.' There were eleven of these, most of which belong to the 'balanced type.' Cases of *han* that fall under the 'balanced type' provide good examples of the differences in doctors' incomes within one *han*. In the case of Himeji *han* (line 2), the difference in income between the highest and the lowest ranks was as much as 380 *koku*.

Table 1.13: Income of various Han doctors

No.	Han	Koku-daka	Year	Number	Income	Note	Type
1	Hachiman ①	27,000	1600–1692	3 4	150–200 *koku* 5–10 *ninbuchi*		polar
2	Himeji ①	180,000	1639–44	26	20 *koku* 4 *ninbuchi* – 400 *koku* 4 *ninbuchi*		balanced?
3	Mito	350,000	1661–72	2 4 7 4 28	500 *koku* 300–499 *koku* 100–299 *koku* *fuchimai* *kirimai*		balanced?
4	Yamazaki ②	10,000	1673–80	1	100 *koku*	actually, *kuramai-tori*	average
5	Yamazaki ①	30,000	1679	1	150 *koku*		high payment
6	Hukuyama	100,000	1688–1703	2	20 *koku* 5 *ninbuchi*		low payment
7	Tanagura	50,000	1693	6 1	5 *ninbuchi* – 250 *koku* 5 *ninbuchi* 100 *koku*		balanced?
8	Tanagura Edo	50,000	ditto	3	15 *ninbuchi* – 200 *koku* 5 *ninbuchi*		balanced?
9	Kohu ①	350,804	1695	2 6 2	200 *pyo* 20 *ninbuchi* – 200 *pyo* 40 *ninbuchi* – 200 *pyo*		
10	Hachiman ②	39,000	1697–1758	5 1	70–100 *koku* 70 *koku*		average
11	Niwase	20,000	1703	? ?	100–200 *koku* 10–30 *ninbuchi*	20 persons in this category 9 persons in this category	balanced?

Social Status of Bakufu and Han Doctors in the Edo Period

#	Domain		Year					
12	Kohu ②	130,609	1719	36		5 ninbuchi – 300 koku		balanced?
13	Himeji ②	150,000	1720	?		200–300 koku		
14	Odawara ①	95,000	1724	2	6	250–300 koku		high payment
						100–200 koku		
15	Odawara ②	95,000	1858	6		42–300 koku		balanced?
16	Hachiman ③	48,000	1759	2		50 koku		low payment
17	Yonezawa	150,000	1809–17	28	7	20 pyo	data for 1868	low payment
						12 pyo		
18	Yoshida	70,000	1830–43	4	2	2 ninbuchi 4 koku – 13 ninbuchi		balanced?
						2 ninbuchi		
19	Ojima	10,000	1856	1	1	2 ninbuchi		low payment
						2 ninbuchi		
20	Izumi	20,000	1862	3	?	4 ninbuchi	Musoku-Deiri-Ishi	low payment
						?		
21	Okabe	20,250	1868	3		8–11 ninbuchi		low payment?
22	Shimotedo	10,000	1869	2	6	50 koku		low payment
23	Ogi	73,250		4		50–99 koku		balanced
				1		40–49 koku		
				13		less than 39 koku		
24	Hachinohe	20,000		1		100–150 koku		balanced
				2		50–100 koku		
				1		6–10 ryou		
				3		2–5 ryou		

Table 1.13: ... continued

25	Shibata	50,000	7	80–170 *koku*	balanced
			4	80–270 *koku*	
			7	4 *ninbuchi* 10 *ryou* – 5 *ninbuchi* 15 *koku*	
			8	3 *ninbuchi* 4 *ryou* – 3 *ninbuchi* 7 *koku*	
26	Sonobe	26,711	2	80–100 *koku*	balanced
			1	50 *koku*	
			1	5 *ninbuchi*	

Note: Based on Kimura et al. (eds), 1988–1990.

Many of the *han* of the 'balanced type' had a large number of *han* doctors and seem to have had an organized ranking system for these doctors. While these *han* gave preferential treatment to *han* doctors who were of high rank or who were from historic families, they also incorporated their *han* doctors' heirs (sons who would succeed their fathers) and doctors practicing in communities into the ranking system by providing them with small stipends, as in the case of Shibata *han* (line 25). This seems to be intended to control and secure medical human resources. Incidentally, as many as fourteen *han* retained doctors who received a high income of 100 *koku* or more.

Finally, let me describe the case of Nagoya *han* with respect to *han* doctors' incomes and its changes and the *han*'s policy. Table 1.14 shows *han* doctors' income situation in Nagoya *han* at two points in time, about 100 years apart. In 1648, the *han* retained twenty-seven *han* doctors, of which seven were *chigyō-dori* members and twenty were *kuramai-dori* members. In 1747, the *han* had twenty-four doctors who were *chigyō-dori* members and ten who were *kuramai-dori* members. Conversely, the average income of these *han* doctors decreased by a little over forty *koku*, from 240.1 *koku* to 198.8 *koku*. The average income of *chigyō-dori* members decreased from 378.6 *koku* to 230.4 *koku* and that of *kuramai-dori* members from 191.6 *koku* to 123 *koku*. In those days, the *han* had to retain competent doctors within the limits of fixed financial revenues (Iwashita 2000: 128). Under these circumstances, we can read the *han*'s intention to give preferential treatment to its doctors by raising their social status through increasing the number of *chigyō-dori* members, who were regarded as higher in rank than *kuramai-dori* members. While the number of *han* doctors increased by seven (26%), the financial resources for doctors increased only by 277.4 *koku* (4.3%). This indicates the *han*'s great struggle to secure doctors.

In lieu of a conclusion

I have attempted to outline the social status of *bakufu* doctors and *han* doctors in the Edo period by focusing on their status positions and economic status. With respect to the status positions of *bakufu* doctors, I took up the issue of palace seating order. As the palace seating order extended with time, the status position of *bakufu* doctors seems to have declined. However, I argue that their positions remained essentially the same, around the middle of all positions. As for their economic status, *bakufu* doctors' average income was lower

Table 1.14: Incomes of Han doctors in Nagoya-Han

Year	Chigyō-dori			Kuramai-dori			a + A	b + B	Average
	a) Total koku-daka	b) Number	Average	A) Total koku-daka	B) Number	Average			
1648	2650	7 (26.9)	378.6	3832.4	20 (73.1)	191.6	6482.4	27	240.1
1747	5530	24 (70.6)	230.4	1229.8	10 (29.4)	123	6759.8	34	198.8

Note: Based on Iwashita, Table 2 (2000: 129). *Chigyō-dori* are those allocated fiefs. *Kuramai-dori* are those payed in rice.

than that of the *hatamoto* class, but was never really low, with an average income of nearly 400 *koku*. In terms of income distribution, there were smaller income disparities among *bakufu* doctors than among *hatamoto* members. I have also shown that resources were distributed reasonably among different ranks of *bakufu* doctors.

As for *han* doctors, their status positions declined generally during the middle and late eras of the Edo period. One of the reasons for this seems to be the incorporation of lower-ranked *han* doctors to the *han* doctors' ranking systems as they expanded with time. The positions held by *han* doctors differed greatly between different *han*. Nearly 30% of the *han* had *han* doctors who held high positions. It is obvious that examples of individual *han* would not reveal the whole picture and discussions from broader perspectives are needed. Something similar can be said in relation to the economic status of *han* doctors. I introduced five types of *han* doctors' income distribution focusing on the differences among different *han*. This attempt to reveal a complete picture would certainly not belittle studies on individual cases. Rather, it helps to clarify the situations of different *han*.[30]

This paper was written as an exploratory essay and as such has many limitations. The analysis I made was based on the assumption that the palace seating order reflected the ranking of vassals. However, I was unable to analyze the meaning of palace seating orders in terms of official positions. It is necessary to conduct a thorough investigation of changes in the palace seating order from the perspective of the ranking of official positions. There is a paucity of data on the status positions of *han* doctors, particularly for the early era of the Edo period. In addition, the true picture of *han* doctors during the Edo period may not be grasped without establishing the status of doctors during the Warring States period. Above all, because I focused on an attempt to elucidate the actual conditions, I was unable to discuss the status of doctors in the context of political and social histories. I will add this to my list of future research topics.

Glossary

ashigaru 足軽
Azuma-no-hanamuke 東贐
Bakufu 幕府
baku-i 幕医
bukan 武鑑
buke ryakkei 武家略系

chigyō 知行
chigyō-dori 知行取り
chōnin 町人
chūgen 中間
daimyō 大名
daimyō azuke 大名預け
denseki 殿席
Dōsan 道三
ex-Emperor Gotoba 後鳥羽上皇 (Gotoba Jōkō)
fuchi 扶持
gokenin 御家人
gokinban tsukamatsuri ishi 御勤番仕医師
hairyō yashiki 拝領屋敷
Han 藩
han-i 藩医
hara-kiri 腹切り
hatamoto 旗本
hōgen 法眼
hōgi 方技
hōin 法印
Honmaru 本丸
hōroku 俸禄
Ieyasu Tokugawa 徳川家康
Masamori Hotta 堀田正盛
hyō 俵
ishi-no-ma 医師の間
jii 侍医
kachi-gashira 歩行頭（徒頭）
kengyō 検校
kobushin ishi 小普請医師
kokudaka 石高
kōtai yoriai 交代寄合
kuge 公家
machi ishi 町医師
Meiyo Burui 名誉部類
Nishi-no-maru 西の丸
oban(-no-)ishi 御番（之）医師
Ofuregaki Kanpō Shūsei 御触書寛保集成
ohiroshiki ryōji 御広敷療治
okachi 御徒
okuishi 奥医師

okujochū 奥女中
omemie 御目見
omemie ishi 御目見医師
omote 表
omoteoban ishi 表御番医師
onmyōji 陰陽師
Ōoku 大奥
osaji 御匙
osōjabanshū 御奏者番衆
ritsuryō 律令
Roan 驢庵
Roan Naritada Nakarai 半井驢庵成忠
rōjū 老中
sarugaku 猿楽
Seiryō Kaibo 海保青陵
sentōtsuki 仙洞附
shōgun 将軍
seppuku 切腹
tamarizume 溜詰
ten'yaku-no-kami 典薬頭
Ten'yaku-ryō 典薬寮
yoriai ishi 寄合医師
tozama-no-ishi 外様の医師
Tsunayoshi 綱吉
Yazaemon Tsuzuki 都築弥左衛門
Yōan-in Manase Masateru 曲直瀬養安院正珪

2 The Curse of the Fugitive Samurai: A Look at Social Stratification and Conflict in Rural Japan

D. K. Andrews

Introduction

The inhabitants of the inland village of Kogata,[1] situated in Japan's Tōhoku region, have for generations on end fought famine, flood, and fire in a climate that is well-known for being less than hospitable.[2] Their community and most of its arable land is wedged between thickly forested mountainous terrain. On the hilltops are tobacco fields, and the river that cuts across the village is lined with the rice paddies on which the community's few thousand residents have traditionally carved out a living. Today, less than 700 households form a village of about thirty neighborhoods.

An entrance, or intrusion, into any given community by an 'outsider' can be a cause of interest, concern, and possibly fear for the community's inhabitants. Yoshida Teigo in his research on the 'stranger' in connection with Japanese folk religion surmised that strangers are 'unknown and unclassified' and therefore present a potential threat in both a 'physical and mystical sense' (Yoshida 1981: 95). This thought-provoking appraisal of the relationship between, 'the established and the outsiders' (Elias and Scotson 1994) leads us to ask, is it possible for the outsider identity to linger on even though the outsiders themselves have become 'known and classified,' being firmly entrenched within the social fabric of a community?

During the course of my research in Kogata, I discovered that a group of six households in two neighboring hamlets derived their status and authority from the peculiar circumstances surrounding the founding settlement in the village. They are known by the term *Ochiudo*, which means fugitive samurai, a reference to the alleged status of their founding ancestors.

Delving into a study of belief and society within this geographically well-defined community (the heart of the village is found nestled in a river valley), I gradually became aware that underlying social tensions within the community occasionally erupt into conflict. Disputes are frequently connected to status relations. And, in this community where heavy emphasis is placed on vertical social relations, villagers believe that three of the more politically influential and socially dominant *Ochiudo* households suffer from *tatari* (curse/retribution).

This study examines social stratification and conflict in contemporary rural Japan, illustrating how social status is perceived, manipulated, and challenged. I argue that the curse of the *Ochiudo* can be comprehended as a technique through which villagers negotiate issues of social disparity within their community.

To understand the relationship between the *Ochiudo* households and the manifestation of the curse, I first describe the pertinent features of the Japanese household, the historical context underlying the *Ochiudo* classification, and some characteristics of *Ochiudo* communities. Then I turn toward a discussion of *tatari* and the social receptivity of the supernatural, highlighting the connection between *tatari* and the *Ochiudo*. Drawing on my research experience, I furnish three case studies of reportedly cursed *Ochiudo* households. In the last part of this study I undertake an analysis of the monumentalizing of the *Ochiudo* identity and the nature of the social conflict in which the *Ochiudo* are embroiled.

The continuity of the Japanese household

In rural Japan, traditional socio-political authority tends to lie with the older and more established households. In this vein, the *Ochiudo* households of Kogata are widely understood by the inhabitants to be among the oldest in the village, believed by some to be founding households. Amid the course of my research, the paradox of the *Ochiudo's* enduring identity as outsiders became apparent. The question posed by the persistence of this identity necessitates an elementary understanding of the Japanese household (*ie*). First, 'The *ie* is always conceived as persisting through time by the succession of the members,' and second, after being established, any given household has the potential to continue indefinitely (Nakane 1967: 1–2). This ideology likewise lends support to the perception that a household's status (*iegara*), in terms of pedigree, is resistant to change. The people of Kogata view a household's status as if it were a palpable heirloom that is passed down over time. Notwithstanding that contemporary examples of the rise and fall of households abound, the standing of households and more particularly that of the main households (*honke*),[3] are perceived by the villagers to be durable property.

Historical context of the *Ochiudo*

Towards the end of the Heian period (794–1185) two feuding clans, the Minamoto and the Taira,[4] engaged in a conflict spanning several decades that culminated in the naval battle of Dan-no-ura (1185) where the Taira were irreversibly defeated.[5] Born out of this historic event, we find that even today the tales of the Taira clan's consequent diaspora live on. These tales have been incorporated into innumerable local histories spanning the length of the Japanese archipelago.

Generally, the term *Ochiudo* evokes the image of a samurai who, losing in a power struggle, is forced into exile. In Kogata the theme of the Taira as noble wanderers is deeply engaging because of the attached romantic mystique. For example, the origin of the village's most worshiped religious object, a bronze statue of a Buddhist saint, is ascribed to a Taira clan lord named Shigemori (1138–1179). He is said to have carried it secured in his helmet on his journey through the hinterlands of Japan.[6] On the grounds of a local temple where the statue is now enshrined stands a nutmeg tree estimated at 700 years of age. Shigemori is claimed to have planted it in commemoration of his arrival in the village. As we will see, this allegorical imagery of Kogata's illustrious heritage has permeated the collective consciousness of the villagers.

Characteristics of the *Ochiudo* community

Takahashi Yuriko's (1980) investigation of *Ochiudo* neighborhoods in the Tōhoku region has revealed that geographic isolation, a specialized trade, consolidated kinship relations, and distinguishable language and customs are common characteristics of *Ochiudo* communities. Following this framework I now proceed to elucidate these categories in the context of Kogata.

To begin with, the *Ochiudo* are often separated from the main population of the village; *Ochiudo* environs are often found in removed mountainous areas or river valleys. In Kogata, two neighboring hamlets have been dubbed *Ochiudo*. Because of their location, several kilometers upstream from the central village in a narrow river valley enveloped by precipitous stone walls, the hamlets were often referred to as 'hidden.'

Moreover we find that the *Ochiudo* often have specialized trades or occupations. They may garner additional income from their mountainous environment. For example, in Kogata *Ochiudo* are known for their involvement in forestry, the production of wood charcoal, and the manufacturing of woven baskets of which they also had the regional monopoly. The inherited skills for this economic industry are credited to the ingenuity of their educated samurai ancestors. Almost all *Ochiudo* neighborhood households participated in this local industry. Because the production of baskets was performed during the non-agricultural winter months, men of the *Ochiudo* neighborhoods refrained from the seasonal migration that other villagers were compelled to undertake. This routine absence of fathers and sons was a taxing burden on both individual households and the community as a whole. Hence the ability of the *Ochiudo* to avoid this seasonal migration created a socio-economic disparity with other villagers.

Additionally, the *Ochiudo* neighborhoods tended to have a relatively high rate of endogamous marriages. Extensive kinship ties within the community can be traced over several generations, contributing to the perception that the *Ochiudo* neighborhoods of Kogata were not only autonomous, but exclusive.

A final characteristic of the *Ochiudo* enclaves is that they are perceived to be distinguishable from the village at large in terms of language and custom. For instance, in Kogata, it is often non-*Ochiudo* individuals who state that the *Ochiudo* dialect differs from that of the rest of the village and reflects the 'high culture' of their elite samurai heritage. Their continued adherence to conservative rules of etiquette within their own community, including the enforcement of strict seating orders at communal gatherings, is said to distinguish *Ochiudo* from other Kogata neighborhoods.

Tatari and the social receptivity of the supernatural

A degree of familiarity with the supernatural resonates in the lives of the villagers of Kogata. Talk of death, which seems to permeate daily conversation, is not considered to be unnatural. It is conceivable that this reflects the community's demographics—the community is steadily aging[7]—the general acceptance of the subject of death and associated phenomena is arresting. Asked why it was his responsibility to make offerings to the dead at his household's Buddhist altar (*butsudan*), a grandfather laughingly replied, 'Because I'm the closest to the dead' (*watashi wa hotoke-san ni ichiban chikai kara*), both in terms of age and social relations. Admittedly, my research has been oriented toward the supernatural and its various manifestations, and villagers have responded to my inquiries regarding the supernatural. Some, for example, have recounted seeing apparitions of the dead walking through their homes or places of work, or even floating above the fields and rice paddies. In addition, my informants have shown a keen interest in the meaning of supernatural occurrences such as a *hidama* (fireball) seen shooting through the early morning sky, which they believe predicts death or calamity in the direction that it vanishes. The people of Kogata have catered to my solicitation for associated narratives, and in doing so have expressed an active belief in the supernatural.

Another deeply rooted belief among the villagers is that 'death comes in threes.' Not just a local expression, this is a belief that underscores how the people of Kogata manage misfortune. As if directed by some supernatural imperative, people die in threes.[8] When a second individual dies, a correlation is made to the first, and it is generally assumed that another death is approaching. Conversations then typically turn toward those at risk, flagging possible future victims.[9] After the third death, villagers will remark, 'As expected, a third person has passed away,' thus reconfirming the logic of a process of supernatural causation. Succession intimates that a prominent characteristic of death in Kogata is the collective social response. What I want to emphasize here is that the depth of the local people's belief in the supernatural is repeatedly observed in the milieu of their social interactions.

There is a common belief in Japan that an unusual cry from a crow may forewarn ill fortune; it may even announce the death of someone within the community. One of my informants, for example, explained that while chatting with a neighbor, they both noticed that crows were cackling in the direction of this neighbor's home. My informant unwittingly joked that the crows had gathered ominously above the neighbor's house and that someone was evidently at death's door. She was shocked, however, to later hear that the neighbor's son had hung himself that very day. Afterwards, when I overheard conversations between his friends and neighbors, I was interested to learn that they directly attributed the suicide to a curse stemming from the father worshipping an excessive number of deities.[10] The son's death was said to be yet the latest chapter in an unfolding tragedy surrounding this household. Even among those who gathered in support of and mourned alongside the father, the definitive explanation for this misfortune was assigned to supernatural causes.

In his work on spirit possession, Yoshida Teigo defined *tatari* as a punitive response to 'a person's disrespectful and impious behavior toward local deities and spirits' and 'a failure to worship deities or spirits properly' (1967: 238). His research also detailed the links between ill fortune and the supernatural (Yoshida 1967: 237). To cite another example from Kogata, a *sake* (rice wine) brewer-dealer who was also the village's largest landholder is currently purported to be cursed. This household has held a prominent position in the village both socially and economically. However, the household head recently died in a fire that engulfed his home. As Yoshida stressed, it has been said in the village that the cause of the fire and his death were directly related to his ceasing to attend the festivals of the tutelary shrine of his neighborhood, a shrine that the man's ancestors had built and had been the principle benefactors of.[11]

By analyzing data collected from cases in Kogata, I concur with Yoshida's findings and conclude that *tatari*, as a form of supernatural violence, can be characterized as deities, spirits of the dead, and other transcendent beings attempting to force a redress for negligent behavior as well as social and moral violations, both past and present, by inflicting illness, injury, death, and other adversity. The beliefs of the people of Kogata actively incorporate the conception of *tatari*. A reliance on supernatural causation to explain the ills that befall members of the community is not uncommon. Receptivity toward an otherworldly explanation is additionally evinced in the case of the *Ochiudo* where the actions of their samurai ancestors are believed to have led to their descendents being afflicted by curses.

The connection between *tatari* and the *Ochiudo*

My research was not limited to, nor did it anticipate the uncovering of, the *tatari* of the *Ochiudo*. Perhaps needless to say, members of the supposedly afflicted households never acknowledged the curses to me. It was through daily conversation with the villagers, which can rightly be described as gossip, that my overall awareness of the association between the *Ochiudo* and *tatari* gradually developed. I should stress that the bulk of information used in this study was gathered from fleeting commentaries and under the breath accusations that infrequently slipped from the mouths of the locals concerning their supposedly cursed neighbors, and as such, it contains emotional sentiments that may contradict the views of other villagers.

Interestingly, be it social, political, economic, or religious, authority in the *Ochiudo* enclaves has been held by historically influential main households. Although the settlement of these households is steeped in legend, their declarations of genuineness were outwardly supported by the possession of samurai weapons, armor, and other antiquities. As I will show, despite this material evidence, the persistence of their outsider status as descendents of fugitive samurai is maintained to a great extent through the exercise of their own volition in the ongoing process of reconstructing an image as entities invested with authority.

Komatsu Kazuhiko has written about legends surrounding the killing of outsiders, after which *tatari* is affixed to the murdering household by their victims. These curses then usher in the decline of the assailant's household and spell trouble for later generations (Komatsu 1997: 60). There is a twist to this motif in the case of Kogata with the outsider as murderer. In this community, it is mostly non-*Ochiudo* villagers that draw a connection between the samurai status of the *Ochiudo* ancestors and the adversity which is said to befall their descendents. Villagers attribute these misfortunes to curses attached to the households. The reason given is that the *Ochiudo* ancestors, in keeping with the authority granted to their social position as samurai, would have slain others. This killing, not atoned for, remains indefinitely bound to their households. Hence, a supernatural reckoning has been placed on the *Ochiudo* of Kogata, transcending the generations, in which the descendents now must bear the burden of their *Ochiudo* identity.

The cases of three *Ochiudo*

The Tamura main household sits at the head of a lineage composed of nine households that is also the largest of the five lineages in its neighborhood. The household head conventionally had final say on any issue affecting the *Ochiudo*, playing a central role in governing the two *Ochiudo* neighborhoods. Its influential position has led other lineages to state that their own roots could be traced to the Tamura household.

Furthermore, the household's political influence extends beyond the confines of the *Ochiudo* neighborhoods. The men of four consecutive generations, dating back to the early 1900s, have served as village assemblymen. The present household head advanced to the position of chairman, and once made a bid for mayor.

The current Tamura household is known throughout the village by its house name *jitō*.[12] Literally translated, this means 'head of the land,' but this title was given to the Tamura household in earlier times for its role as village administrator. The household's status is further supported by the samurai regalia it possesses, which is symbolic of its high position and alleged historic past as descendents of fugitive samurai. One legend relates the story of the lord who lived in the Tamura neighborhood. When he broke the taboo against eating meat, he was imprisoned, and later put to death. This tale is used to reinforce, first, the Kogata *Ochiudo* identity as conservative and authoritarian,[13] and second, it sets the stage for the *Ochiudo* to be linked with *tatari*, for they have murdered.

Stories of this household's 'curse' are told in hushed tones. According to one informant, she was employed to pick apples in the hillside orchards when the other village women acquainted her with the Tamura household's *tatari*. Slanderous gossip to some, they said that this household's samurai ancestors used to 'chop off people's heads.' The question of specifically who they killed, however, remains unanswered.

The supernatural retribution incurred by the Tamura household primarily affects the women of the family. For example the strange, if not neurotic, behavior of the head of the Tamura household's wife is said to be a manifestation of such a curse, as was her early death. Another example is a woman who was rumored to have been locked in the house from an early age because she suffers from some trauma or mental disorder. A local shaman was once consulted to help cure her, but to no avail. With no reports of her death, however, the household's reputation continues to be shrouded by a shameful secret.

In the same *Ochiudo* neighborhood, the main Sano household is positioned at the head of a separate lineage of four households. This household, by maintaining close kinship relations with Tamura, has appropriated a degree of authority and is now often seen playing the role of enforcer for Tamura. As is common among powerful households in the village, the main Tamura and Sano households are linked by kinship, with the younger brother of the former marrying into the latter to become an adopted husband (*muko-yōshi*).

The role of history, whether fictive or not, is pivotal in the formation of many contemporary perceptions of the *Ochiudo* within Kogata. For instance, in accordance with the newly imposed proclamations for the separation of Shinto and Buddhism at the beginning of the Meiji Era (1868–1912), agents of the government reportedly came to the village to confiscate the Buddhist statue that the famous Taira clan lord Shigemori had supposedly bestowed. Although one common story says that a local priest hid the statue to safeguard it, there is another version of the story attached to the Sano household. Having returned home from duty in the army, a young Sano man single-handedly repulsed these custodians by standing bravely before them and announcing himself to be an imperial soldier. By means of such heroic depictions, the reputation of the Sano family as warriors is brought forth to a more recent past.

The Sano household was also famous for its 'Flower Well'. This name derived from the fact that flowers grew in the vicinity of a freshwater spring located on the Sano farm. Used as a means of divination, the upcoming year's harvest could be foretold and consequently the fortunes of farmers, depending on when the flowers first blossomed. This folklore enhanced the *Ochiudo* community's mystique, as if it directly mediated with the supernatural world.

Returning to the manifestation of curses, villagers explain that the *Ochiudo* misfortune is passed down over generations. In the Sano family's case, the villagers suggest that the *tatari* has moved from the mother-in-law to the daughter-in-law. More generally, however, the indications of *tatari* at work in this household have been cited as being the premature death of the household head's wife, arguments between the household head and his son, and the conjugal separation of the son and his wife.

Separated from Tamura and Sano, the main Ogawa household is the top household of its *Ochiudo* neighborhood, with two branch households in its lineage. Like Sano, the members of the Ogawa household do not overtly engage in politics, but instead rally behind Tamura.

In addition to its possession of short swords, unglazed teacups and Buddhist statuary, all of which are recognized as *Ochiudo* items, the Ogawa household boasts a lacquered flute said to be made from the leaves of bamboo grass. It is this flute that has made the Ogawa household famous.

The value of this object is predicated on its supposed origin. The owner of the flute was a defeated Taira samurai warrior who fled to what is now the village of Kogata. This wandering samurai is said to have given the flute in payment for shelter provided by the peasant Ogawa household. Yet in another version, lord Shigemori is said to have been the bearer of this sacred instrument as well as the founder of the Ogawa family line. This prestigious past and its particular features have gained the flute considerable newspaper coverage over the years; however, when the flute was being exhibited at the village museum, an overzealous scholar attempted to authenticate the flute by making cuttings with a knife. He wanted to verify that the flute was a historical artifact and not a fraud. The household head is reported to have been overwhelmed with remorse for his failure to properly protect the flute. After this incident, his health started to falter. To the villagers this was indicative of a curse. The household head had offended his ancestors who had entrusted him with safeguarding the flute. Therefore they manifested their displeasure by inflicting a curse on him. He was also harshly criticized by the local community. He was condemned for exploiting the flute to achieve celebrity for himself.

The household head swore that the flute would not be publicly shown again. His repentant declaration may have allowed him to avoid an untimely demise. Still, he has not completely appeased his critics, for despite the incident taking place some twenty years ago the villagers maintain that his persistent illness is symptomatic of an active curse, and that as long as he has pride in his *Ochiudo* heritage his physical condition will remain incurable.

Ochiudo as commodities

In recent years, a large public works project in the form of a dam forced the abandonment of the old *Ochiudo* neighborhoods. They were relocated to two new subdivisions situated on opposite sides of the *Ochiudo* valley.[14] The flooded valley became a lake, and combined with the dam itself became the latest tourist attraction for the township. The lake was appropriately named after Ogawa's flute, thus locating the *Ochiudo* imagery at the forefront of the village identity. At a nearby Shinto shrine, a carved stone statue has been put in place immortalizing the Taira clan lord Shigemori. As part of a strategy to attract tourists, he has been elevated to the standing of a god, being worshipped by visitors and townspeople alike, and thus capitalizing on the *Ochiudo* legends.

The national government's proposal to build the dam initially sparked a heated opposition movement. A concerted effort was made by all of the *Ochiudo* households to derail the project. After 'persuasive pressure' from the government, however, Tamura suddenly decided to endorse the project and relinquish the lands of the entire *Ochiudo* community; the sole authority to decide the fate of so many bespeaks Tamura's authority. As this was the first time in Japan's history that a deal was brokered before the customary negotiations for compensation and land restoration had been conducted, this unprecedented and unorthodox practice was widely reported both in local and national newspapers.

In large part, the storytelling of the *Ochiudo* legacy is performed by local historians who have enthusiastically collected and recorded related folklore. At the village museum, for example, while visitors gaze at a diorama depicting the 'hidden' valley as it was before the dam construction, the curator and staff entertain them with lectures that highlight the history of the *Ochiudo*.

This is not to say that the *Ochiudo* do not actively participate in their own identity making. They most certainly do. The explicit way in which the *Ochiudo* choose to disseminate their identity is through monumentalization. The diorama in the museum is but one example. They have gone to lengths, exerting heavy-handed political pressure, to ensure its display continues.

Selling their land for the dam significantly enhanced the economic status of all of the *Ochiudo* neighborhood residents. Their new residential areas are frequently referred to as being something like a Kogata version of Beverly Hills, with large homes and wide driveways. These neat rows of residences have become a sightseeing destination. Indeed Tamura and Sano have rebuilt large houses on a commanding elevation overlooking the new residential area, a location that other villagers take to be an affirmation of their superiority. Refusing the domination of these two leaders, a number of households chose to relocate away from their fellow *Ochiudo*. From conversations with the members of these households, I gathered that they seized the opportunity to break free from the often burdensome social relationships that develop as part of living in a close-quartered community.

Along with their homes, the family graves also had to be removed from the construction zone of the dam. Tamura and Sano chose to establish their graves apart from those of other *Ochiudo* and relocated the graves to the temple cemetery within the village center. Thus they have penetrated into the space of the village proper and are said to be testing the boundaries of propriety. Criticized for explicitly flaunting their wealth, Tamura and Sano erected side by side what indisputably became the largest graves. Popular topics of conversation, these towering graves epitomize the current socio-economic disparity felt by locals against the *Ochiudo* neighborhoods. One resident, speaking of her own unfavorable situation, echoed the opinions of many, saying, 'Here is my grave, the grave of the poorest woman in the village, right alongside the graves of the village's richest families.' By this comparison, she implied a discomfort at being forced to live in the shadow of the more economically advantaged Tamura and Sano, who, rejecting harmonious uniformity, instead facilitate dissimilarity with their fellow villagers. Moreover two of the *Ochiudo*, one of whom is Tamura, have also erected stone markers on their graves bearing inscriptions pronouncing their links to fugitive samurai origins.[15] For the *Ochiudo*, these monuments are the marked symbols of their inherent authority as ruling elite.

The main households of the *Ochiudo* neighborhoods were always recognized as being comparably wealthy families of high standing. The dam project simply increased that wealth, magnifying their economic status. People comment that the money from the dam construction caused members of the *Ochiudo* community to get snobbish. As an example, the son of the Sano family is regularly criticized for showing a lack of reserve. He is by all accounts unapologetic. Eliciting antagonism he is called by the name of his neighborhood, in this case a euphemism for '*Ochiudo*,' connoting his alleged self-absorption in his social standing.

In response to the *Ochiudo's* display of wealth the villagers have created new categories by which to reverse their marginalized or subjugated positions. Identifying the *Ochiudo* as cursed can be a form of 'retribution for perceived injustices' (Schnell 1995: 322) for those who lack the ability to address their grievances by other means. Generally, in Kogata open disputes with fellow villagers are strongly discouraged; however, villagers also understand that conflict is sometimes unavoidable. One informant who is in conflict with the Sano household explains, 'You can't fight in the village. But if things get really bad, then it can't be helped.'[16] Working with and assigned below a member of the Sano household, this informant is often harassed and derided for not knowing his/her station, that is, being from a branch house of modest means. Although wanting to confront the offender, my informant refrains from doing so, reluctant to openly oppose the socially powerful Sano family. Instead this informant gossips about the Sano household being cursed and fishes for a sympathetic ear. Being neither able nor willing to overtly confront the social, political, and economic disparity found in the community, a person may choose instead to level the playing field by identifying what they believe to be *tatari*.

Conclusion

I have sketched a rather unfamiliar, although contemporary, picture of Japanese society. Besides offering insight into the present state of supernatural belief, it provides a clue toward comprehending social stratification in modern Japan.

One of the first conclusions of this study is that wrongdoing by both ancestors and their descendents is seen to generate misfortune for the *Ochiudo*. As we have seen, by committing murder the samurai ancestors of Tamura and Sano incurred eternal curses to their family lines. In the case of Ogawa, the household head, being negligent in his duty to safeguard a family heirloom, saw his health suffer. In short, these examples help to frame *tatari* as the alleged source of discord, illness, or death among the family members of these households.

In the case of the Tamura and Sano households, *tatari* was manifested in the wives developing a neurosis, falling ill, and dying. The untimely death of the women (i.e., that they died before their husbands) is also seen to be indicative of supernatural causation. It transpired, however, that there is no social stigma attached to associating with a cursed household, and no ostracism ensues. This leads to the conclusion that the *tatari* of the *Ochiudo* is not deemed to be socially detrimental.[17]

The gossip surrounding the cursed households does not impede social interaction with them. Robert J. Smith has argued that gossip, as a coercive measure, has the ability to reign in social deviation and effect changes in behavior (Smith 1961: 524). This study has attempted to show that the motivation for the labeling of an individual or his household as being afflicted with *tatari* does not necessarily lead to any changes in their behavior or their position in the traditional social order. Rather it is an assertion that the legitimacy of authority and status of the allegedly afflicted parties *may* be contested by other members of the community.

When examining the history of the *Ochiudo,* a tempting point of departure for the researcher would be the analysis of the paradoxical nature of the founding samurai. With the liminal status of outsiders, they allegedly first came to the 'hidden' valley to escape their fugitive status by disguising their nobility. Yet, to merge into the community they would either have had to submit themselves to the established power structure or compel the inhabitants to accept their authority. The latter scenario, as we have seen, is the one depicted in the folktales I heard in Kogata. Nonetheless, it must be emphasized that the villagers need not fully articulate the details of this history. The overall acceptance of the idea of *Ochiudo* and its inherent contradictions can be comprehended in much the same way that Robert J. Smith related that his informants gave him conflicting accounts. In rebuking one villager's account, another informant explains, 'Oh, they like to say that. We don't mind. It doesn't do anyone any harm after all' (Smith 1974: xviii). When I posed the question of his family's authenticity to an elderly member of the Tamura household, he explained that he had been raised hearing stories of his family's *Ochiudo* origin from his parents and grandparents and that he never had any reason to doubt those tales. What would be the advantage for him in doing otherwise? Clearly, for many the act of identifying a case of *tatari* is more relevant than clarifying the extraneous details. One can conclude that villagers interpret their historical realities and then engage each other in a struggle to legitimize or devalue their constructed identities.

Embedded within the dramatic religious context of *tatari*, a sociological aspect can be discerned that reflects the tensions found within the community. Through *tatari* the underlying social conflicts that are rooted in the doctrines of status and authority manifest symbolically. Although *tatari* references fractured relations with the supernatural, it may be observed that *tatari* is perceived by the inhabitants of Kogata as explaining social disparities in the standing of households. Following the lead of other scholars who recognize the curse as a social control mechanism (e.g., Schnell 1997: 1), I propose that *tatari* may be identified as a means by which villagers negotiate issues of status and redress disparity.

Labeling a household as cursed is a political act. In Kogata it is a strategy to downplay the the *Ochiudo's* authority. This designation, however, does not negate their status; instead, it calls into question the legitimacy of their authority. Ann Waswo has pointed out that 'one's social status is determined not simply by income or pedigree but also by how one is treated' (1977: 116). The handling of the *Ochiudo* households as cursed is one way by which to challenge their status.

It is important to note that 'Narratives are not only structures of meaning but structures of power as well' (Bruner 1986: 144). For both the *Ochiudo,* who seek to glorify themselves by evoking a historical past linked to noble samurai figures, and for other villagers, who seek to condemn the subjugating behavior of the *Ochiudo* and address perceived economic disparity by using that same history, the manipulations of the *Ochiudo*'s historical origins 'are the products of contestable human choices and interests' (McCutcheon 2001: 87).

A 'community,' it has been remarked, 'is premised on various forms of exclusion and constructions of otherness' (Gupta and Ferguson 1997: 13). Whether conscious or not, through labeling *Ochiudo* households as cursed, villagers can be seen to be setting the *Ochiudo* apart from themselves. Conversely, through the process of monumentalization, the *Ochiudo* households move to create a 'tangible historic context' (Ivy 1995: 56) in which to assert their genuineness as agents of authority and draw attention to the legitimacy of their being categorically set apart. Ironically, both sides contrive to position the *Ochiudo* outside the normative body of village households.

Glossary

bunke 分家
butsudan 仏壇
hidama 火玉
honke 本家
hotoke-san 仏さん
ie 家
iegara 家柄
jitō 地頭
muko-yōshi 婿養子
ochiudo 落人
sake 酒
tatari 祟り
yagō 屋号

3 Sports Books and the Culture of Inequality in Contemporary Japan: Discourses Emphasizing Effort and their Reproduction

Ryosuke Morooka

The aim of this paper is to analyze the most evident value pattern—the emphasis on effort—in the discourses of athletes in contemporary Japan. By focusing on the way that 'sports books' emphasize the value of effort, this paper explores the social function of these discourses in promoting and disseminating this value.

Discourses of athletes and sports books

Discourses about athletes in contemporary Japan, particularly top athletes, are transmitted to the general public in vast quantities through various types of media. The most common examples include television programs such as sports news and documentaries, newspapers and magazines. The specialized 'sports newspaper,' such as the *Nikkan Supōtsu* and the *Supōtsu Nippon*, is a well established medium that developed soon after WWII due to strong links between newspaper companies and Japanese professional sports, particularly baseball.[1] While many sports magazines have also been published since the war, including *Baseball Magazine* founded in 1946, the number of magazines specializing in sports has increased markedly in the last few decades. The revitalization of this genre was triggered by the launch of *Sports Graphic Number* by Bungeishunjūsha in 1980. Modeled on *Sports Illustrated* of the United States, this magazine has achieved success by combining large glossy photographs with substantial feature articles and interviews about various sports, and has spawned many imitators.

In recent years, the internet has become an important medium for disseminating discourses about athletes. Blogs in particular enable athletes to communicate directly with their audience. For example, the retirement of soccer player Hidetoshi Nakata in 2006 was first announced in his blog; the newspapers reported it on the following day by simply reprinting the blog entry.

My analysis, however, focuses on 'sports books.' 'Sports books' in Japan, also referred to as 'sports-related publications,' is an established and recognized genre although its boundaries have not been clearly defined. Sports books are slower than other forms of media in transmitting information, but they are capable of carrying a more substantial amount of information. Unlike newspaper and magazine articles, which are usually written by reporters, many sports books are written by athletes themselves in their own words, although editors or ghost-writers are frequently involved, and hence are useful sources of information about athletes' views and perspectives.

Today, an enormous number of sports books is circulating in Japan. According to a catalogue of sports books (*Supōtsu no hon zenjōhō*) published by Nichigai Associates, the number of sports-related publications was approximately 20,000 for the period from 1945 to 1991, 10,931 from 1992 to 1997 and 9948 from 1998 to 2002. The number of sports-related publications has increased dramatically since the 1980s as the mass consumption of books in general (a tendency to 'read and throw away') became prevalent. Today there are about 2000 titles published in this genre each year. These numbers suggest the tremendous social impact of sports books.

Why is there such a strong demand for so many sports books? It appears that books about top athletes are being published and read for several purposes. One purpose for reading sports books is to learn techniques and tactics that may help the reader to play a particular sport better. In this case, the readers are typically players or coaches of that particular sport. Another purpose is likely to be simply to satisfy the curiosity of readers. Certain types of nonfiction stories and documentaries are written in response to the desire of fans of a certain sport, team or athlete to learn more than the fragmented information they can glean from news articles. In particular, books of this nature are published in large numbers before and after mega events such as the Olympics and the Soccer World Cup.

Another purpose for reading sports books of particular interest here is to derive ideas or learn lessons for use in non-sports activities. These non-sports activities include study, education, work (management in particular) or life in general. In this case, the athlete is regarded as a kind of 'role model' and his/her story as a 'success story' in life.

Let us look at some of the titles of books written about Ichirō[2] as an example. In the educational field we find *Ichirō wo sodateta Suzuki-ke no nazo* (The secret of the Suzuki family who raised Ichirō) (1995), in the business field we find *Kabu wa Ichirō tōshi de ike—Chōteikinri jidai ni mōkaru sōba senryaku* (Invest in shares in Ichirō style: Market strategy to make money in the age of ultra-low interest rates) (1995), in the management field there is *Shanai de 'Ichirō' wo sodateru hō—sutā jinzai ni hitsuyōna nōryoku to sono minitsukekata* (How to nurture 'Ichirō' in your company: Skills required for a star employee and how to acquire them) (2005), and finally in the 'self-development' field we find *'Ikigai' no moderu wo sagashite—Ichirō no yakyū no 'sekai' wo chūshin ni* (A search for the model of meaningful life: Around the 'world' of baseball of Ichirō) (2005). These titles clearly suggest that sports books are published and read for the ideas or hints they can offer for a wide range of activities other than sport. As my analysis demonstrates, this tendency is not unique to Ichirō-related books, but is common to all Japanese sports books.

Emphasis on effort in sports books

In this and subsequent sections, I analyze the values expressed in contemporary Japanese sports books using the autobiographies of sporting celebrities (players, managers, coaches, etc.)[3] that purport to be self-penned.[4] Approximately 300 autobiographies have been reviewed for this study.[5]

There are three ways in which certain ideas or value patterns are presented or corroborated through sports books.[6] First, the author may assert directly in his/her discourse that a certain idea is the standard that the reader should conform to. Second, the author may present a certain idea as a belief that he/she personally holds. In this case, the author does not preach blatantly, but his/her achievements as a top athlete, or a 'successful person,' can convince the reader. Third, the author may present anecdotes or an account of his/her own experiences that can be used to demonstrate the importance of a certain idea. In this case, it is the reader's interpretation that associates the account in the book with a certain set of values.

Anecdotes and stories that are useful in corroborating socially dominant values are accumulated socially as 'stock of knowledge' (Schutz 1962) that is available in the society. In contemporary Japan, people involved in sports are the main source of such stories, besides historical figures, which are given far more social importance than the stories of movie or TV stars.[7] One interesting characteristic found in sports books is that they frequently quote other stories and refer to other athletes' words and episodes.

An element that cannot avoid attention in the analysis of the values expressed in sports books is the persistent repetition of emphasis on *doryoku* (effort). This persistence appears to be strange in comparison with the magnitude of the changes that Japan has undergone in recent decades. Notions of identity, gender, aging and social order, for example, have changed substantially but the emphasis on effort has been repeated in various forms and continues to dominate other patterns.

The Japanese word *doryoku* can be traced back to the eighth century, later coming into popular usage as a translation of the English word 'effort' (*Shōgakukan's Japanese Dictionary*, second edition, 2001). Its semantic content is not particularly culture-specific. Rather, what comes across as salient characteristics of Japanese sports books are the context in which the word is used and the dominance of the value pattern which it represents. This value pattern, that I generally call 'emphasis on effort' here, is also indicated by using some synonyms: the most general one is *'renshu'* as 'practice'; *'tanren,' 'kurō'* and *'shugyō'* are also popular words for the usage, translated respectively into 'training,' 'hard work,' and 'discipline' in a provisional way, since they carry culturally-specific connotations that require volumes of social and historical explanation.[8]

Although it is difficult, by its very nature, to quantify the degree of its dominance, I would like to refer to a reprint series of books called *Ningen no kiroku* (Records of people), published by Nihontosho Sentā since 1997, to illustrate the pervasiveness of the pattern emphasizing effort. As the most comprehensive collection of autobiographies by modern and contemporary Japanese people who were successful in various fields, this series at present (2006) includes over 170 titles, ten of which are autobiographies of successful athletes born between 1904 and 1940. Some of these athletes are now active leaders in the contemporary sports community. Eight of the ten titles strongly emphasize the importance of effort, while the remaining two describe stories of success achieved through effort. None of these works contain any remark that could be interpreted as expressing doubt about the importance of effort. I do not intend to suggest that the total pervasiveness of this pattern is common to Japanese athletes in general, since these ten books were especially selected for inclusion in this series. However, they do suggest that the pattern is not unusual and that there are certain reasons for reprinting discourses with a strong emphasis on effort today.

The characteristics of this value pattern that I consider to be the most important are that effort is valued both as a means and an end, and that these two aspects are not differentiated conceptually or cognitively. The emphasis on effort as a means involves emphasizing that results can be (or have been) achieved through effort. On the other hand, the emphasis on effort as an end involves the argument that making an effort is valuable in itself, regardless of the results. The latter aspect has two different dimensions, one is praise for making an effort, and the other is blame for not making an effort. In Example 1 below, effort-making is described as if it is one's natural duty as a human.

Example 1: Katsuji Futagoyama (sumo; 1928–):

I think that when one is born as a human, fortunately or unfortunately, one has no choice but to keep making painful effort until one's death. (1978: 70)

A respectable person is respectable not because of this person's success but because of the work (*kurō*) and effort he/she has dedicated on his/her way to success. (1978: 225)

The emphasis on effort as a means is correlated to the notion of equal ability and the deterministic view of the role of effort in achieving results that are often claimed to exist in Japanese society (Takeuchi 1978, 1995; Miyajima 1999; Saitō and Yamagishi 2000). Example 2 is the simplest of such expressions.

Example 2: Kiyoshi Nakamura (track and field; 1913–1985):

Genius is limited, effort is unlimited. (Kimura 1984: 165)

Example 3: Yasuo Yoshida (table tennis; 1933–):

Concentrate on daily coaching, believing that a difference of ability is small but a difference of effort is great. (2000: 237)

Some statements suggest the view that everyone is blessed equally with not only innate abilities but also luck, or that even luck is determined by the level of effort, as Example 4 shows. Though this is not the place to engage in historical arguments in detail, these views regarding luck have some association with the notion of the predetermined harmony of the universe, as some historians find in Japanese society.[9]

Example 4: Yoshio Koide (track and field; 1939–):

> There is no such thing as accidental good luck, like pennies from heaven. (2000: 127)

> Your luck improves as you make untiring efforts or endure hardships. (2000: 129)

Thus, in extreme cases, the emphasis on the value of effort can lead to strict 'effort determinism' which concludes that any result or achievement is a necessary corollary of one's effort. A case in point is Example 5, which argues that effort always ought to produce good results, otherwise the effort 'cannot be' effort 'by definition.' It is important to note that Sadaharu Oh, who has expressed this view, has been the most popular and influential athlete to be widely recognized as a 'role model' in post-war Japanese society.

Example 5: Sadaharu Oh[10] (baseball; 1940–):

> Some know-alls may say coldly, "Sometimes one's efforts bear no fruit." Is it really so? Do one's efforts go unrewarded in some cases? Even if one's efforts did not produce the desired result, the very act of having made effort should always be beneficial in some ways. If they did not produce any benefit at all, one cannot call them effort. (2000: 102)

Deviating patterns and their convergence

There are of course some deviations that challenge the fervent emphasis on effort. Example 6 contains criticisms of an overemphasis on effort.

Example 6: Yasutaka Matsudaira (volleyball; 1930–):

> I think it is wrong to jump to the conclusion that someone has failed because he/she was stupid...or did not make enough effort, without having any consideration for his/her talents or gifts. (1972: 54)

> Effort is the most valuable human act. As Mr [Hirobumi] Daimatsu said, "Where there is a will, there is a way (*naseba naru*)" is an appealing slogan. It is perfect when you are running for a seat in the senate. It is certainly good if everyone comes to believe in this can-do

spirit. But I must say that reality is different. Some things are not that easy in the real world. Truth is, the goal of becoming the best in the world can be achieved only by geniuses who have made desperate efforts. (1972: 83)

In this example, Matsudaira attacks the simple glorification of the value of effort but does not deny the principle of effort-making completely. While he points out that effort is not omnipotent, he states that 'desperate efforts' are needed in the end. Although he may question the excessive emphasis on effort as an end, he must admit the value and need of effort as a means in trying to attain certain goals in the world of sports. As long as there is no clear conceptual distinction between the value of effort as a means and the value of effort as an end, criticisms such as Matsudaira's are insufficient to undermine the pattern of emphasis on effort.

Example 7 below is a quote from another book written by Matsudaira (1977). It reveals that the mechanisms of the concept of effort to elude criticism function within his discourse. In this quote, Matsudaira professes his agreement with Sadaharu Oh, who expresses his deterministic theory of effort in Example 5. Even though the main concept here is 'concentration,' his shift toward de-emphasizing differences in ability and emphasizing effort is quite obvious in comparison with Example 6. This does not constitute a change in his values over time, but is due to the nature of the pattern of emphasizing effort to fuse approval and disapproval for it and thus effectively negate the latter.

Example 7: Yasutaka Matsudaira (volleyball; 1930–):

Concentration is everything, I totally agree [with what Oh says]. Human ability is not so different between individuals. Human strength is not so different between individuals to start with. The most important question is how much one devotes one's ability or energy to a particular work or a particular moment... If one has doubts about one's own ability, try concentrating all one's energy, knowledge and experience upon a single matter. (1977: 191–2)

Example 8 is another of the deviating patterns. Shinkō is an exceptional author in this context because he is what we call a common hero or antihero, known as a wrestler who has taken the longest time in the history of sumo to enter the senior-grade division. His autobiography emphasizes repeatedly that his talent is inferior to other wrestlers.

Example 8: Katsunori Shinkō (sumo; 1950–):

> Unfortunately, part of one's talent or aptitude is something one is born with and no amount of effort can compensate for lack of it. It is unreasonable to even make a comparison... No matter what society one lives in, it is best to know one's own ability, make the utmost effort and make steady progress. (1984: 115–16)

In this example, he first objects to the overemphasis on effort and states the importance of 'talent' and 'aptitude' as determinants of results. In the second half of his statement, however, he argues that the most important thing to do for someone with scant 'talent' or 'aptitude' is to 'make the utmost effort' after all. A tacit message underlying his comment signifies that one should continue making a single-minded 'effort' in one's own role without making comparisons with others. It is possible to surmise a connection to the notion of '*bun/bu*' (the notion that each person has an appropriate role or place which is given to him/her and that he/she must accept) which is also pervasive in Japanese society.

Although space does not permit me to go into details here, there are various mechanisms other than the invocation of the notion of '*bun/bu*' that emphasize the importance of effort while simultaneously recognizing some substantial significance of innate ability. One example is the 'quantitative' de-emphasizing of the ability factor. This perspective argues that there certainly are 'geniuses' but their number is so small that it is not necessary to take them into account.

Example 9: Masayo Imura (swimming; 1950–):

> People tend to think that Olympic athletes are all special people but this is not the case. Certainly there are some gifted people who can only be described as geniuses. However, a majority are not so. They are ordinary people who have made a single-minded effort in order to achieve their dreams. (2001: 58)

While admitting differences in innate ability, such a statement is able to more effectively narrow the focus on effort in practice than can a simple belief in the uniformity of human ability because it excludes the existence of 'geniuses,' who cannot be beaten by any level of effort, from our recognition as irrelevant to 'us' or 'ordinary people as majority.'

Of all manners of cognitive reduction of ability and genius, usage of the somewhat paradoxical expressions, 'the talent to make an effort' or 'a genius for making an effort,' is particularly interesting.

Example 10: Sachio Kinugasa (baseball; 1947–):

> People often talk about professional baseball players as "talented" or "not talented." I think a crucial talent is the "love of training." Big stars like Mr [Sadaharu] Oh, Mr [Shigeo] Nagashima, Mr [Shōichi] Kaneda and Mr [Yutaka] Enatsu have enormous talent. One common talent among all this talent they have is their love of training. (1985: 191)

It is obvious that this statement has reduced the significance of various other talents for the result to a single attribute called the 'love of training' by regarding the 'love of training' as a 'talent' and declaring it to be the most important one. The next example uses a similar pattern of discourse.

Example 11: Takeshi Nakamura (baseball; 1943–):

> Ichirō, called a revolutionary baseball player and now enjoying immense popularity, is described as a genius by many people. However, he is not a genius. I believe he has made achievements by busting his guts and making twice or three times more effort than others behind the scenes... It was his effort that made Ichirō a baseball genius. (2001: 64)
>
> Being able to keep making effort until results are achieved is one type of talent. (2001: 83)

Takeshi Nakamura was Ichirō's high school baseball coach. In Examples 10 and 11, the "geniuses" such as Oh, Nagashima and Ichirō are interpreted by their acquaintances as examples that demonstrate the importance of effort. I have argued that the conceptual structures of such stories converge on an emphasis on effort. The layers of interpretations by surrounding people reinforce the pattern in terms of its social plausibility. In these processes, the emphasis on effort is firmly established as a socially dominant pattern that hardly depends on any individual opinion.

Emphasis on effort as a culture of inequality

This pattern of emphasizing effort leads to disregard for the differences in physical and social conditions by transmitting messages such as 'external conditions do not determine results' or 'only effort can influence results.' Examples 12 and 13 below even manage to transform values by turning disadvantages into 'advantages.'

Example 12: Hironoshin Furuhashi (swimming; 1928–):

> I also feel that people tend to achieve greatness in everything when burdened with some adverse conditions rather than blessed with favorable conditions. I was left with a handicap when the middle finger of my left hand was severed at the first joint at a factory in my junior high school days... After the Second World War, my mother died as soon as I joined the swimming club and it became very difficult to make a living... However, these adversities make people stronger. They provide incentives to do better. In my case, I kept reminding myself when I was swimming that I had to think smarter and work harder than the others because I had these handicaps. I believe this extra effort has resulted in my world record and got me to where I am today. (1997: 185–6)

Example 13: Seiko Hashimoto (skating; 1964–):

> For myself, it was "because of my [lack of] height, I understand the value of effort". If I was blessed with a better physique, I would not have trained as hard as I did... A handicap is a handicap for those who don't do anything about it, but it works in favor of those who make efforts to overcome it. (1994: 206–7)

Based on this value pattern, the success or failure of the individual is solely the result of his/her individual effort and is therefore his/her individual responsibility regardless of his/her physical or social conditions. Someone who has failed is not allowed to use his/her disadvantage as an excuse for his/her failure and can even be considered to be morally 'bad' in light of the value placed upon effort as an end.

This emphasis on effort as a value pattern is functionally similar to the 'individual-as-central sensibility' Michael Lewis (1978) has identified in American society, which perpetuates a 'culture of inequality'. This is a value pattern, typically symbolized by the idea of the 'American dream,' which attributes success and failure entirely to the individual and denies the need to question issues of social inequality. I do not know how pervasive this sensibility actually is in American society. Besides, the American case presented by Lewis and that of Japanese sports books are different in many respects in terms of notions of innate ability and social mobility. However, it is safe to say that the emphasis on effort discussed so far forms the Japanese version of the 'culture of inequality' if we focus on its function as a value pattern and the cognitive attitudes toward social inequality that it can provide.

As mentioned earlier, sports books are written and read for purposes associated with study, education, work (management in particular) or life in general, and the discourses presented in sports books assume that the value of effort is applicable not only to sports but to various other spheres of life in general. It seems that sports books, which are produced and consumed in large quantities and form a major medium in contemporary Japanese society, play a considerable role in forming and maintaining a 'culture of inequality' in society by supplying discourses that repeatedly emphasize the value of effort as a principle that is applicable to life in general.

Sports books and the reproduction of value patterns

In this section, I demonstrate that the characteristic of sports books as a medium, a factor external to the semantic structure of the value pattern, contributes to the reproduction of the emphasis on effort as a dominant value pattern.

The emphasis on effort is very notable in sports books, but it is not universally the case for the values of contemporary Japanese people. There is a certain social selection process in relation to sports books. In other words, discourses in sports books reflect only a particular segment of the experiences of people. The generalization of this value pattern made through sports books, therefore, involves disregarding the diversity of people's experiences.

First, the differences between the experiences in sports activities and ones in other fields of society tend to be ignored, as I have already mentioned. This is important with regard to the issue of inequality because sports are special activities that demand and provide equality and fairness as basic initial conditions. As far as effort is concerned, sports activities are designed in such a way that individual effort has a high degree of relevancy to the result, as Caillois (1990) argues.

This includes not only controlling the conditions for a competition but also pre-selection and grading of participants to the extent that the competition can be realized as a sport. Many competitions are divided into different classes according to the age, weight or disability of the participants, or grouped into different leagues based on past performance. Dividing competitions into men's and women's is one example of such grouping. Example 14 is a case of professional sport leagues.

Example 14: Tetsuharu Kawakami (baseball; 1920–):

> Players who can manage to join the professional league have talents. Some of them fail to capitalize on their talents for various reasons such as lack of training or dedication and injuries. Even though they are all talented, I believe that the difference between greatness and mediocrity is, in one word, dedication (*shōjin*). (1992: 198)

While this example highlights effort by using the word 'dedication' and de-emphasizes talent as a determinant with regard to a special group of athletes who have gone through a selection process for participation in a professional sport, the peculiarity of the conditions for such an experience tends to be ignored by both the author and the reader when the value of effort is put forward as a general principle.

Second, it is not difficult to recognize that a majority of discourses presented in sports books are based on the experiences of elite athletes. Conversely, unsuccessful people are rarely given the opportunity to make a social statement. In fact, their past 'successes' themselves have the effect of enhancing the credibility of their success stories. Since sports are commonly characterized as physical activities, any insights gained in sports are considered 'natural' and tend to be understood as something definitive and universal by those who experience them as well as those who hear about them.

Third, the experience of success tends to be highlighted more strongly than the experience of failure in the discourses of successful individuals. Furthermore, the experience of success gives some meaning to the experience of failure and even glorifies it by doing so. In the case of successful individuals, the experience of failure can be interpreted or presented either as an episode to highlight their triumphant success in the end or as a necessary process for their subsequent success, thus reducing or nullifying the frustrating aspects of the experience of failure.

We must also remember that only discourses suitable for public release are published as sports books. As a striking example, investigative reporter Hiroshi Suzuki makes the following comment in his book about the 'real picture' of Sadaharu Oh who, as we saw in Example 5, is an advocate of effort determinism.

> It is true that Oh has practiced his batting more than others but he also admits, in his private opinion, "Ninety percent of my success as a home run hitter was due to my talent." However, he only continues to tell

people, "Effort is important," out of a genuine concern so typical of him that young, less talented players may stop making effort if he says so openly. (Suzuki 2003: 107–8)

If not to disseminate the importance of effort directly to society, discourses for publication may be chosen from a marketing point of view in order to satisfy the need of readers who wish to confirm the importance of effort and thus find a source of encouragement. In some cases, this may be instigated by the editor or the publisher rather than the athlete. In addition, consideration is given to its compatibility with socially dominant values when an author or theme of a book is selected for publication.

Seen in this light, the emphasis placed on effort by sports books is neither incidental nor a mere reflection of facts, but rather the result of a process of social selection during which these sports books are passed through many filters. By concealing this selection process, the emphasis on effort as a 'culture of inequality' continues to be reproduced as a socially dominant value pattern.[11]

Pragmatic reasons for the culture of inequality

The strong emphasis on effort found in sports books highlights only a specific aspect of human experience, ignores physical and social inequalities, and leads people to the understanding that all significant determinants of the result are attributable to the individual. To put it plainly, this is a misrepresentation of the facts. Nevertheless, it seems that the emphasis on effort and the de-emphasis on inequality cannot be brushed off as simply fallacious: discourses based on these value patterns are 'reasonable' to the extent that they effectively provide powerful incentives for the pursuit of certain goals.

When a certain role behavior is assumed as given, one can manage cognitive and behavioral energy for achievement of results within the role more effectively if one ignores 'unchangeable' conditions and concentrates on 'changeable' factors. While the degree of factual suppression involved in the operation of such value patterns is inversely proportional to the attainability of the goal sought in the role behavior, the choice between a total commitment to it and an attempt to address inequality of conditions relating to the role should be left to the decision of the individual, as long as the possibility of achieving that goal is more than zero. In other words, the emphasis on effort and the corresponding de-emphasis on inequality have pragmatic reasons that cannot be rejected per se. If the recognition of effort is practically required as an incentive for individual behavior is represented as objective facts or employed for forcibly imposing certain role behaviors, it exerts oppressive and ideological effects that serve to conceal social inequalities.

In conclusion, the emphasis on effort as a value pattern is founded on factual grounds in terms of the value of effort as a means on the one hand; on the other hand, it also has psychological reasons for goal-oriented behavior. In fact, this value pattern seems to provide a work ethic as a kind of 'capitalist spirit.' This insight makes it possible to infer that the emphasis on effort and the corresponding de-emphasis on inequality will not be easily overcome. At the same time, these patterns are not immune to change either. While Saitō and Yamagishi (2000) argue that social relationships must be dense enough to allow people to observe and evaluate each other's behavioral processes in order for the value of effort as an end to be socially sanctioned and maintained, increasing social mobility in contemporary Japan is cutting through such social relationships. The future of the value pattern now dominating Japanese society is indeed a very interesting problem.

Clear from its similarity with the American pattern of individual-as-central sensibility discussed earlier, the fact that the pattern of emphasizing effort has rational grounds in relation to goal-oriented behavior and has compatibility or selective affinity with capitalist economic behavior suggests the possibility that similar patterns can be found in contemporary societies other than Japan and America. For the problem of work ethic as well as various other problems the social function that the discourses of athletes or sports books serve in each society is an important topic. Sports are highly internationalized activities. Comparative studies of the discourses of athletes and sports books from various countries would prove fruitful. This study is intended as an initial step toward such a comparative study.

Glossary

bun/bu 分
doryoku 努力
kurō 苦労
naseba naru 成せば成る
renshu 練習
shōjin 精進
shugyō 修行、修業
tanren 鍛錬

Part II: China, Taiwan and Korea

4 Kinship Organizations and Social Stratification in Late Imperial China: A Study based on Lineage in the Pearl River Delta

Yukihiro Kawaguchi

Introduction

The objective of this paper is to examine the formation of kinship organizations and their relationships with the social class structure within and outside village societies in Late Imperial China.[1] I will base this analysis on one of the lineages in the Pearl River Delta in Guangdong Province.

Many anthropologists have already looked at and discussed the social roles of patrilineal kinship organizations and their places in relation to the class structure of the society (Freedman 1958, 1966; Baker 1968; Potter 1968; Pasternak 1972; Watson 1985). Nevertheless, it is worth revisiting the topic in this paper for several reasons.

First, this paper re-examines the intermediary role that lineages had come to perform between the imperial state and the village societies through the people's adoption of the people of the culture authorized by the imperial administration. Lineages in China were especially prevalent and extensive in the southeastern provinces of Fujian and Guangdong. Anthropologists have thus far been of the view that lineage was an apparatus used by those who had acquired power in the frontier to strengthen their positions over other competitors in the development race and, at the same time, to maintain and expand their political and economic interests within their villages (Freedman 1958, 1966: Watson 1985). Their research started as an attempt to apply the lineage theory constructed in Africa to research in China, a far more complex society. Therefore, anthropologists have tried to find a factor—here, the environment as peculiar to frontier regions—that affect the growth of lineages as corporate organizations in China. Their discussion has assumed that whether a kinship organization rises or falls in a given situation is self-evident, determined by the crucial factor. Conversely, sufficient attention has never been paid to the reasons why genealogy was chosen as the means to build social connections that, as a result, brought about the prevalence of highly formalized lineages (*zongzu*).[2] In other words, the researchers have overlooked that a lineage is a cultural form that should be examined in its relationship to the state. This paper reveals that genealogy did not only connect contemporary members but also offered the means by which these people are linked simultaneously to both the past and the state, by taking advantage of the tremendous progress in research achieved by historians since the 1980s (Faure 1986, 1989; Liu 1999; Inoue 2000, 2002, 2004a, 2004b; Ke and Liu 2000; Katayama 2004).

Second, this paper reveals how lineage organizations stood in relation to the social class structure within the lineages themselves as well as in relation to the social stratification both within and without of village societies. Researchers who introduced the segmentary lineage model to China have discussed the mechanism of segmentation within a lineage at great length, but have never specifically examined how lineages were related to the hierarchy of community residents, villages and different ethnic groups. This paper will look at the central Pearl River Delta, where the available data allows us to examine the correlation between formation of lineages and regional development in detail. By diachronically following the dynamics of the correlation, I establish the link between lineages and the political, economic and ethnic strata of a regional society.

China's so-called 'tradition' was established between the fifteenth and sixteenth century. Ever since this time it has exerted considerable influence on systems of thought and practice throughout East Asia. Although the lineage in southeastern China was merely a specific example of Chinese kinship organizations, it is significant in considering kinship and social strata in East Asia in general. This paper thus offers an interesting comparison to Kamizuru's discussion of Taiwan and Honda's discussion of South Korea in this volume (chapters 5 and 6 respectively).

Pearl River Delta and the lineages

Lineages are patrilineal descent organizations. In southeastern China, their corporate nature was remarkably strong. The members of a lineage owned properties jointly, compiled genealogies recording the history of their lineage along with biographical information on each of its members, and performed ancestor worship rites together. Lineages were particularly large and powerful in the Pearl River Delta in Guangdong. The dominant lineage in each village had a 2000 to 3000-strong membership, owned hundreds of hectares of land, built grand ancestral halls enshrining memorial tablets for the dead and performed ancestor worship.

Lineages in the Pearl River Delta had become quite large and highly corporate in a context closely related to the regional development of the times. The Pearl River Delta was on the fringe of the empire and was first settled in approximately the fourteenth century, when the land was formed in the lower course of the river with accumulated mud and sand carried by the water. To survive the fierce competition in the frontier environment, people needed to form organizations and join forces. At the same time, the empire was in need of a system to establish its rule over the frontier, where the population and farm lands were increasing at explosive rates. Lineages were products of the motives of the influential people in the area on the one hand and the empire on the other. The former wanted to establish and expand their power in the frontier during a period of bustling development, while the latter wanted to effectively rule its fringe territory effectively. The two parties thus found a common ground for mutual recognition in the genealogies that represented the essence of the Chinese culture. By the end of the nineteenth century, lineages had become a device to maintain the social system of Late Imperial China, having a close connection with its political, economic and ethnic hierarchy.

In the following sections, I describe how kinship organizations were connected to social hierarchy in China by looking at the Chen lineage in Panyu County, located in central Peal River Delta.

Development in the area

The Pearl River flows across central Guangdong. At the middle and lower reaches of the river and its tributaries are vast low sea-level wetlands, some of which were formed by depositions carried by the river and others that were man-made. In Guangdong these lands are called *satin*. The Pearl River has been slowly building its delta since the New Stone Age, while reclamation work became active in the late eleventh century. In the eighteenth century, a technology was developed to reclaim a shoal where sedimentation had yet to reach the advanced stage and spread. After this time, the scale and speed of the creation of *satin* increased dramatically (Nishikawa 1981: 95–6).

Increased land area corresponded to population growth. Early settlers built their houses and lived on the higher ground of plateaus and hills while reclaiming marshes in the low-lying surrounding area. As the reclaimed land extended south, the population spread in that direction. Those who reached the end of the frontier assumed the task of developing the next frontier. Thus the Pearl River Delta constantly expanded.

Today, the more southward we walk along the lower Pearl River, the further and wider we find the low-altitude wetlands stretch. These *satin*, which had not been reclaimed from water for long, were not populated before the mid twentieth century. Therefore, no village had been formed. Conversely, in the northern part of the delta, where people first settled, villages are believed to have been formed as early as the twelfth century, and the residents of these villages share a common history in that their ancestors migrated from the north around that time. As establishing the time of settlement and founding of a village depends largely on the history narrated by descendants in later ages, it is not necessarily accurate. However, it can be assumed without doubt that the people who reached the delta first settled in the northern hills and advanced southward developing the lower altitude wetlands.

Panyu is located at the approximate centre of the Pearl River Delta. Most of the area that is land today was formed in the twelfth century or later. Before the Song Period, in other words until the eighth century, two-thirds of present-day Panyu was submerged in shallow water dotted with islands. The area that had already been reclaimed was the hills called Shiqiao plateau in the northwestern part of the country. The plateau was blessed not only geologically with sandy mud-based soil rich in nutrients but also topographically with subsided flat hills offering a good water supply. The plateau was rarely subjected to typhoons or floods. As the local saying *Men do gêu gou feo* (People live on elevated hills) goes, those who migrated there at the time are believed to have first settled on the knolls protruding one to two meters out from the plain (Panyushi difangzhi bianzuan weiyuanhui bangongshi 1996: 20).

According to the accepted history today, the Han people first settled in Panyu in 420 CE (in the Dongjin Period). The history also says that the first Han to settle here was the forefather of the Chen lineage of S Village, and that he chose to live where H Village was to be formed near the centre of the plateau. More villages soon followed in the

Figure 4.1: Land formation of Panyu, based on /Panyu county gazetteer/ (Panyushi difangzhi bangongshi, 1995:279) with partial modifications

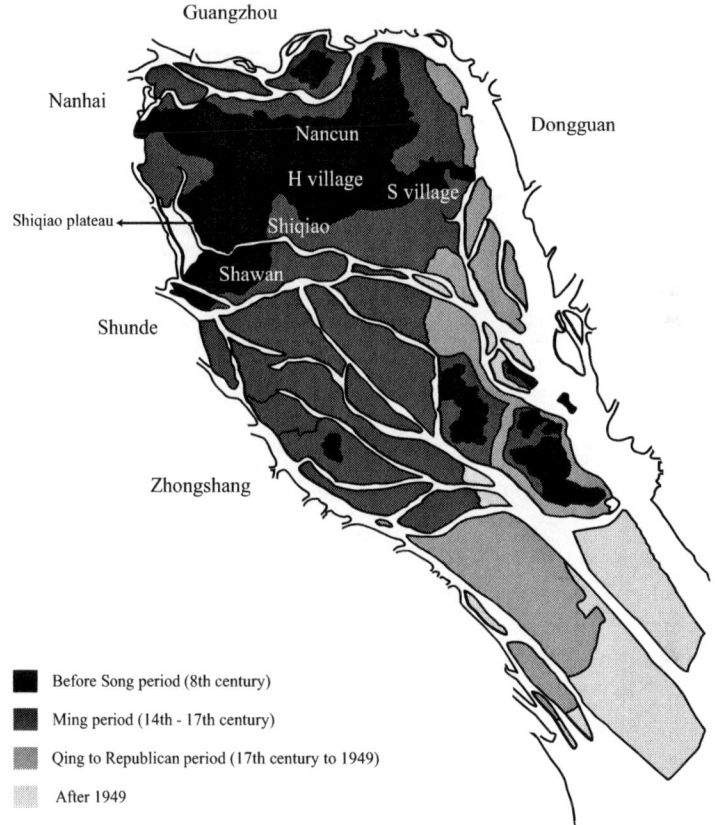

area that surrounded H Village. Most of these villages were probably founded by the tenth century. Many villages in the rest of Panyu were presumably formed in the twelfth century, when the Shiqiao plateau had been populated for two or three centuries. There is no doubt that the development of the area began from the plateau and hills and gradually spread to the surrounding low-lying land. The people who arrived at the southern region when alluvial land was limited and irrigation technology was undeveloped first made their home on the plateau and took the topographical advantage of turning the surrounding vast area of low-lying wetlands and shoals into farmland.

Later in the history, alluvium advanced and increased the land area leading to a greater population influx. The late-comers developed the outer edge of the Shiqiao plateau closer to the coastline and settled there. As shown in Figure 4.1, the centre of development constantly advanced southward. In the twelfth century, or after the Song Period, the spearhead of development had reached the southeastern and southwestern parts of the plateau, where S Village and Shawan are located. In the outer and lower-lying edges of the plateau, villages are mostly believed to have been founded from the Song Period in the eleventh to twelfth century or in the Ming period in the fourteenth century at the latest. To the south of these villages today, there lie vast plains of *satin*, which are even closer to sea level. The sight is a reminder that there was little dry land but an expanse of shallow water when people arrived and that the new settlers shouldered the task of reclaiming it.

In the southeastern part of the Shiqiao plateau, where S Village is located, most of the villages are said to have been founded from the twelfth to the thirteenth century, when alluvium was rapidly in progress but only beginning to form land there. S Village then sat on an island in the sea, which was called Sai Mong Gong or 'a hill to dry fishing nets on.' To the east of S Village is a peak called Lianhuashan, 105 meters above sea level. Although it is a popular tourist attraction today, it was once merely an island in the sea (Panyushi difangzhi bianzuan weiyuanhui bangongshi 1996: 9). In 1375 (under the reign of Hongwu in the Ming Period), the Guangzhou *weisuo* was established. It set up 'nine settlements (Jiutun)' in Panyu and sent 112 families to each settlement. Each family was allocated twenty *mu* (1.3 hectares) of land. Altogether 1008 families received 201 *xiang* and sixty *mu* (1344 hectares) (Zhu 1986: 30–1). The then government encouraged cultivation with the incentive of such a large piece of land. This fact indicates that S Village and its vicinities were still the very verge of the frontier and sparsely populated, despite the rapid increase of the alluvium.

New migrants to and around S Village followed in the footsteps of the early pioneers who had settled in the Shiqiao plateau. They made their homes on the higher ground, which had become land earlier, and vigorously began reclaiming the shoals to the south and the coastal areas to the east at the mouth of the Pearl River. After this time, large-scale reclamation works never ceased in the vast area to the southeast of S Village at the estuaries of the Pearl River tributaries. All the *satins* which we see expanding over the sea surface today were the result of reclamation. During the course of development of the frontier and the establishment of local communities, there emerged people who were gradually gathering strength. They were also active in forming the lineage organizations. These people and their lineage organizations played the decisive roles in establishing societal forms on the newly-opened lands.

Formation of the Chen lineage of S Village

First, I discuss the process in which the Chen lineage of S Village was formed, drawing upon written materials including editions of their genealogy and gazetteers as well as from their oral traditions. As far as the genealogy tells us, the first action of some effect taken by the Chens of S Village as a lineage was the compilation of their genealogy in 1415. Its preface is found re-recorded in the last edition of their genealogy compiled in 1885. It states 'The first person who settled and therefore founded the family was Ping, who became the founding ancestor of the Chens of S Village.' Following the passage, the preface goes on to urge members to have respect for the lineage and emphasizes the importance of keeping genealogical records.

The second edition of their genealogy was compiled in 1509, almost 100 years later. Its preface also preaches the respect for the descent and continues. 'If the origin of the descent is considered, it was Ping, who was the first generation ancestor to settle here.' The prefaces to the two editions of the genealogy both stress the two points; the importance of genealogical descent is emphasized and the first generation Ping is named as the founder of the Chen lineage of S Village. The main aims behind the compilation of the genealogy were to identify the founder of the lineage in the village and to present explicitly the history of the Chens living in S Village since their settlement. Following the compilation of the genealogy, the Chens built their first ancestral hall during the reign of Zhengde (1506–1521) in the Ming Period. The hall was named after the sixth generation forefather called Xingseitong. According to the genealogy compiled in 1885, the Xingseitong underwent extensive repairs from 1669 to 1683 (during the reign of Kangxi in the Qing) to take the shape almost the same as it appeared during the late nineteenth and the early twentieth centuries. The hall occupies an area as large as 2472 square meters. Its interior is covered with elaborate ornaments and carvings. In terms of both size and elegance, Xingseitong is unquestionably one of the most outstanding ancestral halls in the Pearl River Delta, where many large halls were built. It was later selected as one of the four greatest halls in Panyu (*Punyü séidaiqi*).

Hence, we can see that during the fifteenth and sixteenth centuries, the Chens were organizing a lineage at the village level. Forefathers of the founder of Chen lineage in S village were not mentioned in either the 1415 edition or the 1509 genealogy. In the seventeenth century, however, the Chens began to trace their genealogy beyond the village level. The preface to the third edition of their genealogy compiled in 1611 includes a description of the history of the Chens before Ping:

> Our founding father, General Chen Yuande, was originally from Fuqiang in the city of Gongchang, Shanxi Province. During his service to three emperors of the Dongjin, he made a distinguished contribution to defeating the rebel army of Sun En, in recognition of which he was awarded the generalship. Chen Yuande opposed Commander Liu Yu (who took over control in the court). When Liu Yu captured the throne, the general fled to Panyu, Guangdong Province, where he lived in hiding with his two sons, Liang and Gao.
>
> Ping, a twenty-second generation descendant, settled in S Village. By making great achievements and building virtues, he benefited his descendants with his schemes. Ping's line has continued to the fifteenth generation to this day.

Thus, according to this genealogy, the founder of the Chens of S Village, Chen Ping, was a twenty-second generation descendant of the Dongjin's military commander, Chen Yuande. The Dongjin was a period in the fifth century. Chen Yuande fled the capital and settled in H Village on the Shiqiao plateau, which is believed to be the first area in Panyu settled by the Han people. The 1611 genealogy reveals the history of the Chens, which is accepted today and which concords with the official history of Panyu County.

The genealogy also records an action taken by the Chens a few decades before the edition was compiled. In 1569, they went through the necessary formalities to be the official owners of the grave of Chen Yuande:

> Six *li* to the northeast of H Village and two to the southwest of C Village, there is a level round plate-shaped piece of land surrounded by cultivated fields. General Chen Yuande was buried there and later a tree was planted. In the third year of the reign of Longqing (1569) in the Ming Period, a man called Xie Shaotang, who lived in Shiqiao,

tried to make the land his own and pulled out the tree, in the belief that the grave had been left unclaimed. With the authority of our genealogy, we remonstrated with him that the grave belonged to our ancestor. Xie returned it to us and later sold us an adjoining land of two *mu* and four *fen* (sixteen acres). In the sixth year of the reign of Longqing (1572), the land became ours.

Almost concurrently, in the years of the reign of Wanli (1573–1619) in the Ming Dynasty, the elite gentry of the Chen lineage of S Village played a central role in building a hall dedicated to Chen Yuande. In 1674, the Chens of S Village took the initiative in funding and carrying out extensive repair work on the hall.

To sum up, the Chen lineage of S Village started to take the shape of a lineage at the village level in the last half of the fifteenth century. In the last half of the sixteenth century and the early seventeenth century, when they discovered a genealogical link that traced further back from their village founder, the Chens of S village set out to organize a higher-order lineage holding the first generation forefather of the Chen lineage of H Village as its origin.

The Chen descendants of S Village formed a lineage to achieve what was required in the context of the frontier environment of the Peal River Delta at the time, namely, to form an organization for mobilizing strength, to present a legitimate descent as the Han people with a long history of settlement in the area, and to adopt and practice the cultural norms authorized by the imperial government. In the following sections, we will examine each of these factors in this order.

Rise of gentry elite and the need to collectivize

The Chens began to establish a lineage when waves of new migrants were arriving at the Pearl River Delta and vigorously reclaiming land. One of the reasons for forming a lineage is found in the situation faced by those on the frontier. They needed to form an organization and mobilize their collective strength to survive the development competition.

The development of the Pearl River Delta was a process of reclaiming the river system and shallow sea that did not clearly belong to anyone. It entailed fierce competitions over the right to reclaim the land and the ownership of the newly-formed land. Inevitably, influential people with government connections exploited the advantage in the development competition (Sasaki 1959: 171–2). From the mid-Ming Period, the gentry accelerated their development and seizure of *satins* through use of force. In such circumstances, petty farmers, who feared that the land they had reclaimed could be seized by the powerful, often chose to hand-over the ownership of the land they reclaimed to the powerful in exchange for protection and assurance to continue to cultivate the land (Matsuda 1981: 59–60). This is how a gentry with political and economic powers rose at the forefront of development, where new migrants competed for resources. Once they had established a certain foundation in the competition, the powerful people seized more resources by enclosing the lands of smaller operators and squeezing them out.

Let's take a look at S Village and its vicinities again. A different narrative tradition says S Village had been populated by the Guans, Zhengs, Zhus, Zhangs, Gaos, Mas, Cais and Qins as well as the Chens of another descent when the ancestor of our Chens arrived at the village in the Southern Song period in the twelfth century. Our Chens were late comers. At the time, the vicinities of S Village were the very forefront of *satin* development and there were already powerful lineage organizations formed by others. Approximately one and a half kilometers to the northwest of S Village lay D Village. The dominant residents of D Village shared the same family name Chen, but their lineage had no genealogical relationship with that in S Village. According to their genealogy and gazetteers, the Chen lineage of D Village produced a successful *juren* in the civil service examination as early as in the second year of the reign of Hongzhi (1489) in the Ming dynasty, a *jinshi* in 1508, and another *juren* in 1525. It was not until 1543 that the Chen lineage of S Village produced their first *juren*, falling half a century behind the Chen lineage of D Village in the civil service examination competition. The Chen lineage of S Village had to wait until 1880 to see one of their members become a *jinshi*. In the early sixteenth century, the Chen lineage of D Village had already reproduced civil service degree holders and acquired a powerful influence in the local community, where *satin* development was coming into stride.

At the time, the Chens were new-comers in S Village. They faced formidable rivals in the competition for development around the village. As a late starter, the Chens needed to establish as an organization as soon as possible to enter the competition. It was at this time that the Chens began to produce members who succeeded in the civil service examination and became elite government officials. It was generally a few generations down from the founder when a family had achieved such prosperity that it began working towards the formation of a lineage. In Hong Kong's New Territories, for example, prominent families were often prompted to compile their genealogy on such occasions as a member's success in the civil service examination (Segawa 1996: 30). Successful in the exam and with their power on the rise at a time of development competition, the elite members of the Chens embarked upon organizing themselves into a lineage to pursue demesne and reproduce more elite members.

The first member of the Chen lineage of S Village to be successful in the civil service examination was a ninth generation called Chen Linde. Born in 1392, he lived his life in the first half of the fifteenth century. He passed the county examination and became a *shengyuan*. He was awarded the degree of *lingsheng*[3] which honored the most excellent among his peers. The first genealogy of the Chen lineage of S Village was reportedly compiled by him in 1415.

The first member of the Chen lineage of S Village to become a government official was Chen Dayou. He passed the government examination to qualify as a *juren* in 1543 and was appointed as the governor of Xianyou County, Fujian. He later achieved distinguished exploits, leading an army to defeat the Japanese pirates invading the county under his charge. His services were highly praised in many records, including the *Guangdong fuzhi*, *Panyu xianzhi* and *Fujian dongzhi*. It was also Chen Dayou who led the construction of the Chens' ancestral hall, Xinseitong, and another hall dedicated to the first generation Chen of H Village. He not only passed the civil service examination and took on a government post but also left his mark on local history. This outstanding elite member played a vital role in establishing the lineage of the Chens in S Village.

In the fifteenth and early sixteenth centuries, the Chen lineage of S Village produced a succession of bureaucrats and other prosperous men. Having established the lineage, they maintained and expanded their power and were ready for further exploits. This was evident in the fact that the Chen lineage of S Village named its own first ancestral hall after the sixth generation Chen Daoming. Chen Dayou and almost all others who passed the civil service examination to hold government offices descended from this sixth generation Chen Daoming. The descendants in his line formed five segments with the descendants at the ninth generation level as the focal points and became the main force in the Chen lineage of S Village. Conversely, as Figure 4.2 shows, some lines became stagnant and others left the village. To win further development competitions, the weak within the organization had to

Figure 4.2: Genealogical chart of Chen lineage of S village

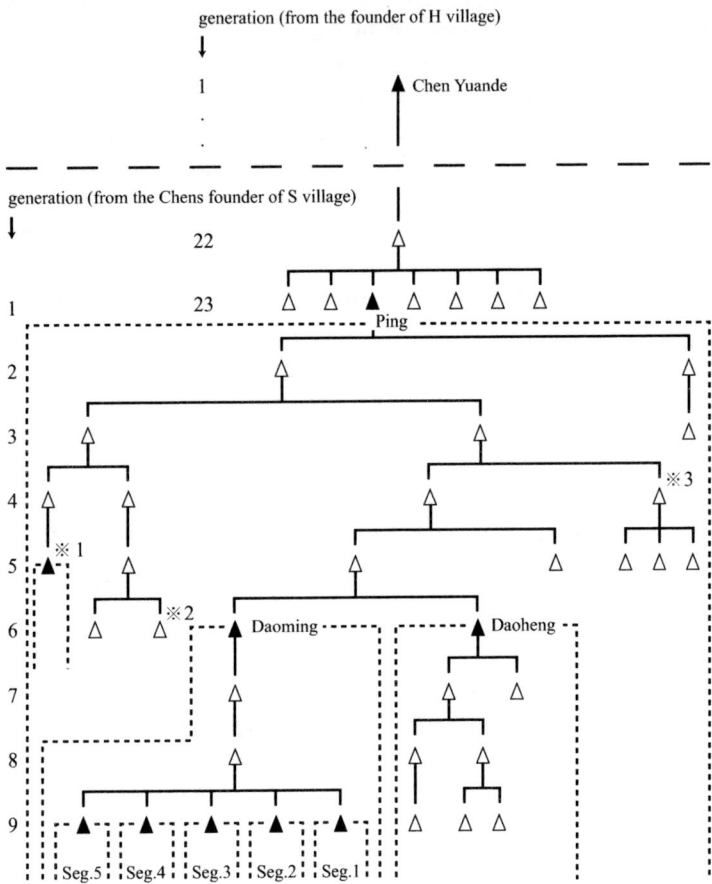

▲   The founder or the focal ancestor of the segment
----   Boundary of the segment
※ 1   Gone to C village (next village to S village)
※ 2   Gone to Zengcheng (northeast of Guangzhou)
※ 3   Gone to Sizhou (Anhui province)

be forsaken, while the powerful needed to join forces and concentrate resources among themselves. In this respect, the genealogical position held by Chen Daoming was extremely crucial.

After the segments were formed, the Chen lineage of S Village transferred the ownership of nearly all of the land they acquired to the name of the Xinseitong to ensure that the descendants from the sixth generation Chen Daoming could continue to monopolize the profits generated from that corporately owned land. Although membership of the Chen lineage of S Village was given to all descendants from the founding ancestor in the genealogy, the membership of the lineage as a political and economic organization became exclusive to those who descended from Chen Daoming after the segmentation. By forming a segment with Chen Daoming as the focal point, his powerful descendants succeeded in consolidating their power and excluding members of other lines from sharing all sorts of the benefits arising out of their position, economic as well as social and political. As far as we can tell from the genealogy and oral traditions, Chen Daoming had few achievements worth mentioning. He was chosen as the focal ancestor not because he was a great ancestor but because he was in a very convenient genealogical position for his descendants.

Thus the powerful members of the Chens of S Village succeeded in uniting themselves by means of setting up a segment under the name of Chen Daoming while segregating themselves from the other descendants of the founding ancestor. After this time, the expansion of the Chens of S Village was unstoppable. Until the early twentieth century, the expanse of land registered in the name of Xinseitong constantly increased, as did the number of Chen Daoming's descendants to pass the civil service examination. Concurrently, the Chens of S Village grew into a lineage unrivalled in the region. Originally, the Chens were late starters both in the village and in the development competition. In the end, however, they emerged as the clear winner of the competition. Residents with other family names left the village or their descendants died out, while the Chens alone prospered as a lineage group and became dominant in the S Village population. By the nineteenth century, the Chens of S Village had become far more powerful than their namesakes inhabiting D Village. They achieved this through a process of further internal segmentation, in which the powerful members formed branch divisions to monopolize the use of wealth and power and to build a system for reproducing civil service degree holders. A lineage organization was an effective device to maintain and expand human, political and economic resources in order to win the competition on the frontier.

Establishing the history of legitimate settlement

As mentioned, one of the circumstances that led to a lineage organization was the environment at the time. Anthropologists from the 1960s to 1980s attributed the formation of large-scale lineages in southeastern China primarily to the frontier environment (Freedman 1958, 1966; Pasternak 1969; Potter 1970; Watson 1985). In practical terms, establishing a lineage involved the formalities of identifying its founding ancestor from generations past and compiling a genealogy, funding the construction of grand ancestral hall(s) with an immense sum of money and regularly performing ancestor worship rites. This indicates that the people of the time in the Pearl River Delta not only formed organizations by means of their patrilineal descent but also that they adopted highly formalized cultural norms and actually practiced them. The focus of this section is the act of compiling a genealogy, a process premised on revisiting and constructing the past in order to establish one's lineage as legitimately Han people, thus placing it firmly within the state, as well as by way of proving their long history of settlement in the area, securing the legal basis for their claims for the use of natural resources.

In the Pearl River Delta environment, where development was rapidly in progress and a few centuries of migration had resulted in a highly concentrated population, it was extremely significant to be able to settle and use resources. Faure, a social historian, calls the rights to build a house in a village, to cultivate land and to use natural resources 'settlement rights.' He says that residents of the community came to claim and maintain these rights as inherited from their ancestors (1986: 1–4; 1989: 6). According to Faure, having one's ancestor registered in the *li jia* tax collection system, introduced early in the Ming dynasty, served as an official certificate of one's settlement rights (Faure 1989: 14). Amidst a constant influx of migrants in the Pearl River Delta, especially in S Village and other communities at the forefront of development at the southern end, early settlers presumably justified their monopoly of resources with an argument equivalent to what Faure called settlement rights. They argued that having an ancestor who had been registered members in the old *li jia* meant that one's family had been living in the village since before the system, thus providing evidence of the firm basis of one's entitlement to the rights to live in and use the resources of the village.[4]

Recent historical studies also revealed that the *li jia* played a significant role in the relationship between villagers and the state. According to Katayama, asserting that one had been registered in the *li jia* and paying taxes to the state was effectively to identify oneself as a Han living in Guangzhou and its vicinity or *Guangfuren* (Katayama 2004: 24). Guangdong in the early Ming Dynasty was still considered to be an outlying region, where Han deserters from the *li jia* lived side by side with non-Han ethnic groups: the Han deserters repeatedly mounted insurgencies against the state and the non-Han groups such as the Yaos, Zhuangs, Dongliaos and Lis continued their long-running rebellions (Inoue 2004b: 13–14). From the fifteenth to the early sixteenth century in the Pearl River Delta, leaders of the development who were building firm foundations for themselves in their villages came under pressure to draw a line between themselves and those outside the framework of state rule, such as rebels and the non-Han ethnic groups. They needed to declare that they were legitimate Chinese people integrated in the state system. For the first time in the history of their relationship with the state, they were being forced to confirm their identity. To do so, they used their position as households registered in *li jia*.

In addition to their position in the *li jia* system, people used genealogies that recorded 'the history' of the kin groups and the villages where they settled to prove that their ancestors had lived there before the Ming period. Historians who scrutinized the genealogies in the Pearl River Delta reveal that a majority of the lineages traced their descent to ancestors in Zhujihang in Nanxiong County (Makino 1985; Faure 1989; Katayama 2004). There is a widely-circulated legend about a wave of migration via Zhujihang. The story has a number of subtle variations but the plot remains essentially as follows: In the southern Song period (1127–1281), a concubine fled the palace to Zhujihang in northern Guangdong Province. Local people gave her refuge. The emperor was furious and sent his army to Zhujihang. To escape from persecution, people went to the County office and obtained official permits to migrate. They scattered in all parts of Guangdong. At their destinations, they reported to the County and created a family register before settling down (Makino 1985: 255–6). By combining one's own descent with this legend, one could prove a few things: that one's ancestor was a Han Chinese originating from northern Guangdong; that the migration from Nanxiong was made with official permission; and that the migration took place in the southern Song period. Thus, one's descent as a Han Chinese was proven, as was the time of migration, with official permission, to the village where one now lived.

As mentioned above, the Chens of S Village established their lineage organization at the village level before they discovered a genealogical tie with the Chens of H Village and set out to form a higher-order lineage tracing back to the founder of H Village on the

Shiqiao plateau. The plateau was the first land that emerged from water in Panyu. The founder of this higher-order lineage was a former central government general who moved to Panyu. His personal history is recorded in gazetteers including the *Guangdong dongzhi*, the *Guangzhou fuzhi* and the *Panyu xianzhi*. The Tongzhi edition of the *Panyu xianzhi* contains a description as follows:

> Chen Yuande was born in Yuandaoxian, present-day Gongchang, Shanxi Province. He was famous for his fearless courage from his childhood. He served Emperors Xiaowudi, Liandi and Gongdi with distinguished records in expedition. During the Rebellion of Sun En, Yuande and Liu Lao defeated the rebels. Due to this achievement, he was appointed *Jianguo dajangjun,* or Grand General for State Founding. After Sun En's death, his comrade Lu Xun regained ground and seized Guangzhou. Yuande was given an order to quash the rebels but he could not accomplish it. Liu Yu intended to seize Jin. Yuande's defiance outraged Liu Yu. He demoted Yuande to a local office in Jinjiang. When Liu Yu usurped the throne, Yuande left government service and moved to Panyu, where he lived in seclusion with his wife and children. His descendants have prospered to this day. The Qianlong edition of the gazetteer compiled by Ren Guo says that Yuande first settled at Shuikeng before he moved to H Village. His descendants live in the present-day villages of S, Chigang, Wenlinggong, Bainichong and Shangmeikeng. (Tongzhi edition, *Panyu xianzhi*: 579)

Whether the personal history of Chen Yuande is correct or not is not important. What is important is that the man actually existed in history and that his move to Panyu to found H Village was recorded as an indisputable fact in history books. This gave the Chen lineage of S Village good grounds for their claim that they were of Han descent originating in central China and that their ancestral history before the settlement in S Village was trustworthy.

The Chen lineage of S Village had to seek the origin of their descent from Chen Yuande of H Village, and not in Zhujihang. This is understandable in the context of their rivalry with the Chen lineage of neighboring D Village. As mentioned, at the time, the Chen lineage of D Village had been producing a good pool of civil service elite. They had already constructed a history that established that their lineage came to D Village via Zhujihang. To compete in the race to develop the area, it was probably vital for the Chen lineage of S Village to establish a history that differed from that of their D Village counterparts and with which they could assert an equally legitimate descent. Although to have a famed general who fled the north in the fifth century to Panyu deviated from the mainstream history of the lineages in the Pearl River Delta, it supported the claim that the Chen lineage of S Village was of Han descent and that their history prior to the settlement was trustworthy. The genealogical link with Chen Yuande was enough to satisfy what was needed for a legitimate lineage history.

For the Chens of S Village, the credibility of Chen Yuande's place in history and role as the focal point in their branching out from H Village were crucially important. The membership of the lineage, therefore, made repeated efforts to ensure that these facts were proven to be true. As they identified Chen Yuande as their forefather, the Chen lineage of S Village became actively involved in the construction of a hall dedicated to Chen Yuande in H Village, with Chen Dayou and his gentry elite as the main driving forces. It was mainly through Chen Dayou's initiative that Chen Yuande's hall was built in the reign of Wanli in the Ming Period (1573–1619). Their genealogy compiled in 1885 includes the following:

> [Chen Dayou] had a wish to build an ancestral hall. After he left the service, he went home to the village. He summoned a meeting of his lineage members and made the proposal. He started action without stint. The ancestral hall was built during the reign of Wanli in the Ming Period, under the supervision of Great Dayou.

The hall underwent extensive repairs in 1674. Records in their genealogy suggest that the Chen lineage of S Village played a major role in these renovations. The repairs were funded by the Chens of H Village and the three villages, including S Village, that had branched out from the H Village Chens. Their contributions totaled seventy-seven *liang*. According to the records of figures and sources of the fund in the genealogy, S Village contributed twenty-two *liang*, the second largest sum after H Village's 27.2 *liang*. The work ultimately cost them 130 *liang* and the balance was made up by a loan from the properties of two branches of S Village. The genealogy also reveals that the epitaph on the stone monument erected to mark the construction of the hall was authored by Chen Wenbo of S Village and calligraphed by Chen Mingyu, also of S Village. Being part of the elite in the seventeenth century following Dayou, Mingyu secured the degree of *lingsheng*, while Wenbo scored *juren*. They both took

Figure 4.3: A picture of the shrine of Chen Yuande and the pine tree he allegedly planted

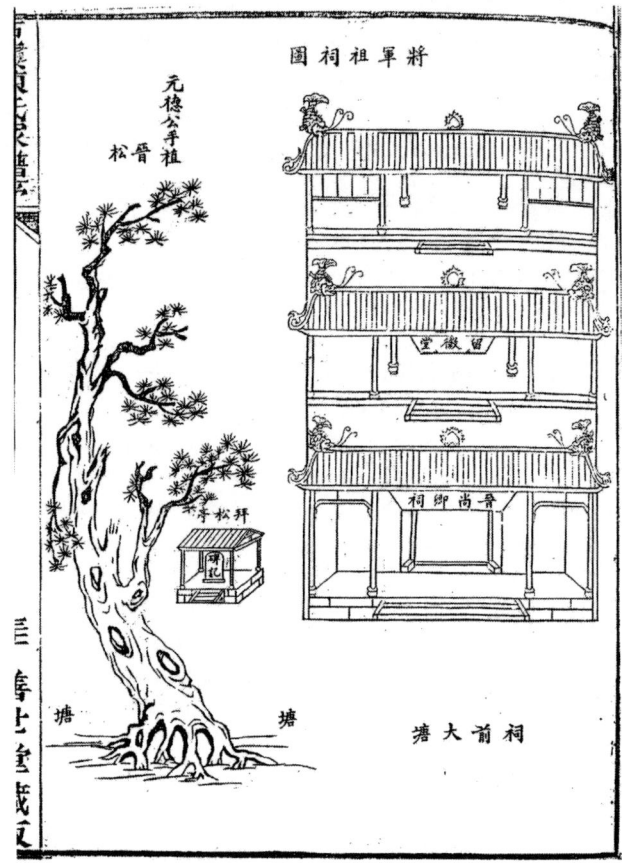

office in the civil service and received mention in a gazetteer (Tongzhi edition, *Panyu xianzhi*: 716). The genealogical link with H Village carried a great significance to members of the Chen lineage of S Village in terms of proving their own history. It is not hard to imagine that the elite of the time enthusiastically involved themselves in the construction of the ancestral hall dedicated to Chen Yuande.

Much attention was also paid to adding more credibility to the historical existence of Chen Yuande. The design plan of the hall included in the genealogy of the Chen lineage of S Village bore the picture of a pine tree said to have been planted by Yuande. Next to the picture, the caption says '*Yuande gong shouzhi Jinsong* (pine tree planted by Yuande in the Jin period)' (Figure 4.3). The genealogy contains a few anecdotes regarding the pine tree. One of them is from a nineteenth century government official who admired the tree. He built a pavilion from which he viewed the precious plant and called for a poem to be written about it. Beginning with '*Qiansui gusong nandejian* (A thousand-year-old pine tree is hard to find)' in its first line, the poem included in the genealogy portrays Chen Yuande's personal history and greatest achievements. The second anecdote is a sequel. A fire in 1862 destroyed the pavilion and the boughs of the pine tree, leaving mysteriously scented embers. They were sold at a high price and the money was used to rebuild the pavilion. These anecdotes were told and recorded in the genealogy because the pine tree reputedly planted by Chen Yuande could effectively give credibility to his existence in history. He is claimed to have settled in the area as early as the fifth century, which was virtually a prehistoric time in the Pearl River Delta. His credibility was directly connected to the legitimacy of the origin of the Chen lineage of S Village. It was only natural that the remote 'descendants' of Chen Yuande worked so obstinately to make his existence 'a historical fact.'

To form a lineage required contemporaries to band together. At the same time, it required them to prove continuity with their past. Genealogy was chosen from a large number of means of social linkage, not only because the frontier environment demanded that people form a group, but also because they were faced with the need to present their legitimate descent and history as Han people.

Our examination of the lineage-forming processes of the Chens of S Village and others in the Pearl River Delta points to highly constructed and negotiated histories that each of the lineages declares as its own past. Yet, at a time when a constant deluge of new migrants inundated the Delta, it was essential to establish a line of descent that, as far as the people of the time were concerned, served to provide proof of continuity between a lineage and its past, which was also acceptable by others.

Leaning toward the orthodox culture

People formed lineages by the means of genealogy in the social and environmental context of the Pearl River Delta in the fifteenth and early sixteenth centuries that demanded that they band together into groups and demonstrate their descent. Lineages, at least as far as the Pearl River Delta was concerned, shared a common set of activities in their process of self-establishment. These activities included constructing ancestral halls, compiling genealogies, maintaining ancestral graves in respectable shape and performing ancestor worship rites. The style in which they performed each of these activities was found to be remarkably uniform throughout the Delta. It was a development in which the intention of the state and the desire of the frontier communities met. The former aimed to impose ideological and religious authority on the fringe areas in order to bring them under its control, while the latter were keen to demonstrate their legitimacy by following the Confucian practices authorized by the central government.

Until the fifteenth century, when the practice began to spread far and wide, building a hall for ancestor worship was open exclusively to high-ranking bureaucrats and not to the general public in village communities. Positive actions by the Confucianists at the time largely contributed to the expansion of this practice. Prior to the seventeenth century, Buddhism, Taoism and shamanism were the main faiths in the Pearl River Delta villages. As these faiths were not approved by the state, their religious institutions were labeled as *yinci* by the officials of Guangdong, who tried to destroy them and went on to spread the orthodox Confucianism (Ke and Liu 2000: 11–12). Across the country since the early Ming Period, criticisms had been made against *yincis* from the perspective of the fundamentalist theory of religious rites based on the doctrines of Zhu Xi (Hamashima 1990: 1339). Particularly on the frontier of Guangdong, the Confucianist elites had been actively disseminating the ideology of the imperial government. Wei Xiao, who was assigned to Guangdong as a *tixuefushi*, an official in charge of the administration of educational matters, in the reign of Zhengde in the Ming Period (1521), destroyed *yincis* and instead ordered people to perform rites of ancestor worship in his campaign to eradicate heathenism in the Guangzhou area, most particularly in the counties of Panyu and Nanhai (Inoue 2002: 2–5, 2004a: 35).

As it was not allowed for people other than high-ranking bureaucrats to perform rites of ancestor worship—in strict accordance with the formal doctrines as described in the classic texts—the Confucianists added new interpretations to the texts, which they endeavored to propagate. Historian Inoue (2000) reveals that a draft on ancestral hall system reform submitted to the emperor by a *libu shangshu* called Xia Yan in the reign of Jiajing (1536) provided a strong case in support of the new Confucian interpretation. Xia Yan proposed that everyone be allowed to perform rites to worship his ancestors, that the descendants of a bureaucrat of *sanpin* rank or above be allowed indefinitely to perform rites to worship the incumbent as the founder of their family and that descendants of a bureaucrat of *sipin* rank or below be allowed to perform rites for four generations. After this time, according to Inoue, Xia Yan's proposals became widely considered as the official view of the Ming government (Inoue 2000: 375). Some genealogies of the Pearl River Delta lineages in the same period express the view that families other than those of a bureaucrat were also allowed to construct ancestral halls (Ke and Liu 2000: 12). This indicates that the Confucianist view was being adopted in the village societies. It was in this context that some central government officials had set out to form a lineage back in their villages after retirement.[5]

The Chen lineage of S Village was no exception. It was established by the elite members that the Chens had increasingly come to produce. During their assignments as bureaucrats and then back home in Guangdong after retirement, they were probably inspired in many ways by the intellectual circles of the day that advocated Confucianist reforms and the propagation of lineages. Among them, Chen Dayou is noteworthy. A former governor of a county in Fujian, Chen Dayou initiated the construction of Xinseitong, the first of the S Village Chen lineage ancestral halls. In the Xianyou County, where Chen Dayou was posted as governor, a movement to destroy '*yincis*' was active in the early Ming Period in the sixteenth century (Kojima 1999: 177–9). The experience in Fujian, which had been a centre of Neo-Confucianism since the time of Zhu Xi, presumably had a great effect on Chen Dayou's post-retirement move to establish a lineage. Inside Xinseitong, a wood block carrying the name of the hall hangs on the wall. The calligraphy is said to be that of Wei Jiguang, who was a Ming dynasty general famed for his achievements in defeating pirates. He was a friend of Chen Dayou. As mentioned earlier, the construction of an ancestral hall in H Village was another of Chen Dayou's initiatives, actively supported by the gentry of S Village, including Chen Wenbo and Chen Mingyu. From this, it is possible to deduce how enthusiastically the elite ex-bureaucrats involved themselves in activities to help establish their lineage, such as the construction of ancestral halls.

Accommodating the government's desire to integrate the newly-forming frontier region into its empire, the elite on the rise demonstrated that their families represented the state-authorized ideology and its practice by building an ancestral hall and forming a lineage. A lineage can be considered as a product of the converging desires of both the state and the residents in the frontier villages: the state presented the extremely stylized cultural norms to be respected, and the elites in the frontier regions adopted and put them into practice. An ancestral hall bearing the name of a distant forefather has represented the contemporary legitimacy of lineage members in the Pearl River Delta in the sixteenth century and since. Those with lineage organizations drew a distinction between themselves and new comers on the one hand and non-Han minorities on the other: they identified themselves as the legitimate Han Chinese who lived their lives in accordance with the state-authorized norms. A lineage was the means they employed to get ahead in the development competition on the frontier and to justify their position of power within the community by using the authority of the imperial government.

Lineage and social hierarchy

I now examine the role of a lineage in the hierarchical relationships, firstly, among residents within the same community, secondly, between villages, and lastly between the majority Han and minority ethnic groups.

Lineage and hierarchy within the community

By the early twentieth century, the Chen lineage of S Village had come to own 33,000 *mu* of land (approximately 2200 hectares) and built more than 100 ancestral halls in the village. The lineage had been formed and strengthened since the fourteenth century by its influential members to become an unrivalled power in the vicinity. It was one of the largest lineages in the Pearl River Delta, where a great number of sizable lineages were found.

The outstanding expansion of the Chen lineage of S Village was largely due to the combined mechanism of segmentation and integration that kept them united as a whole while containing a complicated hierarchy that developed within the lineage. The lineage's common land was almost exclusively run by a few powerful members. They leased out the land and used the profit to obtain more land. They invested in their offspring's education and reproduced the elite. The greater the political and economic influences of the exclusive members grew, the more powerful their lineage became as a whole, which in turn benefited its ordinary members. This system was well established and maintained the unity of the lineage as a whole.

The elite of a sub-segment of the Chen lineage in S Village called Hanxutong was a good example. The sub-segment was formed with an ancestor of the nineteenth generation as its focal point and produced a series of elite members famed throughout the county, including successful applicants of the civil and military service exams, government office holders, those who are mentioned in the local gazetteers or *xianzhis* for their remarkable achievements, and the editors of *xianzhis*. Among the segments and sub-segments within the Chen lineage, Hanxutong was outstanding. Eleven Chens of S Village have passed the civil service examination since the mid-Ming Period. Out of the eleven, four came from the Hanxuton sub-segment, comprised of only thirty-odd members. The only two Chens to have won the highest degree of *jinshi* in the examination were both members of the Hanxutong sub-segment. It was the elite of Hanxutong that led the expansion of the Chen lineage of S Village, which was to reach its pinnacle at the end of the nineteenth century.

It was the elite members of these powerful segments who practically led the whole lineage organization. As their influence increased, ordinary members also benefited greatly. A majority of members earned a living by leasing the rights to use and managing the lineage-owned land, or by tenant-farming. Those who leased the land and tenant-farmers had to pay sixty to seventy-five percent of their crops, which in return entitled them to preferential access to the land and freedom from troublesome negotiation with government officers. A lineage had land not only to farm but also to bury deceased members without families or immediate relatives. It also had facilities called *yiqi* at which to rest their memorial tablets. The lineage built schools and educated its members' children. Every time it held a ceremonial rite, it distributed pork and *mantou* to its members. A lineage sometimes helped old people and widows with their living expenses. At the time when villages were not integrated directly into the state's system of governance, to be a member of a powerful lineage provided one with some degree of security and assurance. It also validated one's superiority vis-à-vis members of other lineages, subordinates of lineages called *hafu* or *seimen*, boat-dwellers and other minorities. For these benefits, a majority of members of a lineage remained within the organization, controlled by only a handful of elite members.

The rites performed by a lineage displayed the authority of its prominent members and the hierarchy within the organization. They were also used to confirm the membership and unity of the lineage as a whole. Between 13 and 15 January every year, families to which a male child was born in the previous year put up lanterns in the eaves and along the lane in front of their house. This custom, called *hoideng*, was an important rite to announce the birth of their son to the community and have him accepted as a member of the lineage. The families visited ancestral halls, starting from those of their smallest sub-segment, then those of larger segments, and finally those of the lineage as a whole. Their sons' names were recorded in the segment's genealogy at each hall, before they were finally added to the genealogy of the whole Chen lineage of S Village at the focal ancestral hall or *da zong ci*. Through this rite, a newly-born male child was formally accepted into the lineage and given membership. Inevitably, because of uneven segmentation, some children belonged to a number of segments at different genealogical levels, while others only received membership from the focal ancestral hall. The moment a baby boy was born, he was at the same time given an equal and uniform membership in the lineage as a whole and a differential position in the stratification as manifest in the unequal internal segmentation

Rites of ancestor worship also enforced unity and division. Powerful members wore a long robe called *cêng yi* and arrived at the ritual site on horseback or in a palanquin. The entire lineage membership took part in the ritual at the grave of or the hall dedicated to ancestors at higher generation levels. Pork, *mantou* and money were distributed among all who attended. Those who had passed the civil service examination and members sixty years old or over received double the share of money and food. The act of rewarding its successful elite and elderly members on a ceremonial occasion characterizes a lineage, which was led by a few powerful members but at the same time maintained its overall unity according to the genealogical principle. After the rite for the whole lineage was over, people went to the hall of their own segment and performed another rite, in which food and money were again distributed. As members of powerful genealogical lines belonged to a number of subordinate segments, they attended more rites and received more food and money. Rites of ancestor worship were another occasion where the membership and unity of a lineage were confirmed and at the same time the disparity in the hierarchy within the organization was displayed. A lineage had in its structure the two contradicting forces of division and unity, which were symbolized and also redressed by the rites.

Stratification among lineages and villages

In the overall unity, overweighing the disparity of the monopoly of political and economic powers by a small number of influential members, the Chen lineage of S Village continues to expand. As the lineage grew into an unparalleled force, villages in the area became politically and economically stratified.

So far in this paper, emphasis has been placed on the reconstruction of the past starting from the time of settlement. However, it will be easier to understand the issue of inter-village stratification by examining its contemporary state, and then tracing its development back.

The office of S Township, one of the twenty townships comprising Panyu District—consisting of seventeen administrative villages—was set up in S Village in 1987 when the township system was introduced. (To be more precise, S Village is now divided into West S Village and East S Village, but this is only a matter of present-day administration.) The entrance of S Village is marked by an arch and is always inundated with bike-taxis waiting for passengers. The streets are lined with markets and shops as well as supermarkets, restaurants, barbers, banks and post offices. Although other villages also have commercial businesses, they are extremely limited in number and scale. Financial, communication and entertainment services are only available in S Village. In relation to the surrounding villages, S Village serves as the centre, both administrative and commercial.

The township office was set up in S Village because a people's commune had been located in the village since the 1950s and, historically, it had been the economic and cultural centre of the area since before the People's Republic of China was founded in 1949. In organizing the collective system, brigades were formed to replace former villages and a number of these brigades were formed into people's communes as umbrella organizations. When the people's commune system collapsed in the 1980s, communes were changed to townships and brigades to villages. Some elderly villagers remember S Village in the early twentieth century as already being a bustling place with one big fair and another smaller one held regularly with streets of permanent shops, where restaurants, wholesalers and other businesses offered services unavailable in ordinary villages or markets. S Village at the time could be classified as an 'intermediate market town' in terms of Skinner's model (Skinner 1964: 24–6), with a commercial scale and function superior to those of a 'standard market town,' enjoying prosperity as the local hub of economic distribution. This indicates that the contemporary social structure of the area—with S Village as its political and economic centre—had been established at least by the early twentieth century. The economic development of S

Village and the expansion of the Chen lineage went hand-in-hand. The increasing economic prosperity of the Chens led to the expansion of the lineage in the form of educating the next generation and increasing common property, which were in turn beneficial to the political and economic resources of S Village. As the Chen lineage of S Village grew into an unrivalled force in the area, S Village developed into an economic and cultural centre for the surrounding villages.

Most of the seventeen administrative villages of today's S Township have two or three lineages each. Fairly large by national standards or even by southeastern Chinese standards, these lineages were equivalent to what Freedman classified as the 'Z type'—a 2000 to 3000-strong membership, with a complicated internal structure of stratification and segmentation with a good amount of common property (Freedman 1958: 132). Yet the Chen lineage of S Village surpassed them by far, in terms of area of land owned, the numbers of family members who passed the civil service examination and the number of ancestral halls constructed in the village. Apparently, S Village performed commercial functions far better than other villages in the area. In terms of stratification of lineages and villages on the Shiqiao plateau, lineages classifiable as super-Z type like the Chens lived in economic distribution hubs such as S Village, while Z type lineages inhabited surrounding villages with lesser economic functions. The four greatest ancestral halls of Panyu included Xinseitong in S Village, Leogangtong of the He lineage in Shawan and Guongdaitong of the Wu lineage in Nancun.[6] Both the Hes and Wus were large enough to be classified as super-Z type. They lived in market towns that, like S Village, served as commercial distribution hubs in the area. In the surrounding area, there were villages with smaller-scale economic functions, populated by Z type lineages. The scale of a lineage was closely correlated with that of its village, and stratification emerged among villages in the Pearl River Delta, particularly in Panyu, where lineages were deeply involved in local development.

Stratification of ethnicities

Until the thirteenth century, the Shiqiao plateau in Panyu encompassed little arable land and was sparsely populated. In the fifteenth century, development began and people started to settle in the area. By the eighteenth century, the geopolitical framework of the local communities were virtually as we find it today. The area including S Village, where the Chen lineage is based, was located at the southernmost end of the land, or in other words at the very verge of the frontier around the turn of the twelfth century. This area later became known as *mentin*, as more land was reclaimed downriver. Compared to the southern wetlands, where reclamation was constantly underway, the *mentin* was older land at a higher altitude. There, migrants had settled and villages had been formed. In each of the villages, a couple of lineages with a 1000 to 2000-strong membership lived. In villages like S, where a larger lineage lived, fairs were regularly held and marketplaces developed into hubs of bustling economic activity. Members of a lineage in the *mentin* district lived together in their village and jointly owned land around the village and newly reclaimed *satin* stretching along the lower Pearl River. They built ancestral halls and shrines and performed rites. By pursuing legitimate cultural practices, they came to share the self-perception as members of the legitimate Han people who belonged to the state. Through this process, the Chens emerged as winners in the development competition and were firmly positioned as a dominant local power.

Lineages in the *mentin* reclaimed and developed *satin*. The newly reclaimed farming land of low altitude was sparsely populated by late-comers who arrived in the Delta after resources had already been monopolized by *mentin* powers. Migrants to the *satin* made a living by fishing, transporting goods, laboring on reclamation works run by *mentin* lineages and tenant-farming the *satin*, which had become common properties of the lineages. Called by their *mentin* counterparts by the derogatory name of '*Dans*,' residents of the *satin* basically lived on boats or simple grass huts called *weigun* scattered around the farmland. In the *satin*, people did not live in such a concentrated manner as to form a village. Therefore, no commercial distribution hub was established and few ancestral halls or shrines were built.

An elderly member of the Chen lineage of S Village describes *satin* people as lacking the custom of recording a genealogy and as ignorant of who their ancestors are. Conversely, members of this and other lineages in the *mentin* area have written genealogies and know their own history. They can assume their position in historical time as a part of the genealogical continuity from their ancestors. It is this very aspect that supports their identity as legitimate Han who had inhabited the area for generations and distinguishes them from *Dans* in the *satin* and new migrants to the area.

As explained above, *mentin* and *satin* are not only geographical concepts but are also indicators, formed in the course of development of the local society, of economic relationships, political hierarchy, social stratification and distinct ethnic groups or *zuqun* that divide the legitimate Han Chinese and the marginal *Dans* (Liu 1999). The close interconnection between the local development of the Pearl River Delta and the lineages formed in this process created ethnic stratification.

Conclusion

Genealogy was the underlying principle of the existence of a lineage. It connected the present with the past and at the same time linked contemporary members descending from a common ancestor. Construction of an ancestral hall and ancestor worship took hold as cultural norms of the Han, thanks to vigorous campaigns driven by the Confucians of the time to spread their doctrine. By forming a lineage, people on the rise on the frontier joined forces and demonstrated their history proving their founder's time of settlement, prior movements and Han Chinese descent, which also gave them contemporary legitimacy. Forming a lineage meant, in other words, maintaining and expanding members' influence in the local society and identifying themselves in relation to the state. Genealogy, rather than faith or locality, was chosen as their means to do so. It was precisely because descent was an essential concept constructed through systematization by the state and reinforced by Confucian arguments that it became recognized by the Han Chinese in respect of continuity and authenticity.

After a lineage was formed in the context described above, typically its powerful members virtually monopolized the use of political and economic resources, which consequently led to the expansion of the lineage as a whole. Although the inner structure of a lineage developed complex stratification, its overall integration was maintained as members benefited from the power gained by their leaders. This was also because the mechanism of division and unity was clearly symbolized in their rituals and at the same time redressed. As regional development progressed, the correlation between lineages and their villages created a social hierarchy in surrounding areas. Lineage membership in effect validated the superiority of its holder over the members of smaller lineages, late-comer migrants and minorities such as boat people, as well as establishing the member's entitlement to live where he lived as a legitimate Han Chinese.

Paternal kinship ties were merely one of many social relationships that the Han could manipulate. In the Pearl River Delta at the time, however, the ties were more than that. This provided an answer to the following question, which Freedman (Freedman 1958, 1966) and succeeding researchers (Potter 1968, 1970a; Pasternak 1969, 1972; Watson1985) fell short of supplying: If the frontier environment required people to form groups, what made them choose the means of genealogy and consequently organized lineages? In the Pearl River Delta, the village elite were attempting to establish their influence within and outside their villages, while the state was aiming to extend its control over the newly-developing frontier. The lineages were a product created where the motives of the two players met with what genealogy had in essence to offer. As the development of the frontier was advanced in correlation with the formation of lineages, kinship organizations and social stratification in the regional society were inseparably bound to each other in the Pearl River Delta.

Glossary

Legend: M = Mandarin; C = Cantonese
Anhui 安徽 M
Bainichong 白泥涌 M
Cai 蔡 M
cêng yi 長衣 C
Chen 陳 M
Chen Daoming 陳道明 M
Chen Dayou 陳大有 M
Chen Linde 陳麟德 M
Chen Mingyu 陳銘玉 M
Chen Wenbo 陳文博 M
Chen Yuande 陳元德 M
Chigang 赤崗 M
Dan 蜑 C
Daoheng 道亨 M
Daoming 道明 M
Dongguang 東莞 M
Dongjin 東晋 M
Dongliao 峒獠 M
fen 分 M
Foshan 仏山 M
Fujian 福建 M
Fujian dongzhi 福建通志 M
Huo Tao 霍韜 M

Fuqiang 伏羌 M
Gao 高 M
Jiutun 九屯 M
Gongchang 鞏昌 M
Gongdi 恭帝 M
Guan 関 M
Guangdong 広東 M
Guangdong dongzhi 広東通志 M
Guangfuren 広府人 M
Guangzhou 広州 M
Guangzhou fuzhi 広州府志 M
Guangzhou weisuo 広州衛所 M
Guongdaitong 光大堂 C
hafu 下夫 C
hoideng 開燈 C
Han 漢 M
Hangxutong 行恕堂 C
Hongwu 洪武 M
Hongzhi 弘治 M
Huang Zuo 黄佐 M
Jiajing 嘉靖 M
Jianguo dajiangjun 建国大将軍 M
Jinjiang 晋江 M
jinshi 進士 M
juren 挙人 M
Kangxi 康熙 M
Leogangtong 留耕堂 C
Li 俚 M
Li 礼 M
li 里 M
li jia 里甲 M
Li Yizhuang 李義荘 M
Liandi 歷安帝 M
liang 両 M
Liang 亮 M
Lianhuashan 蓮花山 M
Libu shangshu 礼部尚書
lingsheng 廩生 M
Liu Lao 劉牢 M
Liu Yu 劉裕 M
Longqing 隆慶 M

Lu Xun 盧循 M
Luo Yuchen 羅虞臣 M
Ma 馬 M
mantou 饅頭 M
men do gêu gou feo 民多居高阜 C
mentin 民田 C
mu 畝 M
Nancun 南村 M
Nanhai 南海 M
Nanxiong 南雄 M
Panyu 番禺 M
Punyü séidaiqi 番禺四大祠 C
Panyu xianzhi 番禺縣志 M
Ping 評 M
Qianlong 乾隆 M
qiansui gusong nandejian 千歲古松難得見 M
Qin 秦 M
Qing 清 M
Ren Guo 任果 M
沙田 satian M
    satin C
sai mong gong 晒網崗 C
sanpin 三品 M
seimen 細民 M
Shangmeikeng 上梅坑 M
Shawan 沙湾 M
Shanxi 陝西 M
shengyuan 生員 M
Shiqiao 市橋 M
Shuikeng 水坑 M
Shunde 順德 M
sipin 四品 M
Sizhou 泗洲 M
Song 宋 M
Sun En 孫恩 M
Taiquanxiangli 泰泉鄉礼 M
Tixuefushi 提學副使 M
Wanli 万曆 M
Wei Jiguang 威継光 M
Wei Xiao 魏校 M
weigun 圍館 C

Wenlinggong 文嶺崗 M
Wu 鄔 M
wuxi 巫覡 M
xiang 項 M
Xianyou 仙遊 M
Xiaowudi 孝武帝 M
Xia Yan 夏言 M
Xie Shaotang 謝紹唐 M
Xinseitong 善世堂 C
Yao 徭·猺 M
yiqi 義祠 C
yinci 淫祠 M
Yuan Changzuo 袁昌祚 M
Yuandao xian 猨道県 M
Yuande gong shouzhi Jinsong 元德公手植晉松 M
Zhang 張 M
Zheng 鄭 M
Zengcheng 增城 M
Zhengde 正德 M
Zhongshan 中山 M
Zhu 朱 M
Zhu Xi 朱熹 M
Zhuang 獞·僮 M
Zhujihang 珠璣巷 M
zongfa 宗法 M
zuqun 族群 M

5 Common-Surname Tong-ism in Contemporary Taiwanese Society
Hisahiko Kamizuru

Introduction

Taiwan has been troubled by two stratification issues. First is the longstanding provincial origin problem. The mainlanders who came to Taiwan with the Chinese Nationalist Party, which has ruled the country for many years, have been at the center of political power for nearly half a century and have enjoyed preferential treatment, particularly in the world of bureaucrats, teachers and military officers. Conversely, the native Taiwanese people, who have been residents of Taiwan since before the Second Word War, and their descendants, looked to the world of business for their livelihood. Thus a social division was established between the mainlanders, who dominated politics and the bureaucracy, and the native Taiwanese who dominated the economy. Although the provincial origin problem is no longer as serious as previously, it is still an important social issue facing Taiwanese society.

The second issue relates to income disparity. According to 2005 data (Taiwan Tsūsin 2006), there was almost a six-fold gap between the average incomes of the top 20% (NT$1,794,000 = US$54,700 approx.) and the bottom 20% (NT$298,000 = US$9100 approx.) of the income distribution table. There was also a large regional gap, with the average annual income in the nation's capital city of Taipei being about NT$1.14 million (US$34,800) while the average annual income in the less developed eastern county of Taitung was less than half of that amount. According to 2004 data (Taiwan Tsūsin 2006), there was nearly a twofold gap between the salaries of the managerial staff (about NT$63,000 = US$1900 per month) and the service industry clerks (about NT$31,000 = US$940 per month). The 2005 data shows that the monthly salary of customer attendants in the service industry was even lower, at about NT$18,500 (US$560 approx.). Some have obtained citizenship of other countries such as the USA and transferred their assets out of concerns about political instability, and some have built mansions in mainland China to take advantage of economic disparities. On the other end of the scale, there are elderly women who sell chewing gums for NT$10 (about thirty cents) each night at hawker centers.

In Han-Chinese society, there is a concept called common-surname 'tong-ism' which links people of different economic and social standings. Tong-ism is a unifying principle that promotes interpersonal relationships based on a common attribute. The origin of the term is the Chinese word 'tong,' which means 'sameness' or 'commonality.' This principle was mentioned by Fried (1962) in the 1960s. According to Fried,

> T'ungism applies to people drawn together because they speak the same Chinese sublanguage, come from the same province, come from the same county, come from the same town, or have graduated from the same middle school or college, or are members of a particular class year or any of these. (cited in Cohen 1968: 287)

It is typically translated as 'togetherness'. Cohen explains that 'The bond of t'ungism thus might cut across ties of kin, class, and residence' (Cohen 1968: 287). In short, there are many bases for tong-ism, and having the 'same surname' is one of them.

Chinese anthropologist Fei Xiaotong argues that 'relatives are theoretically bound to fill each other's needs and provide mutual assistance' in the Han-Chinese kinship system (Fei 1991: 81). This is also applicable to the Han-Chinese in Taiwan who consider that people with a common surname must give each other assistance.[1] Even if their lineage is not known, people with a common surname are considered to have a common ancestor and are regarded as relatives.[2]

An organization based on the common-surname tong-ism relationship is called *zongqinhui* in Taiwan. The common-surname association 'as the largest kin group, enables people to form sustainable relationships with strangers with the same surname according to the norms of kinship' (Horie 1988: 61).

However, in contemporary Han-Taiwanese society, common-surname tong-ism is used by people to build personal connections based on a sense of togetherness as the 'same clan' and the image of mutual assistance while maintaining differences in economic and social standing. It does not serve to reduce differences in fiscal and social status.[3] I begin by analyzing the dual nature of common-surname tong-ism (emphasizing closeness and harmony while acting in accordance with personal interests) in contemporary Taiwanese society,[4] using the Liu Surname Association of Taipei City as the primary example. I then critically discuss the perception that Han society is primarily kinship oriented.

Common-surname associations in Yushan

With three hundred years of history, Yushan is the oldest and was once the most prosperous district in Taipei. There were three common-surname associations of Liu in Yushan after the Second World War. During the 1970s, representatives of a common-surname association of Liu in the Philippines visited the Liu associations in Taipei. In response, the executives of the three associations in Taipei proposed to pay a return visit. However, private overseas travel was restricted in Taiwan at the time, and existing common-surname associations were not eligible to apply for travel as they were incorporated foundations. Therefore, it was decided to set up a new body that satisfied the necessary requirements. Thus The Liu Surname Association of Taipei City was established.

The main difference between the new Liu Surname Association and the preexisting three common-surname associations was that any Taipei resident with the surname of Liu (any man or woman with the surname of Liu, whether married or unmarried, and any woman who married a man with the surname of Liu) was eligible to join the former, whereas the executives of the other associations had screened applicants. The Liu Surname Association charged a joining fee of NT$500 (about US$18) and no annual fee, at the time of my research in the mid-1990s. Its supporters donate thousands to tens of thousands of *yuan* each to provide operating funds for festivals and events. The Association's financial base is weak, however, due to a lack of property or other assets that produce regular income.

The Liu Association had its heyday during the 1970s and 1980s. According to its executives, the sources of this prosperity included overseas travel, which triggered its formation, and the support of prominent people. For example, the company president of a distributor for a leading Japanese corporation supported the activities of the Association (such as the world congress) by making multimillion-(NT)dollar donations. However, the executives of the Association complain that 'young people have stopped joining' since overseas travel restrictions were eased and a former president of the organization passed away in the mid-1990s. When I began my research in 1994, the Liu Surname Association had around 120 members, about half its peak membership. The membership size has not changed significantly to date (as of 2006).

The core leadership of the Liu Surname Association includes a politician, a college operator, a company owner and a director of one of Taiwan's leading temples. There is also a company worker whose father was a former director of the Association and a self-employed builder. There are about twenty executives, who are all males, mostly aged between forty and sixty. The general membership includes company workers, shop owners, public servants and their wives, most of who are in the same age group as the executives. Although anyone with the surname of Liu can join there are no impoverished people among its members.

The current activities include various exchange programs, rituals or ceremonial events and mutual assistance programs. Its exchange programs include:
1. a joint congress of all Liu common-surname associations in Taiwan;
2. a general meeting of the Liu common-surname associations of the world;
3. exchange activities with a Liu common-surname association in Korea.

The Liu Surname Association has poured its efforts into the development of various exchange meetings since its establishment. It facilitated the formation of new Liu common-surname associations in various parts of Taiwan and became the driving force behind the (annual) hosting of the joint congress of the Liu common-surname associations in Taiwan. At one joint congress I attended, the Liu common-surname associations in all counties except Taitung County gathered and jointly commemorated some prominent historical figures with the surname of Liu, honored members over the age of eighty, and discussed the running of the joint congress.

The Liu Surname Association of Yushan, together with the aforementioned Philippine common-surname association, was actively involved in the establishment of the world general meeting of the Liu common-surname associations. It took the lead in hosting the inaugural world general meeting in Taiwan in the early 1980s. Since then, the Liu Surname Association has produced a secretary-general of the world general meeting and played a leadership role in the organization. The world general meeting is held annually by the common-surname associations of each member country in turn.

The Liu Surname Association of Yushan conducts exchange activities with a Korean Liu common-surname association. Although it is acknowledged by its members and others that they are Koreans, the Korean association participates in the world general meeting because their ancestors are believed to have migrated from China to Korea about 2000 years ago.[5] The Liu Surname Association provided the starting point for their ongoing exchange. During the early 1980s, members of the Korean Liu common-surname association visited the Liu Surname Association of Yushan in search of their ancestral roots. They have continued their relationship and the Liu Surname Association of Yushan sent a delegation to the world general meeting held in Korea.

The rite of ancestor worship is conducted in the ancestral hall on the lunar New Year and in spring and autumn. These events are mainly run by the Liu Dazutang Surname Association, which was one of the parent bodies of the Liu Surname Association, but the latter is also involved. The joint rite at the ancestral hall is conducted for eminent figures in the history of the Liu who became government officials in successive Chinese dynasties.[6] In addition, individuals can enshrine other ancestral tablets. Any Taipei resident with the surname Liu can purchase spaces for ancestral tablets on the altar of the ancestral hall, and many of the purchasers place the ancestral tablets of their grandparents and parents there. The Liu Surname Association has five rows of such spaces available for purchase, with the middle row the most expensive (NT$200,000 = about US$7300 as of 1996) and the ends the cheapest, still at a considerable cost of NT$50,000 (about US$1825). The scale of the ceremony is much larger in spring and autumn than on the lunar New Year and the rite of ancestor worship takes nearly an hour to complete. A banquet is held after the rite.

At the time of my research in 1996, the Association was awarding scholarships to three academically excellent children of members twice a year (NT$2000 = about US$73 per scholarship) as part of its mutual assistance activities. In addition, the Association notifies its members of other members' or their children's weddings and funerals and sends flowers.

However, these activities do not necessarily appeal to the Taiwanese people today. The ability to travel overseas, which in the past underpinned the attraction of its exchange activities, has lost its attraction with the liberalization of overseas travel. The rite of ancestor worship is of special benefit only to Christians: Christians are banned from offering such rites by themselves, but can resolve their religious conflicts by having the Association offer the rites on their behalf. The scholarship of NT$2000 is not very helpful; the average starting salary of a university graduate was around NT$30,000 (about US$1000) per month in 1996. While Taiwan's common-surname associations provide assistance for members' funerals (Horie 1988: 59–60), the Association does not do that. Notification of ceremonial occasions is not effective in attracting membership because it does not provide any economic benefit.

People often try to locate the raison d'être of common-surname associations in Taiwan in terms of their function as vote-gathering organizations during an election or umbrella groups for corporate management (Ye 1978; Ishida 1996: 141–59; Horie 1988), but the Liu Surname Association does not serve any such function. As I elaborate below, one election candidate with the surname of Liu visited a ceremonial event to solicit votes during my stay. I was told later, however, that no one had voted for him. Therefore it is unlikely that the Liu Surname Association is useful in this regard.

Despite the apparent lack of appeal, the Liu Association's raison d'être lies somewhere other than the oft-proclaimed activities or functions mentioned above. The Association offers its executives opportunities to acquaint themselves with new local elites. Yushan had a large influx of new residents after the Second World War, to the extent that pre-war local elites complained that they did not know who lived in Yushan any more. At the same time, being in the southwestern part of Taipei City, Yushan was left behind in the post-war development efforts—which centered on the eastern area—and was regarded by Taipei as a 'backward' county. Unlike the pre-war era, many of Taipei's elites moved to other areas to live. In these circumstances, the Liu Surname Association has provided a convenient place to meet Taipei's new elites since any Taipei resident with the surname of Liu was eligible to join. The executives from Yushan were able to not only meet these new elites but also cleverly select beneficial acquaintances through the Association or other common-surname associations (Kamizuru 2004). This was made possible by the perception of closeness attached to the 'common surname' on the one hand and the pragmatic approach the executives have taken in handling matters on the other. I examine personal relationships within common-surname associations more specifically in the next section.

Personal relations within the Liu Surname Association

A general characteristic of common-surname associations is an atmosphere of closeness. For example, Ishida, a researcher of Taiwanese common-surname associations, once visited the Shi Surname Association in Tainan through an introduction by the Shi Surname Association in Taichung. The Shi Surname Association of Tainan warmly welcomed Ishida on the basis of that introduction alone and gave him a lot of information. Ishida says that this is because of trust between members of the same clan. He also reports that the Shi Surname Association in Taipei performs welfare services and provides 'scholarships, emergency aid for members, celebrations and visits for special occasions such as weddings and funerals, and various entertainment activities.' Personal relations within surname associations are conducted for the purpose of 'deepening friendship' and members are 'very closely' connected (Ishida 1996: 286).

The closeness between members is also stressed by members of the Liu Surname Association in Taipei. Many of its executives say that members must help each other and avoid talking about politics which may lead to conflicts.

Some members actually expect mutual support when they join the Liu Surname Association.[7]

> Case 1: Liu Qinan (an employee of a small size company), member of the Liu Surname Association, came to Taipei from an area north of Taipei about thirty years ago. When I asked him why he joined the Association, he replied, 'I felt unconfident because I came from the countryside and I thought people with a common surname would help me if I encountered any problems.'

This anticipation of mutual support is particularly strong among ordinary members. Once they join, they find activities that generate a sense of closeness between members that may suggest the possibility of mutual support. The rite of ancestor worship and the banquet are examples. Members' economic or social standing does not matter before their ancestors. The only thing that matters is their distance from the ancestors, that is, their age. At the ancestral ritual of the Liu Surname Association in spring and autumn, therefore, symbolically important acts such as 'reading ancestors' teachings,' 'reading auspicious sayings from ancestors to descendants' and 'offering incense to ancestors' are performed by older members rather than the executives. At the joint congress, elderly members are always honored in a ceremony. Kinship and equality before ancestors are emphasized on these occasions. However, these rituals are run by the executives. The executives, not the older members, make decisions regarding the operation of ceremonies and manage the proceedings on the day.

The banquet after the rite is an occasion to cultivate friendship. I have personally observed it twice and it had a very congenial atmosphere. Although it appeared to foster a sense of togetherness on the surface, it was not quite the case in reality. Closer scrutiny revealed that members were merely sharing the same space and close relatives and friends formed separate groups based on pre-existing relationships to have their meal together. The executives often formed their own group and ate together. After the meal, they left the table in groups. There were no activities to promote friendship during the meal. Individual members almost never shared a table with strangers unless they were executives.

These examples suggest the activities of the Association have two opposing vectors. They project closeness between members by generating a sense of togetherness among participants in one sense. At the same time, they make participants aware of the distance between ordinary members and executives in terms of the practical operation of the organization. An important element in generating this duality is the double standard of personnel selection for activities. To create a sense of togetherness in activities, age is the only criterion based on the concept of 'equality before ancestors.' To create a sense of distance, people are differentiated on the basis of individual ability and merit: only a few are selected to become executives. The former is concerned with equality and the latter is concerned with individual differences.

The coexistence of the emphasis on closeness and the pragmatic approach are evident in every aspect of the activities and personal relationships of the Liu Surname Association. Election campaigning is one such example.

> Case 2: At the end of 2004, Liu Yongchun (President of the Rotary Club), whom I had known for more than ten years through the Liu Surname Association, offered me a chance to see a parliamentarian with the surname of Liu. He told me, 'I supported him in the recent election because he had the same surname. Now he has been elected to the parliament, I am going to see him next week. I must ask him first

but you can come with me if he agrees.' I did not hear from him after that and I was not able to see the parliamentarian.

This case appears to suggest that the common surname is useful during election periods. As mentioned, however, this is not necessarily the case. The election at the time was a fierce battle between the ruling party and the opposition party. The ruling party proposed to move further towards Taiwan's independence and strengthen its own identity. The opposition party took the position that Taiwan should improve its relationship with mainland China and tone down the emphasis on a separate Taiwanese identity. One Liu, whom I have known for over ten years, was a fervent supporter of the ruling party and disliked the opposition party intensely. His older sister was a supporter of the opposition party and used to say that she did not talk about politics with her brother because they always ended up arguing over the election. Liu Yongchun voted for a candidate with the same surname who had a similar political view to his own. He never supports a candidate with a different political credo even if they share a common surname.

The next example also demonstrates that a common surname is not necessarily effective for gathering votes in an election.

> Case 3: Liu Yisheng (aged mid-seventies at the time of my research) was a retired company owner and an executive of the Liu Surname Association. A man with the surname of Liu who was running for a Taipei City Council election attended a meeting of the Association. He was there to ask members of the Association to vote for him. After the candidate finished his speech, I asked Liu Yisheng, 'Will the members vote for him?' He replied, 'Having the same surname, I may be expected to vote for him, but I will not vote for him.' He told me that he would not vote for him because he only turned up to campaign for the election and the other executives had no positive feelings toward him either, for the same reason.

Although those who have a common surname are supposed to help each other according to the norms of the Association, their actual voting behavior reflects their normal day-to-day behavior. They do not cast their votes indiscriminately on the basis of a common surname alone. The emphasis on closeness and the pragmatic approach are both visible here.

The next example (not a direct example about the Association) shows that this is also the case in business.

> Case 4: Liu Debao (aged mid-seventies at the time of my research) was one of the top executives of the Liu Surname Association who had started a Japanese agency business after the war, then built up his own construction company in Taipei. He was a director of a finance company before his retirement. He said that he got on well and did business with ordinary people rather than his relatives and people with the same surname. When I asked him if he had ever hired someone because of a common surname, he replied, 'I employed my younger brother once but it did not work out, so I gave him money to leave the company.' He said that he had never employed anyone else with the same surname.

It is his view that even brothers should be asked to leave if they are detrimental to the operation of a business. He considers that kinship must be separated from business. This view is also applicable to the common surname.

There are stories of people being hired through the Association. Case (5) is an example.

> Case 5: Liu Denghui was a director of a well known temple in Taipei and also an executive of the Liu Surname Association. One day, I visited a cultural facility managed by the temple. The administration manager of this facility also had the surname of Liu. Liu Denghui told me that he got to know this person through the Association and offered him the position when the latter retired from his previous job.

This story makes the common surname appear useful in terms of finding employment. However, there have been many retirees at the Association other than the administration manager. In fact, the manager discussed in Case (5) was known to Liu Denghui through other channels, too. And Liu Denghui chose him because of his honest character and thought he could ask him to take the job which was almost volunteer work for the temple.

Cases (4) and (5) above demonstrate that people do not employ others simply on the basis of sharing a common surname. Furthermore, the main supporter of the Association at its peak was the owner of a distribution agency for a Japanese corporation. I have never heard that he had ever promoted someone within his company because that person had the same surname. Members I met at the Association all said, 'Business is business.'

The following is an example of a case where surname-based connections were sought but did not work out.

> Case 6: One person with the surname of Liu was trying to sell his water filter products through the Liu Surname Association. He often told me how bad the quality of Taiwan's tap water was and how good his filters were (the water was drinkable without boiling, etc.). He made the same sales pitch to other members too. However, I have never heard of anyone, including myself, buying his products. I have known him for over a decade but I have not heard of a single sale to members of the Association to date.

It appears that what is exchanged at common-surname associations is a variety of information rather than actual products or jobs.[8] The next case is a typical example.

> Case 7: The Liu Surname Association of Taipei once hosted a world congress in Taipei. A high government official with the surname Liu provided helpful advice on bureaucratic formalities. An executive of the Association who received his advice (a top director of Taiwan's famous temple) said, 'The high official has the common surname. He readily gave us a lot of information.' However, the executive had known the high official through other channels (temple and government dealings) as well, and their connection was not based solely on sharing a common surname.

As mentioned earlier, an important function of the Liu Surname Association was to provide a place for the Yushan-based executives to meet newcomers to Taipei City. It was also a place where they would find people who might be useful for themselves or the organization.

> Case 8: Liu Zhenan was born in the countryside in the central region of Taiwan. He came to Taipei to look for work at around the age of twenty. His career shows that he has been very successful: he is now the owner of a college. He has been involved in the Liu Surname Association for several decades. He met a member of the Association through work who told him about the ancestral hall in Yushan. He visited the ancestral hall and joined the Liu Surname Association. About ten years ago, he became interested in the world congress of the Liu common-surname associations and attended one in that year

with the executives of the Association. Immediately after that, he was nominated for directorship of the Association and took up the position. He has also been admitted to the Liu Dazutang Surname Association and has now become an executive.

Since the Liu Dazutang Surname Association owns the ancestral hall on which the principal address of the Liu Surname Association is located, it is more important than the Liu Surname Association for the Yushan-based executives. Members of the Liu Surname Association are not admitted to the Liu Dazutang Surname Association immediately: they have to be assessed as to whether they are the right sort of people to be part of the Dazutang. In other words, the executives of the Association screen and select prospective members of the Dazutang from its own membership. On my enquiry, one Yushan-based executive who nominated Liu Zhenan to the directorship of the Association and membership of the Dazutang explained to me that his nomination was made after an assessment of the nominee's character, based on his involvement in the world congress and in the preparations for the event. More specifically, his keen involvement in the common-surname association and adherence to the objectives of the Dazutang were recognized. Liu Zhenan, on his part, told me that the reasons for his being nominated to the directorship of the Association and a member of the Dazutang were 'social status, character and money; and money is particularly important.' As the owner of a college, he had sufficient social status and financial means. He considered that the leadership of the Liu Dazutang Surname Association rated these two factors highly.

The above case shows how the Liu Dazutang Surname Association brings in people of high social and economic standing, but we should not overlook the fact that sincere commitment is also highly valued.

Similarly the exchange of information is carried out in informal relationships. It is desirable for executives to associate with each other on equal footings. For example, marriage, burial and other ceremonial occasions must be conducted in a suitable manner and the guests must make suitable monetary offerings. The executives must maintain face and those who cannot afford to do so due to lack of financial means or time are gradually excluded from the upper echelons of the Association.

Case 9: I once asked my close acquaintance, who was one of the executives (Liu Yisheng in Case 3), about another executive whom I had not seen for a long time. He said, 'I have heard that his business is not going well lately. That is probably why he cannot attend. He has lost face. Not just here but he did not turn up at a wedding of one of the executives the other day.' I asked him, 'Don't people with a common surname help each other in such a situation?' He said, 'We don't do that. We are all different.'[9]

The Surname Association in this example does not project the image of permanent, close ties. Instead, we see people assess each other, present their own values and build relationships through various exchanges.

Another notable aspect of the activities of the Association is the frequency of exchanges among the executives. In comparison with the scarcity of Association-wide activities that can be attended by general members, the board meeting is convened once a month without fail. Although it is a meeting, the executives hold discussions over drinks and a sumptuous meal. The overt purpose of the meeting is to discuss the past activities and future plans of each member of the association, but little time is spent on these subjects. They mainly talk about each other's latest news, the state of the economy, etc. One executive told me that they were not supposed to talk about matters that might be offensive to others. This comment clearly demonstrates that the board meeting of the Association is held for the purpose of cultivating intimate ties among the executives. This is indicative of the importance attached to this aspect of the Association's activities, that is, the promotion of closeness between the executives. The Association's executive board of directors does not change significantly at each election. Many of those who leave the board of the Association tend to join the boards of the other three Liu associations in Taipei.

A lot of information circulates within the Liu Surname Association, but what is significant is the fact that circulation is limited to certain groups of people, namely the executives. They identify influential people among new members, elevate them to the executive level and cultivate relationships with them. Newly cultivated relationships are then grafted onto already established networks of relationships with others. Using these networks of relationships, the executives introduce people whom they consider to be suitable to their acquaintances in other organizations (for example, directors of a financial institution or a temple). By the same token, high government officials give advice on immigration and other bureaucratic matters to the executives of the Liu Surname Association.

One executive commented on the activities of the Liu Surname Association: 'They are not thinking about the Association seriously. The executives just get together and enjoy eating and drinking together.' Another executive said, 'It is fine by me because I am an executive but I think there are very few benefits for ordinary members, to be honest.' These remarks clearly demonstrate the characteristics of the true state of activities of the contemporary Liu Surname Association. On this basis, it is too one-sided a view to regard the activities of the Association as aiming to unify all members or to foster closeness among them. We need to turn our eyes to the dual functions of the Association: uniting and differentiating.

Common-surname Tong-ism and contemporary Taiwan

As discussed, common-surname tong-ism in contemporary Taiwan has the dual capacity to emphasize closeness and harmony while adopting a pragmatic approach to fostering relationships. In other words, common-surname tong-ism in this context functions as a device to form relationships on the pretext of blood relations by using patrilineal kinship-based ideology underpinned by closeness and harmony, but in fact enabling personal relations to be established with a large number of people in various areas that are not shackled by norms of kinship. This reality is different from the traditional image of patrilineal kinship, the main purpose of which is closeness and mutual assistance. This difference appears to stem from the fact that, as R. Watson explained in her study of Hong Kong in the 1980s, Chinese society, including Taiwan, is structured by the systems of the State and the market economy, and family background does not govern production or consumption nor form the foundation of society (R. Watson 1985: 173–4).

In his study of lineages in southeastern China, Freedman explains the main reason for the continued existence of lineages in a stratified society as follows: 'The humble member of a lineage owning large corporate resources was still in a better position than his analogue in a poor lineage' (Freedman 1958: 127). Very large lineages collected taxes on behalf of the government, settled internal disputes in accordance with their own rules, leased land to poor farmers and conducted rites of ancestor worship using common property. He argued that economic, prestigious, political and legal benefits obtainable through a powerful lineage motivated its members to remain with the lineage. Members of the lower stratum were able to work the communally-owned land of the lineage, behave as part of the lineage with successful examinees of the national civil service examination, and gain protection from powerful members of the lineage if they got into difficulties (Freedman 1958: 127–30). Here, we can observe the way people in different strata are linked by mutual interests. Members of the lower stratum act as constituent parts that support the large scale of the lineage, and the upper stratum members provided various facilities to their lower stratum counterparts.

However, the Liu Surname Association of Taipei did not collect taxes on behalf of the government, did not settle internal disputes in accordance with its own rules, and did not lease land to poor farmers. In contemporary Taiwanese society, taxation and legal proceedings are conducted by the apparatus of the state. The same applies to welfare. According to the Ministry of Finance, the Taiwanese Government has implemented various programs under its social welfare policy, including financial assistance to low income families, allowances for elderly members of low to medium income families and welfare benefits for elderly farmers. The existing income disparity would increase by 1.26 times without these provisions. Membership of the Liu Surname Association does not provide its members with any benefits in this regard, and the Association does not conduct any activities that may lead to a reduction in the income gap.

With regard to prestige, Segawa argues in relation to the revival of lineage organizations and activities in mainland China, that contributing one's own money to the restoration of ancestral halls, graves and other lineage or branch monuments or towards the repairs of village roads and bridges has been the way to convert financial wealth into social prestige by elevating personal wealth to a relatively more public domain (Segawa 2004: 222). However, Taiwan's common-surname associations are not functioning well in this regard, either.

The establishment of common-surname associations in Taiwan was triggered by the Chinese renaissance movement, initiated by the KMT Government as part of its anti-Communist Chinese policy measures in the 1970s. It was encouraged by the government partly to demonstrate that the Republic of China was preserving traditional Chinese culture and partly as a tool to create ties with other countries in order to counter its isolation in the international community. Many of the surname associations in Taiwan were founded during that period and attracted interest from the public, partly due to the government's support.

The renaissance movement ended a long time ago and common-surname associations can no longer attract people's attention as they once did. In Han-Chinese society, the ability to attract attention is one of the important elements that support the prestige of a social organization (Serizawa 1993, 1999; Pan 2002a, 2002b), but contemporary common-surname associations in Taiwan are lacking in this respect. Religious organizations, temples, the Lions Club, the Rotary Club and other organizations that exist in a relatively more 'public domain,' to borrow Segawa's terms, attract more attention from the community than do kinship-based organizations such as common-surname associations.

Another factor that characterizes the nature of Taiwan's common-surname tong-ism is the fact that the core industry of Taiwan is commerce rather than agriculture. Freedman points out the importance of farming in terms of the sustainability of lineages (Freedman 1958; see also Baker 1968). Potter noticed that lineage organizations were developed in the south rather than the north and pointed out the importance of high farming productivity for sustaining various lineage activities (Potter 1970).

However, farmland ownership is not an attractive source of wealth in contemporary Taiwan. Now that secondary and tertiary industries have become the mainstay of the Taiwanese economy, farmland is not perceived as a wealth-creating asset. Farming is thought to generate a relatively small income relative to the labor required. Urban and industrial land that can be bought and sold, not farming land, reap enormous profits. Such land holdings are not given away to siblings (after the estate is divided) nor leased to strangers in the way that farmland is. Some patrilineal kin groups or common-surname associations own real estate including land, but this is merely in the form of fractional ownership by which each stakeholder owns a portion of the property. It is shared ownership by wealthy members rather than communal ownership by the whole group in question.

In contemporary Taiwan, wealth acquisition depends largely on success or failure in the market rather than in agricultural production. People tend to think that patrilineal kinship-based familism must be important in Taiwan because of the prevalence of family companies and preferential treatment of mainlanders in the bureaucracy. However, with the advancement of democratization and market principles, those who lack ability are excluded and nepotism is strongly condemned as corruption in Taiwan.[10] Acquisition of wealth largely depends on ability to read the market, specialist skills and education. The question of how to utilize available information and resources is far more important in the market than in the world of farming and there is little room for consideration of kinship in this competitive environment. We saw an example of this in Case (4) above.

This phenomenon is not limited to Taiwan but is ubiquitous in any Chinese society where wealth acquisition depends largely on market performance. For instance, Sonoda reports a case in Hebei Province, China, in which a person jointly financed and managed a business with his brothers and cousins but he replaced them when the initial contract period of three years had passed because the business was not making a profit. Sonoda argues that such a case cannot be explained satisfactorily by the concept of familism (Sonoda 2000: 262–4).

A similar case was reported by Sasaki Mamoru (1993), who studied merchant families in northern China. For example, the head of one merchant family jointly managed a shop with his brothers and at the same time ran his own shop selling almost the same range of products. He was faced with the question of how to strike a balance between his own shop and the jointly owned shop. In the end, he took advantage of his position as the head of the family and gave priority to the profitability of his own shop while trying not to harm the business of his family-owned shop. In this example, a man runs his own business separately from his brothers and puts this enterprise before his family business. He does not treat his own shop and the family shop equally just because he is in business with his brothers (Sasaki Mamoru 1993: 92–120).[11] In other cases reported by Sasaki, merchants would not help their brothers who suffered economic downfall. Some would not only refuse to help but would also try to minimize damage to the family fortune threatened by their brothers' misbehavior (Sasaki Mamoru 1993: 92–120).

Additionally, J. Watson points out that economic and social benefits other than land have significance for the survival of lineages (1975). For example, lineage ties are useful for migrants from Hong Kong to England in terms of gathering information about the host country or management of land and assets left behind in the home country.

As mentioned earlier, however, information does not guarantee success. In Taiwan, people emigrating overseas tend to cash in their land and other assets and transfer the money to a bank in the host country. I have never heard of a common-surname association managing assets on behalf of its members.

Common-surname tong-ism in contemporary Taiwanese society does not function as a means to find employment, to obtain status or position, or to secure one's livelihood unless one has necessary ability.[12] Common-surname associations do not mediate disputes. Nowadays, these matters mostly come under the jurisdiction of the government. In Taiwan, partnership and employment relations among siblings can be severed if they are not suitable as partners and employees. Wealth acquisition requires individual ability and effort rather than reliance on personal relations based on common-surnames.[13] In light of Sasaki's case studies discussed above, this is not limited to the Han-Chinese in Taiwan.

Conclusion

Although I personally do not know of any case of successful social elevation achieved through common-surname tong-ism, it is not my intention to argue in this paper that it does not exist. However, it should be pointed out that the perception of common-surname tong-ism based on the overtly promoted and/or proclaimed image of closeness and harmony as we have seen above is misleading. The interpretation that common-surname tong-ism is an important device to enable social mobility based on the values it emphasizes is too far removed from reality. No one is catapulted into wealth or treated equally by people of other social strata on the basis of common-surname tong-ism.

Common-surname tong-ism connects people across different economic and social status groups, but *how* it connects them is the question. Based on the above discussion, there are broadly three ways to make such connections in contemporary Taiwan. First, common surnames are used as a device to create personal relationships as discussed above. There are many ways through which personal relationships are formed in Taiwan such as work, hobbies, school and local community but common surnames still have the capability to turn a total stranger into a 'relative' even today. There is no doubt that one's ancestors and place of origin are important parts of a person's identity in the Han-Chinese society of Taiwan, and therefore the common surname provides a commonality with others and an opportunity to create relationships among those without previous acquaintances.

Second, common-surname tong-ism is used as a model to explain a complex relationship in simple terms. As I have suggested, the rhetoric about 'having a common surname' often does not explain anything. In a parliamentary election, 'having a common surname' is not the reason why someone decides to vote for a particular candidate.

A shared political belief (which relates to one's perception of the State and self-identity) is more important—sharing a 'common surname' is merely used by way of simple explanation. It is the same in the case of a high government official providing information. Personal relations are built on double and triple levels of association, but having a 'common surname' tends to provide an overtly satisfactory explanation. People still assess each other and consider their own interests even in a common-surname relationship, but the 'common surname' has become an acceptable explanatory model that conceals the real reasons behind the relationship. The explanatory model is premised on a norm that emphasizes mutual assistance between relatives, as Fei Xiaotong argues (Fei 1991), and the perception among the Han-Taiwanese that people sharing a common-surname are real relatives rather than quasi-relatives. Thus, the 'common surname' has become an important model that explains one's relationships and actions without stating actual reasons in Taiwan.

Finally, common-surname tong-ism provides a domain in which people act on principles other than merit and competition. As we can see in the rite of the Liu Surname Association, one's distance from ancestors, namely age, is an important element which cannot be overcome by individual efforts. It was the primary reason that relationships between people with a common surname were considered to embody 'closeness and harmony.' The 'closeness and harmony' is the objective of the Liu Surname Association and is the basis for explaining membership and members' actions on the pretext of a 'common surname.' This idea offers a sense of values that differ from those prevalent in the real world dominated by competition and bargaining.

At the same time, however, such a view is not fully compatible with the pragmatic aspect of the common-surname association. In fact, pragmatic and conciliatory relationships coexist in the common-surname association. What is significant is that the latter obscures the former to take priority as the purpose of the organization. It bears a certain similarity to R. Watson's argument that 'there is little doubt that the egalitarian ideology of the lineage plays an important role in bridging the gap between rich and poor' (R. Watson 1985: 54).

Common-surname tong-ism allows people of unequal standing to establish personal relations based on the togetherness of belonging to the 'same clan.' However, it is this togetherness which makes the formation of unequal personal relations possible as we have seen in the Liu Surname Association. Focusing on this duality, we will need a closer investigation to find out who is making use of personal relations based on common-surname tong-ism and for what purpose. This will provide an opening to break free from an easily formed stereotype that sees the Han-Chinese society as one based on kinship.

Glossary

Zongqinhui 宗親会
renqingzai 人情債

6 Reproduction of Status Traditions and Social Prestige in the Provincial Society of Colonial and Post-colonial Korea: A Case Study of Namwŏn

Hiroshi Honda

Introduction

The purpose of this paper is to examine how various cultural traditions linked to the pre-modern social status structure have been reproduced in the provincial society[1] of colonial and post-colonial Korea, based on a case study of Namwŏn, North Chŏlla Province, situated in the southwestern part of the Korean Peninsula. Furthermore, this paper analyses the meaning of these traditions in the context of the local elite since the end of the Chosŏn era and the newly emerging forces, and examines how these practices were tied to social prestige.

The most well-known traditional local force in the provincial society of Korea, particularly in the rural area, are so-called *yangban*.[2] The characteristics of the typical provincial *yangban* are as follows: they are the descendants of the *chaeji-sajok*, who settled in provincial rural villages generally after the sixteenth or seventeenth century; they worship the significant achievements of their ancestors; they abide by Confucian norms; they had been living as a group in their localized core (see Shima 1978) and its neighborhood until depopulation began in the mid-1960s; they have formed a patrilineal kinship organization called *munjung* to carry out projects to devoutly honor their ancestors; and they have enjoyed superior social prestige. Their ancestors, *chaeji-sajok*, were originally the landed gentry. The *chaeji-sajok* belonged to the upper-class and enjoyed various legal and social privileges, but after the modern reformation of the state's administration starting with the Kabo Reforms of 1894, most of these privileges have been lost. By then, many *chaeji-sajok* families were no longer economically upper-class, and some became landed or tenant farmers or even farm laborers. Yet, in terms of their relationship with ancestors, they collectively retained superior social prestige as the *yangban*. Conversely, such prestige held currency only within the geographical boundaries of provincial *yangban* communities where the base of their own *munjung* was localized (usually within the bounds of a pre-modern county); their claims for high prestige were not always accepted if they were bankrupt and left their original place (Goldberg 1973). Meanwhile, as demonstrated by the considerable difficulties faced by emergent forces in asserting and gaining acceptance for social prestige equal to that of the *yangban*, this 'prestige' and the status group founded on it were highly exclusive. In terms of social anthropological studies in post-colonial Korea—which began in earnest during the 1970s—the social organization of the *yangban* and the cultural traditions they supported have been among the foci of ethnographical research (Itō 1986).

While the social prestige of the *yangban* has already been discussed in several studies (e.g. Suenari 1987; Okada 2001), I would like to contribute my historical research on the period from the end of the Chosŏn era to the colonial era, including some data on the Namwŏn area, in order to articulate the reproduction of *yangban* status traditions and prestige. In doing so, I address the issue of the middle-level local elite and emerging forces who did not rank as highly as the *yangban* but still enjoyed far more prestige than the so-called *sangmin* (commoners). In particular, I focus on the case of *rijok* (patrilineal kin groups consisting of agnatic descendants of *hyang-ri*, or local functionaries), which hereditarily produced local functionaries in charge of administrative duties at local bureaucratic offices during the latter half of the Chosŏn period. The social status of *rijok* was lower than that of the *chaeji-sajok*, but wielded considerable power in real politics as local forces. For several reasons the *rijok* remains rather inconspicuous in the provincial society after the modern reforms, especially in the colonial period (1910–1945) and the days after Liberation in 1945. There have also been very few ethnographical studies on the *rijok* in the field of anthropology of Korea since the 1970s. However, after I Hunsang's pioneering study (1990) on the *hyang-ri* and *rijok* in the late Chosŏn Dynasty, the body of research on their historical profile and modern changes in their modes of existence is slowly growing (e.g. Yŏnse Taehakkyo Kukhakyŏnguwŏn 1999). Some researchers have begun to emphasize the importance of the *rijok* in understanding the political process in the provincial society (Kim Kwangŏk 2000). I have been conducting case studies on the state affairs of the *rijok* in colonial and post-colonial Namwŏn by unearthing the literature and gathering oral histories (e.g. Honda 1999, 2004). In this paper, I elucidate status traditions and social prestige for intermediate power holders or agents who are neither *yangban* nor commoners, drawing upon examples of the leading figures of the *rijok* families supplemented by cases of other emerging forces.

I begin this discussion by clarifying the status structure and its foundations in the context of provincial society of the late Chosŏn Dynasty. I then consider what kind of status prestige was enjoyed or pursued by those who belonged to the *yangban* class and the intermediate classes respectively.

Before closing this introduction, it is important to briefly illuminate the main subject area of this case study. Namwŏn is situated in the midlands of North Chŏlla Province in the southwestern part of the Korean Peninsula. It has thrived through the ages as a transport hub where roads to South Chŏlla Province and South Kyŏngsang Province meet, and as a farming region with fertile soil. Namwŏn was one of the larger local administrative counties which belonged to a higher level of the administrative structure during the Chosŏn era. As the economic and geopolitical importance of the coastal plain area—with its large expanse of farmland—increased within colonial Chŏlla Province, the relative economic status of Namwŏn declined. Still, the development of an urban area took place relatively early in Namwŏn Ŭmnae,[3] which was a core administrative settlement with one of the largest marketplaces in the province. Namwŏn's *rijok*, as mentioned above, were mostly those who had lived in this *ŭmnae* for generations, and came to occupy diverse economic niches as the urbanization and development of the *ŭmnae* progressed. In contrast, the *yangban* who descended from the *chaeji-sajok* were based in the rural area. Except for those who migrated to the *ŭmnae* or cities, rural *yangban* generally continued to earn their living by farming well into the colonial period. These differences in economic bases are considered to have some subtle effects on the establishment of their respective social prestige.

Status structures in the late Chosŏn period

To understand status structures in the late Chosŏn period, it is important to first determine which social entities or categories should be treated as status groups, and then to identify the corresponding entities or categories in the provincial society of the late Chosŏn period. This question has already been critically discussed by a historical sociologist, Kim P'ildong (1991). I define the concept of status based on his argument and identify the fundamental characteristics of various status groups of the late Chosŏn period.

According to Kim P'ildong (1991), there are three common elements in conceptualizations of the concept of 'status.' Firstly, status is an expression of social hierarchical relationships (i.e., a social stratification system). Secondly, status often legally defines social privileges and discrimination. Thirdly, status is hereditary and hence carries attributive connotations (Kim P'ildong 1991: 496). The three classes of clergy, aristocracy and citizenry or peasant under the French ancient regime, or the Edo Japanese classes of warrior, farmer (peasant), artisan and merchant (in addition, *eta* and *hinin* (outcasts)) can be understood based on this understanding of status. In contrast, the difficulty with the provincial society in the late Chosŏn period lies in the fact that the system of attribution to hierarchical ranking, generally hereditary groups or categories associated with social privileges or discrimination was not necessarily legally defined as a single and whole system. These days, some researchers of the status system view 'social status' as status groups or categories based on some kind of social agreement, and differentiate it from the legally defined 'legal status' (Kim P'ildong 1991; Chi Sŭngjong 1991; Yoshida 1998).

In light of these arguments, Kim P'ildong proposes the following four requirements as indices for the theoretical framework needed to explain the status system in the Chosŏn era (Kim P'ildong 1991: 454–6).

1. We must clearly define the concept of status.
2. We must clearly recognize the fact that Chosŏn's status system was part of a dynamic process. In particular, we must correct our past tendency to try to reconstruct its basic structure from historical facts in the early Chosŏn period.
3. Since different status categories were established in different circumstances, the determinants that applied to each of them were also multidimensional. The overall structure of Chosŏn's status system must be understood as a combination of different factors and dimensions.
4. We must understand the 'scenes of everyday life' in which the status system functioned specifically and separately. The status system primarily functioned in its relationship with the state, but also in the context of a 'society' (local community) of ordinary people which was relatively distinct from the state.

In this paper, I focus on requirements 3 and 4 in an attempt to develop a picture of the status structure in the late Chosŏn period. Firstly, the most comprehensive differentiation of citizens provided by state law was that between *yangmin* and *ch'ŏnmin*. The former were those subject to *yangyŏk* (duties for the dynastic state imposed on freeborn people, including taxation, provision of daily necessities and precious goods to the king and dynastic offices, military service, labor service etc.) and eligible to sit for *kwagŏ* (civil service examination[4]). The latter were 'despised people,' not subject to *yangyŏk* and not eligible to sit for *kwagŏ*. The *ch'ŏnmin* were divided into slaves (*nobi*) owned by public offices (public slaves) and those owned by private individuals (private slaves) (Yoshida 1998: 216–19). Among the *yangmin*, those who possessed official ranks and posts and those who were granted the *yuhak* status were exempted from *yangyŏk* duties. The *yuhak* originally referred to the students of Sŏnggyungwan, the highest seat of Confucian education, who were preparing to sit for the final civil service examination (*munkwa*), but the meaning of the term changed later as I discuss below (Yoshida 1998: 220).

Sajok signifies the family of *sadaebu* (office holders), that is, the family of those who possess dynastic offices or grades of officers. Since the middle Chosŏn period, those who entered the civil service had virtually been limited to *sajok* lineage members and therefore *sajok* became a status in the aforementioned sense as the lineage that produced state officials (Yoshida 1998: 218). As a result, the title of *yuhak* with *yangyŏk* exemption came to be used as an honorable title for *sajok* lineage members who did not possess grades of officers or dynastic offices (Yoshida 1998: 220).

Alternatively, some *sajok* members settled in the provincial society and built power bases during the sixteenth and seventeenth centuries. They gradually came to form a thick social stratum, conceptualized as the *chaeji-sajok* by social historians (cf. Miyajima 1995). The *chaeji-sajok* initially produced some lineage members who passed the civil service examination and became state officials, but the numbers undertaking this gradually declined over time. Rather, they maintained their superiority over other classes as the virtuous people who were model practitioners of Confucian ethics through the compilation of *hyang-an* (the *sajok* register for each local administrative county) or through the administration of *hyangsadang* (local agency) and *hyangyak* (village contract)—devices of self-governing institutions. It was generally after settlement and the establishment of power in the provincial society that *sajok* descendants gathered to live in particular settlements (farming villages) or regions where their apical ancestors or outstanding family members settled. They thus formed the so-called *chipsŏngch'on* (a settlement of a particular patrilinial kinship group), then organized a type of association called *munjunggye* to promote the institutionalization of patrilineal kinship. In this process, the ranks of *chaeji-sajok* were gradually established in each county. Distinguished *sajok* lineages were referred to by their clan name,[5] preceded by the name of their *chipsŏngch'on* or *segŏji* (the localized core of a patrilineal kinship group). For example, distinguished *sajok* lineages in Namwŏn were referred to collectively as 'Ch'oe-No-I-An,' that is, the lineage of Sangnyŏng Ch'oe which descended from fifteenth century civil official Ch'oe Hang and settled in Tundŏk-pang, the lineage of P'ungch'ŏn No which descended from sixteenth century civil official No Shinjin and settled in Huch'ŏn-ri, the lineage of Chŏnju I which descended from Ch'unsŏngjŏng who was a great grandson of Hyoryŏngdaegun, the second son of King T'aejong, and settled in Tundŏk-pang, and the lineage of Sunhŭng An which descended from late Koryŏ-era councilor An Hyang and settled in Naegi-ri. In the local society, they are customarily referred to as the Tundŏk Ch'oe lineage, the Huch'ŏn No lineage, the Tundŏk I lineage and the Naegi An lineage, respectively. The *yangban* in colonial and post-colonial provincial society are basically the descendants of these *chaeji-sajok* lineages.

A large majority of *yangmin* were people called *sanghan*, *sŏin* or *yang* who had a duty to do military service as part of their *yangyŏk*. They were the so-called *sangmin* (freeborn commoners). Others who performed administrative work at local bureaucratic offices as part of their *yangyŏk* were, although small in number, a powerful presence in local politics that could not be ignored. These local functionaries were called *hyang-ri* (or *sŏri*). The position of *hyang-ri* can be divided into three ranks: head officials called *hojang* (and *ibang*, which became an equally important rank later on), the heads of six offices, each of which handled distinctive functions (both the offices and their heads were called *yukpang*),[6] and lower-level officers in charge of day-to-day affairs called *kak-nim* and *chesaek*. Chief functionaries (*suri*) such as *hojang* and *ibang*, and even *yukpang* heads in part of the counties, were supposed to be selected exclusively from particular lineages in each county. This can be regarded as one type of social status. Such lineages are referred to as the *rijok* (or *ijok*) in this paper. Some *rijok* familes have a long history. For example, *suri* families in Kyŏngju and Andong of Kyŏngsang Province hereditarily produced *hojang* and *sangsomun* (which later became *ibang*) as local ruling families during the Koryŏ era, some descendants of which obtained dynastic offices in the early Chosŏn period and became founding ancestors of *sajok* lineages, while the rest of the families produced leading local functionaries throughout the Chosŏn era. Conversely, the pre-sixteenth century history of *suri* lineages in some of the other counties, such as the *rijok* families in Namwŏn mentioned below, are rather obscure.

Other than the *hyang-ri* and the *rijok*, status groups positioned between the *sajok* and the *sangmin* included the *sŏjok* (descendants of illegitimate sons of the *sajok*), the *chapkwa chung-in* families that lived in the capital city of Hanyang and produced foreign language specialists, medical officers and astrologists through the technical civil service examination, and the capital *sŏri* who worked as administrative functionaries at Hanyang's bureaucratic offices. Some researchers call these mid-level status groups *chung-in* (middle people) collectively. It should be noted that each of these status groups came into existence in unique circumstances: for example, it was the illegitimacy of their origins in the case of the *sŏjok*; the inferiority of the bureaucratic ranks they came to monopolize in the case of the *chapkwa chung-in*. On the other hand, since the eighteenth century, many non-*sajok yangmin* people began to assume the title of *yuhak* (entered as such in their family registers (*hojŏk*))—the honorable title for the *sajok* without office—in order to avoid burdensome *yangyŏk*. It is doubtful that they were treated on par with the *sajok* in the provincial society, but it could be that they were permitted to use the title officially because they had achieved some form of improvement in their economic or political standing.

I will not go into details here but, when considering the status structure in the late Chosŏn period, it is important to take other status groups into account, including the *ch'ŏnmin* (public slaves and private slaves), the *mu* (shamans and priests who were not necessarily the *ch'ŏnmin* but nevertheless discriminated against), hereditary entertainers, Buddhist monks and artisans, each of which had its own basis of existence. The example of the self-styled *yuhak* people shows that changes in legal status were not necessarily linked to changes in social status. In this sense, Kim P'ildong's argument that Chosŏn's status structure should be understood as a combination of different factors and dimensions is significant.

In the next section, I provide an overview of Namwŏn's *hyang-ri* and *rijok* in the late Chosŏn period, before moving on to a discussion of status traditions in colonial and post-colonial times.

Namwŏn's *hyang-ri* and status traditions

According to the registers of late Chosŏn *hyang-ri* and *muim* (military and police functionaries) passed down to the association of elderly descendants of Namwŏn *rijok* (Namwŏn Elders' Association), chief functionaries in the ranks of *hojang* and *ibang* were almost exclusively produced by males whose surname (*sŏng*) was either I or Yang. As far as I could cross-check with genealogical records, the surname of I came from either of four branches of the Yŏngch'ŏn I clan, and Yang came from either of two branches of the Namwŏn Yang clan. Many of the heads of six offices were also produced by these six leading families, although approximately ten other surnames were also found. These ten surnames were likely to be ranked next to the leading families (referred to as 'minor families' here). In the case of military functionaries (*kungwan*), however, 41% of chief military and security functionaries (*haengsugungwan*) came from eighteen non-*suri* families (including the abovementioned minor families). Analyzing the military functionaries' register in Kyŏngju of Kyŏngsang Province, Takeda identifies a high proportion of non-*suri* clan names among military functionaries (thirty-nine clan names accounting for 19%). Takeda suggests that it was 'perhaps because of the requirement for their involvement in military affairs that an individual aptitude for military duties was considered more important than lineage or status' (Takeda 1989: 420–2).

To find out how these *rijok* families were treated in the community, particularly by the *chaeji-sajok* lineage members, it is useful to examine a local dispute that arose in the late nineteenth century Namwŏn over *samaan* entries. *Samaan* was a register of those who passed the recognized scholar (*saengwŏn*) and advancing scholar (*chinsa*) examinations. Since the register was compiled by the *chaeji-sajok* people, however, only those who were members of the *chaeji-sajok* lineages were allowed to have their names entered. In 1892, I Kyuhwa, I Ch'ŏlsŏp, I Hongsŏp from the Yŏngch'ŏn I clan who had passed the *saengwŏn* and *chinsa* examinations demanded to be registered in the *samaan*. The *chaeji-sajok* lineages of Namwŏn declined to register them on the grounds that it was a well-known fact that the Yŏngch'ŏn I was a *hyang-ri* clan which historically had produced Namwŏn County functionaries. The *chaeji-sajok* side wrote to the head of Namwŏn County (*namwŏnbusa*) and argued that the assertion that I Ch'ŏlsŏp and others were descendants of I Kŏn and his son I Hakchŏn, who had been pupils of a renowned scholar, was wrong because: (1) I Kŏn and I Hakchŏn did not leave any direct descendents; and (2) the Yŏngch'ŏn I of Namwŏn had been a *hyang-ri* clan from the beginning, and none of their clan-members were traced to the *chaeji-sajok*. The families of I Kyuhwa, I Ch'ŏlsŏp and I Hongsŏp were direct descendants of I Ch'ŏnnam, who settled in Yongdam village, Wŏnch'ŏn-pang (Chuch'ŏn District, Namwŏn City today) in the seventeenth century, instead of settling among the *rijok* families in Namwŏn Ŭmnae. According to members of another family which settled in Unbong County adjoining Namwŏn County, their family line within the Yŏngch'ŏn I clan was regarded as being above the *hyang-ri* level. Nevertheless, from the viewpoint of the *chaeji-sajok* lineages, as long as they were part of the Yŏngch'ŏn I clan living in Namwŏn County, they did not deserve the same level of treatment as the *sajok* because they were members of *hyang-ri* clan (Kim Hyŏnyŏng 1993: 142–5; Kuksap'yŏnch'anwiwŏnhoe 1990).

Since the late nineteenth century, there has been a noticeable change of inclination among the *rijok* families in Namwŏn, in that they have sought to form or restructure their own cultural traditions rather than demand equal treatment from the *sajok* status group. An example of this is the reinforcement of the organizational, financial and ritual aspects of Nogyeso—the association of *rijok* elders mainly consisting of retired *hyang-ri* and *kungwan* functionaries (Honda 2004). Another example is evident through the refinement of the rituals and finances of Namwŏn Kwanwangmyo, a shrine for Guan Yu (Kwan U in Korean), a Chinese Shu Dynasty general whose spirit reportedly appeared during Toyotomi Hideyoshi's second invasion of Korea in 1597 and rescued Korea from the crisis (Honda 2006). Yet another example can be seen in the empowerment of the financial base for Sŏnwŏnsa, a Buddhist temple reportedly constructed to remedy the geomancy (*feng shui*) deficiencies of Namwŏn Ŭmnae, followed by the establishment of its peace prayer rite (Honda 1999: chapter four). Nogyeso touted the practice of Confucian decorum as its aim and enjoyed the patronage of the Namwŏn county head during the late Chosŏn period. At Namwŏn Kwanwangmyo, a ceremony to express gratitude for the manifestation of Gwan Yu's spirit and to praise the loyalty and righteousness personified by him was conducted as an official rite presided over by the kings until the end of the Chosŏn era. Sŏnwŏnsa also had the support of the Namwŏn County Head. However, the Namwŏn-based *sajok* lineages never played an active role in these associations or ceremonial facilities. At the same time, the involvement of *rijok* families in the maintenance and operation of local rituals and key facilities in the Namwŏn area, particularly in the *ŭmnae*, became noticeable. For example, the rebuilding of facilities for the protection of important *feng shui* sites within Namwŏn's *ŭmnae* area was led by someone from a *rijok* family of the Yŏngch'ŏn I clan who had held *hojang* and *ibang* posts (Honda 2004). It is important to stress that the formation and restructuring of cultural traditions, which is an important factor in examining the establishment of the *rijok* as a status group in the colonial period and after, occurred during this period and that it occurred in a place where the hegemony of the *chaeji-sajok* status group could hardly reach.

Modern social changes and the *chaeji-sajok*

Among a range of factors that underpinned the existence of various status groups in the late Chosŏn period, the legal status system, the public service appointment system and the administrative structure closely related to the first two systems underwent the most dramatic changes, amid a backdrop of political and economic upheaval, from the end of the Chosŏn era to the early colonial period. The Kabo Reforms, which began in 1894, can be considered to be the first of such changes. During the reform process, it was declared that the bureaucratic recruitment system of *kwagŏ* examination would be abolished, lineage and class distinctions between *yangban/sangmin* and civil/military would be removed, *nobi* slavery would be abolished and the *ch'ŏnmin* would be freed (*Kwanbo* [Korean Government Newsletter] 28 June 1894).

It appears that the distinction between *yangban* and *sangmin* as social status groups was mostly maintained in provincial communities even after the abolition of the legal status system and the *kwagŏ* examination. In these provincial villages the descendants of the *chaeji-sajok* lineages continued the communal activities of each *munjung*, based on localized cores such as *segŏji* or *chipsŏngch'on*, and also carried out social exchanges and other activities honoring Confucian traditions with members of other *yangban* lineages. According to the study by Chi Sŭngjong and others on the situation of the *sajok* clans in the Tansŏng area of Kyŏngsang Province during the social upheavals following Korea's opening to foreign trade and diplomatic relations with Japan (1876) and the Western Great Powers (1882), descendants of the *chaeji-sajok* reproduced the prestige of '*yangban*,' even after the Kabo Reforms, through the cultural practices of the *sajok* in the realms of community, lineage and family, and everyday life (Chi Sŭngjong *et al.* 2000). Reports by Odauchi (1923) and Zenshō (1935) also confirm the fact that each of the local *sajok* lineages, as well as the community of the county-based *sajok* as a whole, was a politically and socially dominant group in the provincial society, particularly in the central and southern parts of the Korean Peninsula, during the colonial period. According to a field survey of central and southern rural villages conducted by Suzuki (1944) in the early 1940s (towards the end of the colonial era), the majority of the *nongja* and *noja* (private slaves who belonged to the *sajok* households) had migrated to other regions over a period of approximately thirty years and had disappeared from the local scene, but there were still clear distinctions between the *yangban* and the *sangmin* in various spheres of life, including social customs, kinship and marriage (e.g., Wŏnju County in Kangwŏn Province, Chech'ŏn County in North Ch'ungch'ŏng Province and Yŏngju County in North Kyŏngsang Province). Descendants of the higher-ranking *yangban* still enjoyed considerable prestige, and the *sajok* lineages were further divided into subgroups such as the *sajok* and the *hyangjok* (Wŏnju County) (Suzuki 1944: 29, 32–3, 167).

According to a local historiography published in 1960, at least 20% of the memorial halls to honor lineage ancestors in Namwŏn were built in the early twentieth century (almost half of the memorial halls for which the year of construction is known). The *chaeji-sajok* not only actively carried out ancestor worship activities in each *munjung*, but also continued to maintain collective activities as *yangban* and *yurim* (Confucian intellectuals) within the boundary of the former county for which educational facilities such as Namwŏn Hyanggyo and Yangsajae[7] served as local bases. In particular, an association called Chonsŏnggye was established in 1919 to provide financial support for Namwŏn Hyanggyo and attracted a large membership of 2078 people, consisting mainly of descendants of the *chaeji-sajok* lineages (Honda 1999).

In his discussion of rural society in colonial Korea, Kim Ikhan views the leaders and core members of rural self-government organizations as the local gentry who are generally small- to medium-scale landowners in economic terms, belong to a social class that historically succeeds the *chaeji-sajok* family lines, mainly live in rural areas, lead or manage the settlement's self-government, have academic backgrounds, and enjoy high prestige in their communities (1996: 2). This class of local gentry has also produced the promoters of new education and activists for enlightenment and independence campaigns.

The *yangban* and *yurim* had nation-wide social networks beyond the boundaries of former counties. Ryu Mina's study on Kyŏnghagwŏn, a Confucian educational institution in colonial Korea, points out that the local *yurim* conducted educational activities in each county in close collaboration with their central base of Kyŏnghagwŏn[8] (Ryu 2004, 2005).

To summarize the argument so far, it is clear that even after the abolishment of the legal status system under the Kabo Reforms and after the beginning of colonial rule, the *yangban*, who were the descendants of the *chaeji-sajok* lineages, and the *yurim*, who assumed the role of practitioners and educators of Confucian traditions in local communities, maintained social prestige. This prestige derived from status traditions through the practice of Confucian traditions individually and at home, the worshipping of ancestors mainly through *munjung* activities, the promotion of Confucianism within each of the former counties, and the reproduction of nation-wide social networks of *yangban* and *yurim*. As mentioned above, the status system in the late Chosŏn period is considered to have two broadly defined bases—legal and socioeconomic. Particularly in the case of the *chaeji-sajok*, which gradually lost access to positions and offices in the central government, it is suspected that their status-based prestige became increasingly dependent on their social capital (social networks) within and beyond the local community, and their economic capital (superior financial power) and cultural capital (the maintenance and refinement of Confucian traditions). Therefore, as long as the reproduction of their social, economic and cultural capital was even partially possible, the social prestige of the *chaeji-sajok* could also be reproduced even after the abolishment of the legal status system and privileges.

How, then, did the non-*yangban* local elite and the newly emerging forces find their way into status traditions during and after the colonial period, without having such extensive social networks or superior cultural capital? Further, in what form were they able to pursue prestige? After examining the social and economic changes in colonial Namwŏn, I will discuss these questions in relation to the examples of some members of the *rijok* families.

Social and economic changes in colonial Namwŏn

Throughout the colonial period, Namwŏn was principally an agricultural region but, in comparison with inland mountainous counties of the same province, it did have slightly better-developed non-agricultural industries—particularly commerce and manufacturing. This was due to the fact that Namwŏn Ŭmnae had prospered as a trading center for a long time due to its location as the hub of land transport within the three provinces of North and South Chŏlla and South Kyŏngsang and also due to the fertile farming zone surrounding it, as mentioned above. Namwŏn Ŭmnae's market place (*ŭmnaejang*) was still one of the largest in North and South Chŏlla Provinces during the latter half of the 1930s where petit-merchants and local peasants traded mainly agricultural and industrial products and daily necessities every fifth day. The employment statistics in the Korean census of 1930 provide a glimpse into the industry structure at the time. The proportion of full-time farmers in the working population reached 70–80%[9] in most of the fifteen districts (*myŏn*) of Namwŏn County. Namwŏn District, the county base including the *ŭmnae*, was the only district with less than half (46.9%) of the population engaged in agriculture. Instead, it had a higher proportion of manufacturing and commerce workers (Chōsen Sōtokufu 1933). The data confirms that *ŭmnae* residents worked in a relatively diverse range of jobs, while those in other districts were largely engaged in farming activities.

In rural Korea from the 1920s to the mid 1930s, so-called polarization took place in the farming sector where extensive and capitalistically managed farms of large landlords emerged on the one hand while the number of landed and landed-cum-tenant farmers gradually decreased and were replaced by a rapidly growing number of tenant farmers on the other. Though this did not occur in Namwŏn to the extent that it did in the western plains of the North Chŏlla Province, Namwŏn also had considerably high proportions of landed-cum-tenant farmers and tenant farmers—26.1% and 64.0%, respectively, according to 1935 statistics (18.8% and 76.0% for the entire North Chŏlla Province) (Matsumoto 1998: 102–9). There were no prominent landowner families in Namwŏn, such as the Koch'ang Kim family in Koch'ang, North Chŏlla Province (Eckert 2004) or the Tongbok O family in Hwasun, South Chŏlla Province (Hong Sŏngch'an 1992). There were, however, some landowners with an annual income of several thousand *sŏk*, just below the level of *mansŏkkun* (wealthy landowners who received more than 10,000 *sŏk* of rice per year in farm rent). After the mid-1920s, the Pak family in Unbong District represented by Pak Hŭiok who was the largest landowner in colonial Namwŏn, the Chŏnju I family of Samae District and Yu Sidong, also of Samae District, wielded considerable economic power as large rural landowners. It is apparent that the economic domination over the farming majority by a small number of landowners escalated in rural areas.

There were small- to medium-scale landowners in Namwŏn Ŭmnae, too, although their holdings were far smaller than those of their rural counterparts. On the other hand, during the colonial period, a substantial number of migrants from mainland Japan (*naichijin*) came to live in the *ŭmnae* and some of them became powerful landowners. Yang Kyŏngsu was the leading landowner among the Korean inhabitants, while Hosoya Motosuke and Suwa Zen-emon were known as the two major Japanese landowners in Namwŏn Ŭmnae.

Due to administrative boundary changes in 1914, former Namwŏn County (except the areas ceded to neighboring counties near the end of the Chosŏn period) merged with Unbong County and this merged county seat was sited in Namwŏn Ŭmnae. The county head was a Korean bureaucrat sent from the Government-General. Other county officers consisted of both Japanese and Koreans. Districts, or subdivisions of the county (*myŏn*) were presided by *myŏngjang* (heads of *myŏn*), and their offices were staffed by the secretaries and other clerks who were generally local Koreans. Judging from their surnames, members of prominent *sajok* lineages of each district were appointed to the office of the head, except the two former *ŭmnae* districts, Namwŏn and Unbong. In Namwŏn District, the first head was Yang Chaeyŏng from one of the Namwŏn Yang lineages—one of the leading *rijok* families of Namwŏn Ŭmnae. The second head was Kim Hyŏnsŏk from the Kimhae Kim clan who belonged to one of the minor *rijok* families and was also appointed to the first mayor of Namwŏn Township when the district was promoted to the township (*ŭp*) in 1931.[10] In Unbong District, the office of the head appeared to be assumed mostly by members of the Unsŏng Pak family—a *suri* family of former Unbong County.

In broad terms, the local gentry, including large landowners, appear to have exercised a considerable control economically over the Korean farmers who accounted for the overwhelming majority of the rural population, whereas the *ŭmnae* was comparatively more heterogeneous in not only its industry structure but also its population composition. Since the 1930s, the proportion of immigrants in the Namwŏn District's population was substantially higher than that of other districts in the county,[11] including the Japanese who accounted for over 5% of the whole population.[12] The population growth rate was also markedly higher.[13]

While the *ŭmnae* was the ancestral home for many members of the leading and minor *rijok* families, and large groups of descendants of each family continued to live there during the period of colonial rule, the localized cores of the *sajok* families, which had a higher status, were located in the rural area. It is true that some descendants of the *sajok* families moved to live in the *ŭmnae*. They did not, however, wield as much influence as they did in their localized cores. Many of the remaining ceremonial facilities of the former dynasty and local government in the *ŭmnae* were placed under the control of the *rijok* members. It seems that it was the migrants from mainland Japan who were becoming a rival force to the *rijok* as far as the *ŭmnae* was concerned. The number of *rijok* households in the *ŭmnae* is estimated to have been around 200 during the 1920s and 1930s, but the number of Japanese households reached 125 in 1921 (Chōsen Sōtokufu 1921) and increased to 232 by 1936 (this figure is for the whole Namwŏn Township) (Chōsen Sōtokufu 1936). It is likely that the Japanese were exceeding the *rijok* not only in number but also in terms of economic power.[14] They also enjoyed a privileged position in the colony as they were migrants from the suzerain state.

Intermediate agents, status traditions and social prestige

The emergent intermediate agents who were neither *yangban* nor commoners were positioned between the ruling and subordinate classes. They were mediators who typically played the role of brokers or coordinators between the bureaucracy, powerful agents and the community, that is, those who operated in the interface between them and were generally referred to as *yuji* locally (see Honda 2007). These intermediate agents were not the direct inheritors or beneficiaries of the *yangban* status traditions. The emergence of this kind of agent would not have been a phenomenon restricted to the *ŭmnae*, the population of which continued to grow more diverse both economically and ethnically during the colonial period. Even in the rural area, non-*chaeji-sajok* landowners were emerging. However, I limit my discussion to situations occurring in the *ŭmnae* as I am unable at this stage to expand the scope of this study to the rural areas. My discussion will instead center on *rijok* family members, with several additional remarks on other new emerging forces, due to limitations of available data.

First, I examine the relationship between the intermediate agents in the *ŭmnae* and the status traditions by looking at the case of a Nogyeso hall reconstruction by the *rijok* family members in the early 1930s. I thus elucidate the driving force behind the reproduction of *rijok* status traditions at the time.

Reproduction of the *rijok* status tradition

Case One: The reconstruction of Ŭpsŭngjŏng

Ŭpsŭngjŏng was the meeting hall for Nogyeso—an association of Namwŏn *rijok* elders as mentioned above. According to *Ŭpsŭngjŏng Kisa*, which was the record of the circumstances surrounding its construction (Ŭpsŭngjŏng Tablet, October 1871), work began in March 1865 and was completed in July 1866. According to *Yangnojŏng Chunggŏngi*, which recorded the reconstruction of the hall (Ŭpsŭngjŏng Tablet, autumn 1931), it was originally used as the facility for learning and archery. Martial arts were banned, however, and the hall was seized by the government when de facto colonial rule by the Japanese Resident-General began in 1906. Seven elders (I Wŏnjo, Yang Tongyun, Chŏng Inung, Kim Pongp'il, I Pyŏngmuk, Yang Ch'ilyun and No Chŏngsu) successfully petitioned for the return of the hall in the name of their association. The hall was renamed Yangnodang (the hall for elders) at that time. Of the seven elders, two with the surname of I and two with the surname of Yang were members of Namwŏn's leading *rijok* families. The other three most probably were members of the minor *rijok* families. One of the seven had served as *hojang* and *ibang*, another as *hojang*, a third as *haengsugungwan* and a fourth *hyŏngbang*, *hobang* (heads of two of the six offices of local functionaries as mentioned above) and *tosŏwŏn*.[15] Thus, more than half of the seven elders had been top or high-level local or military/security functionaries. This suggests that leading figures of the *rijok* families were strongly interested in this facility.

According to the record, the reconstruction plan was proposed by I Hadŏk, a member of the Nogyeso, in the spring of 1930 when the condition of the building deteriorated some sixty years after construction. Since this was a 'major undertaking,' however, it was not implemented in that year. In the summer of 1931, I Hyŏnsun and others from Sogyeso (an association of younger members of the *rijok* families) visited Nogyeso to discuss the reconstruction proposal. The incoming mayor of Namwŏn Township (head of Namwŏn District at that time) Kim Hyŏnsŏk,[16] former Namwŏn county head Im Chinsŏp, I Hadŏk and several other Nogyeso members met and decided to proceed with the reconstruction as follows. Firstly, Nogyeso would make a contribution commensurate with its financial capacity and the remainder of the expense would be supplemented by Sogyeso's financial assistance, but the fund thus raised would not be enough to cover the cost nor could it be raised in a short period of time. The incoming mayor, Kim Hyŏnsŏk, agreed to loan the initially required fund (possibly, from the coffers of Namwŏn District) based on *changin* which probably refers to long-term interest rates in order to start the project immediately. Fortunately, I Hadŏk had some surplus funds for *po* (a type of irrigation facility) and, together with the proceeds from the sale of three *turak* (one *turak* = approximately 660 square meters) of the Nogyeso's rice paddock, a sufficient amount of funding was secured. The reconstruction began in April and was completed in June on the lunar calendar.

Let us look into the background of each individual involved in this case. I Hadŏk was a former *hyang-ri* from a leading *rijok* family of the Yŏngch'ŏn I clan. He was born in 1860 and became the Namwŏn *hojang* in 1891. He was clearly one of the prominent local figures in Namwŏn Ŭmnae who had strong connections with the bureaucracy as he was a member of the Privy Council during the period of the Great Han Empire (1897–1910). As for connections with the modern industrial sector, he was a member of the founding committee for the Namwŏn Financial Union when it was established in 1908.[17] He made a donation of ten *yen* to the flood victim relief group organized by the Namwŏn Youth Association and the Namwŏn Bureau of the *Tong-a Ilbo* Newspaper in the aftermath of a major flood disaster in 1920. He also played leading roles in the management of various *rijok* associations and donated thirty *ryang* (Korean currency equal to about 3 to 6 *yen*) to Nogyeso for its financial consolidation in 1916.

Kim Hyŏnsŏk was born in 1881 to a *rijok* family of the Kimhae Kim clan. He is from a minor family but married a daughter of the third son of Yang Kyŏngik, who was a *hojang*. He held the office of the head of Wangch'i District in Namwŏn County from 1919 to 1930, then became the second head of Namwŏn District after the sudden passing of his predecessor Yang Chaeyŏng (born in 1881) at the end of 1930 or in early 1931. Kim Hyŏnsŏk became the first mayor when Namwŏn was upgraded from district (*myŏn*) to township (*ŭp*) in November 1931 and remained in office until August 1934. Although the aforementioned tablet record states that he became the mayor in the summer of 1931 (April to June on the lunar calendar), his official appointment was later than that. In the modern industrial sector, he became president of the Taebang Financial Union (founded in 1930) in March 1931, immediately prior to his appointment to the office of mayor. He was also the leader of a group of thirty people who applied for the approval of the Namwŏn Industrial Union, granted by the Government-General in May. He continued to serve as the president, representative and director of the Union after that time.

I Hyŏnsun was born in 1890 to the Yŏngch'ŏn I clan, but was of a different *rijok* family from that of I Hadŏk. His father, I Tonsik, was seated on the post of *ibang* in that year and was instrumental in the founding of Kwansŏdang (public elementary-level school) in the south of the *ŭmnae*. Unlike I Hadŏk and Kim Hyŏnsŏk, I Hyŏnsun had never held a public office nor, reportedly, was he comfortably well-off. He began to be involved in various community service activities as a volunteer in the early 1920s. In 1921, he played a leading role in the establishment of Namwŏn Kwŏnbŏn (a female entertainers' union). I Hyŏnsun successfully recovered Punwijŏng, an archery facility in the south of the *ŭmnae* requisitioned and used as a sericulture laboratory (or a plant nursery) since 1914, from the government and brought its reconstruction into fruition in 1925. In August 1926, he was elected to the position of council president at the general meeting of the Namwŏn Youth Association held in Namsajŏng (another name of Punwijŏng). When the decision to restore Kwanghan Pavilion, used as the regional law court at the time, was made in November 1926, I Hyŏnsun mounted a campaign to have a shrine erected for Sŏng Ch'unhyang, the heroin of a *p'ansori*[18] (Korean opera) piece called *Ch'unhyangga* (the story of Ch'unhyang), on the site together with the *kisaeng* (female entertainers) of Namwŏn Kwŏnbŏn (see Case Two below).

While members of Nogyeso and Sogyeso, including the above three, were mostly members of the *rijok* families who resided in Namwŏn Ŭmnae, it appears that former Namwŏn county head Im Chinsŏp had no initial connection with Namwŏn. He was born in 1853, passed the *mugwa* military bureaucrat examination in 1879 and served as a military official in various positions of the Chosŏn Dynasty until the end of the 1890s. After becoming a member of the Privy Council, he became the head of various counties in North Chŏlla Province from the Residency-General period until the 1910s. It is likely that he cultivated friendships with leading figures of the *rijok* families while he held the office of Namwŏn County Head for a relatively long period from 1914 to 1919. In fact, *Yangnogye Chungch'anggi* (the record on the reorganization of the elders' association) states that he attended a function after the meeting of Nogyeso in the spring of 1918 and made a donation of twenty five *ryang* (Ŭpsŭngjŏng Tablet, May 1918).

As mentioned, until the generations of the seven elders who petitioned for the return of Ŭpsŭngjŏng in 1906 (born between 1839 and 1852) and I Hadŏk (born in 1860), former *hyang-ri* and *muim*, or career civil/military/security functionaries, played central roles in the reproduction of status traditions for the *rijok* families. In contrast, the next generation was led by people from a variety of backgrounds, including local officials such as Kim Hyŏnsŏk and volunteers with no particular occupations such as I Hyŏnsun. As another example, Kang Taehyŏng (born in 1871), who played a leading role in Nogyeso's activities after 1930, was a former *hyang-ri* but he operated a pharmacy of Chinese medicine and became a small landowner during the colonial period.

Furthermore, there were those who were deeply involved in the activities of Nogyeso and *rijok* status traditions even though they were not members of the *rijok* families, such as former Namwŏn county head Im Chinsŏp, and the abovementioned *ŭmnae* landowner Yang Kyŏngsu (not part of the above example but joined Nogyeso later and became a leading member). While the reasons for this are unclear, it is likely that Nogyeso functioned as a salon for non-*yangban* leading figures of Namwŏn Ŭmnae. Conversely, not all members of the *rijok* families got involved in the reproduction of these status traditions. For example, Yang Hanyŏng was from a *rijok* family of the Namwŏn Yang clan and the older brother of the first Namwŏn District Head, Yang Chaeyŏng. He was the principal (*chigwŏn*) of the county Confucian academy in 1914 and was deeply involved in Confucian traditional activities rather than *rijok* status traditions. Some of the left-wing political leaders who came to prominence immediately after the liberation were from a *rijok* family of the Namwŏn Yang clan as well. In terms of political orientation, the conservatives were not the only people of influence in the clan.

These examples clearly indicate the presence of people among the *rijok* family members who were involved in community welfare activities while attempting to reproduce unique status traditions distinct from higher-status cultural traditions inherited and produced by the *yangban* and *yurim*. This suggests a possible means for the intermediate agents to pursue social prestige.

Intermediate agents and status traditions/community development

While some intermediate agents, such as the Nogyeso philanthropists of the *rijok* families, were actively involved in the reproduction of highly exclusive status traditions in colonial Namwŏn Ŭmnae, which was becoming socially and economically more heterogeneous, other agents were beginning to participate in the formation of a new local culture with a combination of different status traditions and modern culture, reflecting the growing heterogeneity of this community. I consider the case of the restoration of Kwanghan Pavilion and the establishment of the shrine for Ch'unhyang (Ch'unhyangsadang) with the accompanying festival, which began as a commemorative ceremony in 1931 (cf. Honda 2007).

Case Two: The establishment of the Ch'unhyang Festival

Kwanghan Pavilion is an old pavilion situated at the southern end of Namwŏn Ŭmnae. Its origins date back to the beginning of the Chosŏn era. It has been rebuilt and repaired many times since it was burned down during Toyotomi Hideyoshi's second invasion of Korea. Kwanghan Pavilion was renowned for its scenic beauty and attracted and entertained many men of letters during the Chosŏn period. With the start of the Residency-General period, however, the building came to be used as a regional law court with limited public access. In 1926, the then heads of Namwŏn County and Namwŏn District (Yang Chaeyŏng, mentioned earlier) lobbied the authorities for the return of the pavilion. A new law court was built elsewhere in the township and Kwanghan Pavilion was restored to its original state.

At the time of the restoration of Kwanghan Pavilion, female entertainers of Namwŏn Kwŏnbŏn began to campaign for the construction of a shrine to honor the heroine, Sŏng Ch'unhyang, of a *p'ansori* piece called *Ch'unhyangga*. It was a love story set in Namwŏn, depicting the meeting, separation and reunion of the daughter of a female entertainer, Ch'unhyang, and the son of the Namwŏn County Head, I Mongryong. Its didactic storyline as well as its fascinating and vivid love romance proved popular and quickly became accepted as a classic. Since the modern Western-style theater and cinema were introduced to Korea, *Ch'unhyangga* has been turned into many stage plays and movies. Kwanghan Pavilion was the place where Ch'unhyang and Mongryong met for the first time in the opening scene of the story.

The extensive restoration of Kwanghan Pavilion began in October 1930 and was completed in May 1931 at a total cost of 4500 *yen*. The construction of the shrine for Ch'unhyang was undertaken at the same time and was also completed in May 1931 at a total cost of 2000 *yen*. The reconstruction of Ŭpsŭngjŏng in Case One above was undertaken almost in tandem with the completion of these two buildings. While I Hyŏnsun played an important role in the construction of

Ch'unhyangsadang and the reconstruction of Ŭpsŭngjŏng, each of the three projects was driven by a slightly different body of agents, some of whom played important roles in more than one project. A framed tablet showing the list of important persons involved in the repair of Kwanghan Pavilion (*Kwanghallu Chungsu Pangmyŏng*, September 1931) hung in the pavilion cites the then Namwŏn County Head as the leader and former District Head Yang Chaeyŏng as the proponent, and states that sitting District Head Kim Hyŏnsŏk oversaw the completion and former *chinsa* I Subong supervised the project. The names of Namwŏn's *rijok* family members on many of the framed poem tablets hung in the building after its completion suggest that the project attracted broad interest from local men of letters, including *rijok* family members, although it was led by local administrators.

According to a newspaper article at the time (*Tong-a Ilbo*, 27 May 1931), the ceremonial event in 1931, which became an annual festival called Ch'unhyang Festival, had a wide-ranging program—from traditional arts, Korean martial arts and Confucian poetry events (the all Korea *p'ansori* contest organized by the Namwŏn union of female entertainers, the all Korea archery tournament at Namwŏn Kwandŏkchŏng, and the contest of letters organized by the Confucian Association) to 'modern' entertainment and sports of Western origin (the moving pictures festival at Namwŏn Theater and the South Korea singles tennis tournament organized by the Namwŏn Bureau of the *Tong-a Ilbo* Newspaper). The article reported that 100,000 people were expected to attend the festival. Even allowing for exaggeration, the ceremony and entertainment clearly drew a great deal of interest from local residents. Let us look at the organizers of the various events. Namwŏn Kwŏnbŏn was the union of female entertainers, as mentioned. Performing in *p'ansori* and other forms of entertainment had been considered a vulgar occupation before the colonial period, and such performers must have been treated with contempt even at the time of the first Ch'unhyang Festival. Conversely, the Confucian Association was a group of local intellectuals who were practitioners of Confucian traditions, and most were from the *chaeji-sajok* lineages. Namwŏn Kwandŏkchŏng was another name for Punwijŏng, mentioned earlier, and the organizers of the archery tournament would have included young and middle-aged *rijok* members such as I Hyŏnsun. Since Punwijŏng was probably used as the meeting hall of Sogyeso, the facility was likely to have been managed by its members. In addition to these status groups, entertainment events were sponsored by the Namwŏn Theater, owned by budding entrepreneur,

Ch'oe Tuil (who later became an owner of farmland holdings and donated large sums of money to Namwŏn Junior and Senior High Schools after the liberation), and the nationalist newspaper *Tong-a Ilbo*. This newspaper had been an active supporter of literacy education, and had been involved in the promotion of new ideologies as well as the nationalistic activities of the youth associations, such as the campaign to buy home-made products.

According to subsequent newspaper reports, the memorial service for Ch'unhyang at the shrine—officiated by the female entertainers and with various forms of entertainment—attracted a large number of visitors every year. Particularly in 1939, when a portrait of Ch'unhyang by famous painter Kim Ŭnho—commissioned by former governor of North Chŏlla Province and general manager of the Shokusan Bank, Hayashi Shigeki—was hung at the shrine, a crowd of about 30,000 reportedly came to the consecration ceremony. Over 100 female entertainers from Sunchŏn (South Chŏlla Province), Chŏngŭp (North Chŏlla Province), Taejŏn (North Ch'ungch'ŏng Province), T'ongyŏng (South Kyŏngsang Province), etc, performed songs and dances at the ceremony. The Namwŏn Commercial and Industrial Association, Namwŏn District Office and various newspaper bureaus jointly organized a Korean wrestling tournament, a tennis tournament, a Korean swing festival, an archery tournament and a female entertainers' song contest as part of the 'initiatives for prosperity' of Namwŏn. Hagyesa of Seoul distributed about 1000 copies of Ch'unhyang's story for free, and the crew from Chosŏn Yŏnghwahoe in Seoul filmed the day's proceedings (*Tong-a Ilbo*, 21 and 27 May 1939).

The generative process of a local culture, through blending various status traditions and old and new cultures in the name of the 'prosperity' of the Namwŏn region, can itself be regarded as an example of the modern creation of tradition. To employ the line of argument articulated in this study, however, this process can be interpreted as a case in which the creation of a more heterogeneous, unifying and receptive new culture based on locality rather than status groups, unlike the old (mutually exclusive) status traditions, attracted the involvement of a wide range of agents, including intermediate ones. Curiously, I Hyŏnsun played a part in the creation of this local, unifying culture beyond the walls erected by status traditions while endeavoring to reproduce the *rijok* status traditions. I Hyŏnsun earned a high reputation and prestige in the local community for his deep 'love of his home province.' There were also people like Ch'oe Tuil of the Namwŏn Theater among the intermediate agents, who donated his accumulated wealth to education after the liberation and earned respect in the local community. The *yangban* prestige, based on the legitimacy of lineage and the pursuit of Confucian traditions as well as the power of patrilineal groups, boasted its ethical superiority but had a highly exclusive quality (*rijok* status traditions also excluded non-*rijok* descendants in principle). Alternatively, the pursuit of prestige through contributions to local culture can be characterized as a more open approach.

Cultural traditions of the *yangban* intellectuals: a frame of reference

To conclude my discussion on status tradition involvement and the possible pursuit of prestige for intermediate agents, I re-examine the role of the *yangban* intellectuals' cultural traditions as a frame of reference for the assessment of status traditions and social prestige.

For the descendants of Namwŏn's *rijok* families, the activities of Nogyeso, which formed the foundations of their status after the Kabo Reforms and their involvement in the Namwŏn Kwanwangmyo rituals and the Buddhist temple, closely linked to *feng shui* of the *ŭmnae*, were all part of social practice closely linked to the cultural traditions of the *sajok*. Nogyeso was modeled on a similar type of *sajok* association and the objective of its activities was to 'practice proper manners of behavior (*ye*)' by 'nursing the old (*yangno*)' and 'caring for the dead (*songsa*).' It is obvious from its articles of association—stipulating training for undutiful children and the performance of Confucian rituals—that its activities were strongly influenced by Confucian ideology (Honda 1999: chapter three). A member of Nogyeso was required to be a virtuous person in principle. Kwanwangmyo, as a hall for militants (*mumyo*), was elevated to a status level on par with the shrines for Confucius and other Confucian teachers and sages at the time of King Sukchong (1674–1720). It was used as a ceremonial hall for an official rite to celebrate loyalty and righteousness embodied by Guan Yu, as well as to express gratitude for the manifestation of his spirit during Toyotomi Hideyoshi's two invasions of Korea (Honda 2006). The high level of compatibility between *feng shui* and the Confucian traditions in Korea has been discussed by many authors such as Janelli and Janelli (1982).

However, the *chaeji-sajok* had never been involved in the Nogyeso activities. Considering that intellectuals were perceived as superior to militants by the regent class of the Chosŏn Dynasty, it is true that the rite of Kwanwangmyo was regarded as a fringe practice from the point of view of *yangban* cultural traditions. It is also easy to imagine that their involvement in the rituals and operation of the Buddhist temple could never become part of the mainstream practice of the *sajok* cultural traditions in view of the inferior status of Buddhism in the Chosŏn Dynasty, which upheld Confucianism as its national virtue, particularly in the later period. In other words, the traditional cultural capital of Namwŏn's *rijok* families could derive a greater value from the core Confucian traditions of the *sajok* cultural traditions, but it was a marginal cultural tradition in which the *sajok* themselves were never actively involved.

As the donations and contributions toward the restoration of Kwanghan Pavilion suggest, the image of the ideal intellectual upheld by the *yangban* was also recognized by non-*yangban* local elites and philanthropists as the kind of person any successful person should aspire to become. Many framed poem tablets and various stone monuments at Kwanghan Pavilion, Ŭpsŭngjŏng and Punwijŏng demonstrate that intermediate agents placed importance on knowledge and training in Chinese writing and classical literature as the most effective means to express their prestige. Anyone who was active as a local *yuji* had a pen name; a requirement for a man of letters. When a major landowner from a *sajok* family built a pavilion, not only the *yangban* and *yurim* people in and outside of Namwŏn but also some leading figures from the *rijok* families of the *ŭmnae* contributed their works to the commemorative book of poems. Though not an example from Namwŏn, there were some intermediate agents involved in both the intellectual tradition and industrial promotion during the colonial period or soon after the Liberation. Among these were the descendants of the Hŏ clan from Chindo in South Chŏlla Province, which had produced many leading painters of *namjongmuninhwa* (an orthodox style of painting by Chinese men of letters) in the Honam Painting Circle. Hŏ Paengnyŏn established a tea manufacturing business while being an active painter in Kwangju, the capital city of South Chŏlla Province. His younger brother, Hŏ Haengmyŏn, founded a paper mill after working in the secretariat of the Chindo County Office and the South Chŏlla Provincial Office, and also helped found Kwangju Technical High School of Agriculture (cf. Ishizuki 2004).

It is worth noting that in the colonial provincial society, the *yangban* and *yurim* traditions were still used as important prestige evaluation standards by those blocked from pursuing prestige linked to the status of *yangban*, despite the fact that new types of local elites were emerging outside of the local gentry class and that the urbanization of the *ŭmnae* was gathering pace. We must remember that the pursuit of prestige by the intermediate agents was characterized by the restraints placed by these 'superior' cultural traditions as well as its competitive relationship with them.

Conclusion

I have discussed how the local elite and the new emerging leaders were involved in status traditions of pre-modern origin and how these traditions were related to their pursuit of social prestige in the provincial society of colonial and post-colonial Korea, based on the case of Namwŏn, North Chŏlla Province. In particular, my discussion focused on various intermediate agents who did not belong to either the *yangban* or the commoner class. There were two approaches for the pursuit of prestige in Namwŏn in the context of the development and urbanization of the *ŭmnae* in the colonial era. One approach was through the highly exclusive status traditions underpinned by pre-modern cultural traditions. The other was through the local culture, which incorporated various status traditions as well as modern culture, was firmly grounded in the region and open to a wide range of status groups. Although the reproduction of such status traditions and the pursuit of prestige were competing with the 'superior' cultural traditions of the *yangban* and *yurim*, they were also severely constrained by them in certain respects.

We must wait for an accumulation of further historical ethnographic studies in order to ascertain whether these two approaches and the constraints of the *yangban* and *yurim* culture had the same effects on intermediate agents in other regions. However, I tentatively suggest the possibility of substantial variances depending on the social, economic and political structures of each region. In the case of Namwŏn, the local gentry class was the pillar of *yangban* and *yurim* cultural traditions in the colonial period and held considerable political and economic power in the rural area, while the *rijok* class adapted to the increasing urbanization and industrial and demographical heterogeneity in the *ŭmnae* and maintained a certain level of power. Conversely, the cultural hegemony of the local gentry would be weaker in regions in which greater levels of hierarchical shift and economic control by non-local landowners were occurring in rural areas. Or, the formation and reproduction of *rijok* status traditions would be slower in regions in which the political and economic base of the *rijok* families were weak to begin with, or in regions where the *rijok* leaders who were more adaptive to urbanization had migrated to other regions early, leaving only the maladapted in the area. In some regions, *rijok* groups were absorbed into the *yangban* and *yurim* groups. Conversely, in regions with a highly urbanized *ŭmnae* dominated by Japanese migrants and the new elite, the creation of local culture could have taken a different form from that which occurred in Namwŏn Ŭmnae. From this perspective, it is perhaps best to conclude that the case of Namwŏn's intermediate entities came into existence under circumstances unique to Namwŏn.

Yet, it is also possible to identify more general aspects in this case. Firstly, as discussed at the beginning of the paper, the reproduction of status traditions and social prestige after the modern reforms was enabled by the fact that various status groups and categories in late Chosŏn were established on different sets of social and economic bases and were not totally defined by the legal system. Further, the *chaeji-sajok* in particular existed as a status group firmly tied to its economic, social and cultural capital. Another factor that made the reproduction of the *yangban* and *yurim* cultural traditions possible, especially in the colonial period, was the fact that the authority of such cultural traditions and their supporters was, in a way, exploited for the purpose of social stability under colonial rule, instead of becoming the target of criticism (Ryu 2004, 2005). It was also important that agricultural production based on an oligopoly of a small number of landowners, including the local gentry, formed the main part of the industrial foundation of local communities in the central and southern regions. Alternatively, the effects of social change under colonial rule gain more importance when considering status traditions and social prestige for the intermediate agents. It appears that each of the intermediate agents, who did not have a common economic foundation as did the local gentry, found the possibility of reproducing different status traditions and pursuing prestige through their respective economic, social and cultural capital and also through their interactions with other intermediate agents and the *yangban* and *yurim* class. The case of Namwŏn's *rijok* and new elites can be interpreted as one example of such an approach.

Although I was unable to address this issue directly in this paper, the various exclusive status traditions that coexisted in colonial Namwŏn and the more open local culture that emerged at that time have undergone dramatic changes since the Liberation, particularly through the process of industrialization. The rural-based cultural traditions of the *yangban* and *yurim* had survived the demise of the landlord system under post-colonial agriculture reforms of the 1950s, mainly through the activities of the local *munjung*. Now these traditions are faced with the threat of extinction as a result of extreme depopulation and aging due to industrialization and urbanization. Conversely, the cultural traditions of the *rijok*, practiced mainly by retired elderly people after the Liberation, became more akin to activities for socializing than social activities for the retention of status traditions, as their offspring migrated to larger cities for schooling and work. Some of their cultural traditions, such as Kwanwangmyo worship, could not be easily popularized and fell into decline when the formation of a national culture and its dissemination in provincial society took place in the process of industrialization. In contrast, local festivities such as the Ch'unhyang festival were actively used by the centralist government as a tool to mobilize local residents for the purpose of national unification. Finally, it is clear that the pursuit of prestige based on pre-modern status traditions itself is becoming marginalized as modern meritocracy spreads to the middle and lower classes in provincial society through the process of industrialization. Still, considering that the reproduction of pre-modern status groups and forms of prestige continued until recently in Korea, and that it perhaps took very different forms depending on region, this is an important example through which to study the reproduction of social hierarchy and status distinctions in the processes of modernization.

Glossary

Legend: (J) = Japanese; (C) = Chinese; (No mark) = Korean
An Hyang 安珦
Andong 安東
Chaeji 在地
chaeji-sajok 在地士族
chaeji-yangban 在地両班
chang-in 長引
chapkwa 雑科
Chech'ŏn County 堤川郡
chesaek 諸色
chigwŏn 直員
Chindo 珍島
chinsa 進士

chinsasi 進士試
chipsŏngch'on 集姓村
Ch'oe Hang 崔恒
Ch'oe Tuil 崔斗一
Ch'oe-No-I-An 崔盧李安
Chŏlla Province 全羅道
Chŏng Inung 鄭仁雄
Chŏngŭp 井邑
Chŏnju 全州
Chŏnju I 全州李
ch'ŏnmin 賎民
Chonsŏnggye 尊聖契
Chosŏn 朝鮮
Chosŏn Yŏnghwahoe 朝鮮映画会
Chuch'ŏn District 朱川面
chung-in 中人
Ch'unhyang Festival 春香祭
Ch'unhyangga 春香歌
Ch'unhyangsadang 春香祠堂
Ch'unsŏngjŏng 春城正
Confucian Association 儒林団
do 道
eta 穢多 (J)
feng shui 風水 (C)
Guan Yu 関羽 (C) ('Kwan U' in Korean)
Great Han Empire 大韓帝国
haengsugungwan 行首軍官
Hagyesa 学芸社
Hanyang 漢陽
Hayashi Shigeki 林茂樹 (J)
hinin 非人 (J)
Hŏ 許
Hŏ Haengmyŏn 許行冕
Hŏ Paengnyŏn 許百鍊
hobang 戸房
hojang 戸長
hojŏk 戸籍
Honam Painting Circle 湖南画壇
Hosoya Motosuke 細谷元助 (J)
Huch'ŏn-ri 後川里
Hŭksong District 黒松面

Hwasun 和順
hyang-an 鄉案
hyangch'on 鄉村
hyanggyo 鄉校
hyangjok 鄉族
hyang-ri 鄉吏
hyangsadang 鄉射堂
hyangyak 鄉約
hyŏngbang 刑房
Hyoryŏngdaegun 孝寧大君
I 李
I Ch'ŏlsŏp 李喆燮
I Chŏnggŭn 李正根
I Ch'ŏnnam 李天南
I Hadŏk 李河德
I Hakchŏn 李学伝
I Hongsŏp 李弘燮
I Hyŏnsun 李炫純
I Kŏn 李健
I Kyuhwa 李圭和
I Mongryong 李夢龍
I Pyŏngmuk 李炳黙
I Subong 李洙鳳
I Tonsik 李惇植
I Wŏnjo 李元祚
Ibaek District 二白面
ibang 吏房
Im Chinsŏp 林震燮
Kabo Reforms 甲午改革
kak-nim 各任
Kang Taehyŏng 姜大炯
Kangwŏn Province 江原道
Kim Hyŏnsŏk 金鉉奭
Kim Pongp'il 金鳳弼
Kim Ŭnho 金殷鎬
Kimhae Kim 金海金
kisaeng 妓生
Koch'ang 高敞
Koch'ang Kim 高敞金
kongbang 工房
Koryŏ 高麗

kungwan 軍官
kwagŏ 科挙
Kwanghallu Chungsu Pangmyŏng 広寒楼重修芳名
Kwanghan Pavilion 広寒楼
Kwangju 光州
Kwangju Technical High School of Agriculture 光州農業高等技術学校
Kwansŏdang 官書堂
Kyŏnghagwŏn 経学院
Kyŏngju 慶州
Kyŏngsang Province 慶尚道
Lü Dajun 呂大鈞 (C)
mansŏkkun 萬石꾼
mu 巫
mugwa 武科
muim 武任
mumyo 武廟
munjung 門中
munjunggye 門中契
munkwa 文科
myŏn 面
myŏnjang 面長
Naegi-ri 內基里
Nagata 永田 (J)
naichijin 內地人 (J)
namjongmuninhwa 南宗文人画
Namsajŏng 南射亭
Namwŏn 南原
Namwŏn City 南原市
Namwŏn Commercial and Industrial Association 南原商工会
Namwŏn County 南原郡 (南原府)
Namwŏn District, or Namwŏn-myŏn 南原面
Namwŏn Financial Union 南原金融組合
Namwŏn Hyanggyo 南原郷校
Namwŏn Industrial Union 南原産業組合
Namwŏn Kwandŏkchŏng 南原観徳亭
Namwŏn Kwanwangmyo 南原関王廟
Namwŏn Kwŏnbŏn 南原券番
Namwŏn Theater 南原劇場
Namwŏn Township, or Namwŏn-ŭp 南原邑
Namwŏn Yang 南原梁

Namwŏn Youth Association 南原青年会
namwŏnbusa 南原府使
No Chŏngsu 魯鼎洙
No Shinjin 盧臣禛
nobi 奴婢
Nogyeso 老契所
noja 奴者
nongja 農者
North Chŏlla Province 全羅北道
North Ch'ungch'ŏng Province 忠清北道
North Kyŏngsang Province 慶尚北道
Pak 朴
Pak Hŭiok 朴禧沃
Pak T'aeyŏng 朴台榮
p'ansori 판소리
po 湺
pongwan 本貫
P'ungch'ŏn No 豊川盧
Punwijŏng 奮衛亭
pyŏngbang 兵房
rijok 吏族
ryang 両
sadaebu 士大夫
saengwŏn 生員
saengwŏnsi 生員試
sajok 士族
samaan 司馬案
Samae District 巳梅面
Sandong District 山東面
sanghan 常漢
sangmin 常民
Sangnyŏng Ch'oe 朔寧崔
sangsomun 上詔文
segŏji 世居地
Shokusan Bank 殖産銀行 (J)
Shu Dynasty 蜀 (C)
sijo 始祖
Sogyeso 少契所
sŏin 庶人
sŏjok 庶族
sŏk 石

sŏng 姓
Sŏng Ch'unhyang 成春香
Sŏnggyungwan 成均館
songsa 送死
Sŏnwŏnsa 禅院寺
sŏri 胥吏
South Chŏlla Province 全羅南道
South Kyŏngsang Province 慶尚南道
Sukchong 肅宗
Sunchŏn 順天
Sunhŭng An 順興安
suri 首吏
Suwa Zen-emon 諏訪善右衛門 (J)
Taebang Financial Union 帯方金融組合
Taejŏn 大田
T'aejong 太宗
Tansŏng 丹城
Tong-a Ilbo 東亜日報
Tongbok O 同福呉
T'ongyŏng 統営
tosŏwŏn 都書員
Toyotomi Hideyoshi 豊臣秀吉 (J)
Tundŏk-pang 屯徳坊
turak 斗落
ŭigwan 医官
ŭmnae 邑内
ŭmnaejang 邑内場
ŭmyangsa 陰陽師
Unbong County 雲峰郡 (雲峰県)
Unbong District 雲峰面
Unsŏng Pak 雲城朴
ŭp 邑
Ŭpsŭngjŏng 揖升亭
Ŭpsŭngjŏng Kisa 揖升亭記事
Wangch'i District 王峙面
Wŏnch'ŏn-pang 元川坊
Wŏnju County 原州郡
yakkwan 訳官
yang 良
Yang 梁
Yang Chaeyŏng 梁栽英

Yang Ch'ilyun 梁七潤
Yang Ch'unmo 梁春模
Yang Hanyŏng 梁翰英
Yang Kyŏngik 梁敬益
Yang Kyŏngsu 梁慶洙
Yang Tongyun 梁東潤
yangban 両班
yangmin 良民
yangno 養老
Yangnodang 養老堂
Yangnogye Chungch'anggi 養老契重創記
Yangnojŏng Chunggŏngi 養老亭重建記
Yangsajae 養士斎
yangyŏk 良役
ye 礼
yebang 礼房
yen 円 (J)
Yŏngch'ŏn I 寧川李
Yongdam 龍潭
Yŏngju County 永川郡
Yu Sidong 柳時東
yuhak 幼学
yuji 有志
yukpang 六房
yurim 儒林
Zhu Xi 朱熹 (C)

Part III: Southeast Asia

7 Women's Community Activities in the *Kampung* of Jakarta[1] and Social Stratification

Ayami Saito

Introduction

Residential areas in the urban environment in Indonesia are called *kampung*. It is commonly understood that most of the inhabitants are of low socio-economic status and the housing is generally substandard in quality (Krausse 1975: 1). In fact, however, the inhabitants of *kampung* are of diverse social classes or strata. The purpose of the present paper is to analyze the state of stratification within *kampung* by focusing on the social classes of participants in *posyandu* which is a local healthcare activity organized mainly for monitoring the bodyweight of children under five years of age. It is conducted regularly in many *kampung* communities, typically once a month.[2] Its participants usually include children, their chaperons (their mothers in most cases), medical officers and female volunteers called *kader* who organize the event.[3]

In previous studies on Indonesia, local resident organizations that were established under Suharto's regime and their activities, including *posyandu*, have tended to be negatively evaluated as having been imposed from above (Kurasawa 1998: 122; Wieringa 1993: 17). In contrast, I have emphasized the positive implications of these community activities for the local residents and have demonstrated that *posyandu* activities help to empower the *kader* volunteers who provide the services (Saito 2006b). However, since my previous discussion focused solely on *kader*, the question remains as to whether such empowering functions relate only to the *kader* volunteers without benefiting others. In other words, it is yet to be clarified whether such local healthcare activities contain hierarchical disparities or inequalities. This is where the subject of this paper comes to the fore: are there disparities or inequalities between the *kader* providers on the one hand and the recipients of the services who are also participants in local healthcare activities on the other?

In this paper, female *kader* volunteers and mothers of children who are recipients of the service are compared and analyzed.[4]

In examining stratification in *kampung* by focusing on *posyandu* activities, a comment by one *kader* informant seems to provide a clue. In replying to my question as to why she decided to work as a volunteer, she said, "*Saya ingin mengabdi kepada masyarakat selagi saya masih mampu*" (I want to dedicate myself to the people while I am still *mampu*). The word *mampu* literally means 'well-to-do' or 'wealthy.'[5] The questions guiding my line of inquiry can be paraphrased as follows, using my informant's expression: Are *posyandu* activities structured in such a way that the 'wealthy' support the 'non-wealthy'? And if that is the case, who are *mampu* and 'non-*mampu*'?

In this paper, I clarify how the stratification of *kampung* has been dealt with in previous studies and try to find clues as to the concept of stratification used in this study. I then outline the general condition that exists in the study area, and finally analyze stratification based on occupation and income.

Social stratification in *kampung*

The theme of stratification in *kampung* itself is not new. It may not have been the central theme, but this issue has often been dealt with in previous studies (Konno 1999; Logsdon 1974). In this section, I begin by recapitulating how the hierarchical aspects of *kampung* were viewed in previous studies and consider appropriate indicators to be used in the current study.

Occupation is frequently used as an indicator in the analyses of social classes/hierarchy in the *kampung* of Indonesia. Classification according to white-collar and blue-collar work is particularly common. What does *kampung* look like in this light? According to Konno, there are two classes in *kampung*—the middle class, including the new middle class (private sector white-collar workers, consultant professionals, public servants, military officers, and small to medium size trading and manufacturing business owners) and the populace (farmers, craftsmen, laborers and miscellaneous workers) or the subordinate class. Konno suggests that in particular the mid- to lower-strata of the middle class 'have become the leading class in *kampung*' (Konno 1999: 312–13, 324).[6] In a broad sense, it is possible to say that white-collar workers take the positions of leaders while blue-collar workers are non-leaders.

Martha Gay Logsdon (1974) places more emphasis on the hierarchical nature of community activities than does Konno, despite not using the white-collar/blue-collar distinction. She analyzes stratification between the leaders of RW (*rukun warga*: a unit of neighborhood organization), those of RT (*rukun tetangga*: sub-units of RW) and the rest of the residents. She argues that the class differences between RW leaders and residents is clear, while that between RT leaders and residents is not. In comparison with residents, the age, education level and social class of RW leaders are higher, whereas those of RT leaders are not markedly different from those of residents (Logsdon 1974: 56). Logsdon's argument on the existence of class distinction between RW and RT leaders and residents is interesting. However, since specific criteria for class distinction are not provided in her study, it is difficult to apply them to today's *kampung* to test her argument (Logsdon 1974: 55).

Can we find the kind of class structure identified by Logsdon in Jakarta's *kampung* of today, using Konno's white-collar/blue-collar classification? To be more precise, is there any class distinction between RW and RT leaders or RT leaders and general residents. Or based on broader classification, is there a class distinction between RW and RT officials or RT officials and general residents? And does the occupation-based stratification correspond to the notion of *mampu*?[7] Now that the initial question has been elaborated, let us begin the hierarchical analysis of *posyandu* participants.

Study area and method

This study was conducted in a suburban *kampung* located in Cibubur sub-district (*kelurahan*) C Zone, Ciracas district (*kecamatan*), East Jakarta City, Jakarta Special Capital District. I have conducted interview surveys on *posyandu* in C Zone since 2002. As of 2002, C Zone covered an area of forty-five hectares and consisted of fifteen RTs and 1317 households, or 5367 residents. Statistical information on changes that have occurred in C Zone since the 1970s was not available. According to statistical data on the sub-district and comments by residents, C Zone was a rural suburb after independence (Saito 2006b: 83). However, a population influx from Central Jakarta and various areas of Java Island increased its population sharply during and after the 1970s.

The *posyandu* program in C Zone in 2002 included about 350 children under the age of five on its register (Saito 2006a: 59). Due to limitations of research scale and time, only one RT (C1 Zone with a high proportion of newcomers among residents) was selected for this study. Fifteen recipients who participated in *posyandu* relatively frequently[8] were interviewed using a questionnaire in March 2006.[9] C1 Zone had ninety-nine households, or 459 residents, on its register.[10]

The selection method for *kader* was somewhat more complicated than that for the recipients involved in this study. My research in 2003 identified twenty-eight *kader* volunteers who participated in the activity almost every month in C Zone (May 2003), and data was gathered from twenty-seven of these *kader* regarding birth year, occupation, education, family structure, the year they moved to Cibubur, the year they became *kader*, etc.[11] Among these twenty-seven, those who were still active *kader* as of February 2006 were screened for the latest study based on the following criteria: the *kader* (1) has been working as a volunteer for a relatively long period; (2) holds an official position (leader, treasurer, or secretary) in *posyandu*; and (3) is recognized by the *posyandu* leader as a 'dedicated' *kader*. Thirteen people who met one of the three criteria above were considered to be the core members of the *posyandu* and were interviewed in February and March 2006.[12]

Data about the husbands of participating *kader* and recipients, including their income and other attributes, were basically gathered via interviews with their 'wives.' However, the husbands of some of the *kader* were also interviewed. The following comparative analysis is made mainly between thirteen core *posyandu* members, including their husbands, and fifteen recipients.

RW *kader* and RT *kader*

In order to compare RW-level officials, RT-level officials and residents as did Logsdon (1974), it is necessary to distinguish between RW-level *kader* and RT-level *kader*.

Kader in C Zone are generally appointed at the RW or RT level. Many scholars have pointed out that many of the office-holders of Jakarta's RT and RW are men, and usually their wives become the leaders of women's groups called PKK (*Pemberdayaan dan Kesejahteraan Keluarga*: Family Welfare and Empowerment). It is also the case in C Zone that when a married man is appointed as a RW official, his wife is expected to become a PKK leader and a *kader*. In this paper, PKK officials (head, vice-head and treasurer) at RW level, including those who participated to meet such an expectation, are regarded as RW-level *kader*.[13] There are five such women in the subject area and I was able to interview four of them.[14] Conversely, RT-level *kader* are selected from RT and participate in *posyandu* as RT 'representatives'.[15] The remaining nine *kader* are the RT-level *kader*.

In short, the three groups—RW *kader*, RT *kader* and recipients—are compared below. Most important is the comparison between both *kader* groups and the recipients. While this study aims to compare the women, the majority of them are housewives (*ibu rumah tangga*) without their own wage earning activities,[16] and therefore the occupations of their spouses are compared instead. Their spouses are referred to as RW husband, RT husband or recipient husband.

Posyandu participants and stratification

Occupation

As mentioned, previous studies have generally used occupation-based classificatory methods for social class analysis. I first try to see whether there is a class distinction between RW *kader*, RT *kader* and recipients from the standpoint of occupational differences of their husbands, particularly in terms of white- and blue-collar occupations. For this purpose, the occupational classification of SSM survey (eight old categories)[17] has been used. The result is that the ratio of white-collar workers is highest among RW husbands at 100.0%, followed by RT husbands at 66.7% and recipient husbands at 16.7%. Conversely, the ratio of blue-collar workers is highest among recipient husbands at 83.3%, followed by RT husbands at 33.3% while there is no RW husband engaged in a blue-collar occupation ('no answer' and 'unknown' are excluded).[18] These results may appear to suggest a class distinction between *kader* on the one hand and the recipients on the other, with RW *kader* standing higher than RT *kader*.

What we need to remember here is that, while *kader* are chosen and appointed as such due to their social standings, the position as recipients is largely determined by the stage in their life course: they become recipients because they have children who need health-care. Furthermore, although the number of recipients in our sample is only fifteen, they stand for 350 recipients registered in *posyandu*, making this category more representative of the whole population of this *kampung*. If recipients as a whole appear to occupy lower class positions in comparison to *kader*, it is because a majority of the *kampung* residents are blue-collar workers in lower income levels, one reason why *kampung* are often compared to slums. However, it is not that all the residents in *kampung* are poor, a theme to be examined in the next section.

Income

Table 7.1 shows the distribution of the husbands of RW *kader*, RT *kader* and the recipients in our sample in terms of their income levels. It shows that, while one third of the recipient husbands earn less than 750,000 rupiah per month, another one third earn more than 1,250,000 rupiah per month, unmistakably demonstrating that the residents of the *kampung* are of various economic standings, and that the recipients of *posyandu* services come from all income levels.

During my interviews, both *kader* and recipients often remarked that public employees have *enak* ("nice") occupations. According to them, the working hours of public employees are not strictly regulated, and, in addition to various kinds of fringe benefits not available to those in informal sectors, they are assured to have *lumayan* (tolerable or moderate). Granting that public employees include people of widely different standings, we may safely assume that, when the residents of *kampung* speak of public employees as having tolerable or moderate income, they do not have high officials in mind. As of 2006, the basic starting salary of public employees with high school diploma is around 800,000 rupiah per month (Perpres 2006), which, according to *kampung* residents, is sufficient to support a family of a couple with several children. Looking at Table 7.1 in this light, we realize that this is within the lowest income level in which *kader* husbands are included. If *kader* say they take up their role because they are *mampu*, we may infer that the income bracket between 750,000 and 1,000,000 rupiah is the lowest level at which one can regard oneself as *mampu*.

Taking the income distribution of recipient husbands as representative of the residents of *kampung* as a whole, one third of the residents are at the level of barely *mampu*, another one third less than *mampu* or poor, while the remaining one third belong to the level of unmistakably *mampu* or wealthy. Hence we may conclude that the residents of *kampung* comprise not only the poor but people with widely different income levels. Nonetheless, if the general impression is that *kampung* residents are poor, it is either because of the poor one-third, or because what is regarded as barely *mampu* with tolerable income in *kampung* is still lower against the nation-wide standard.

As for RW *kader* husbands, only one of the four is at the income level of "barely *mampu*", while the other three earn more than one million rupiah per month, and especially two of them—one former engineer and one public employee—have monthly incomes of approximately five million rupiah, which qualifies them as definitely wealthy.

Finally, let us look at RT *kader* husbands. All of them have incomes over 750,000 rupiah, and thus qualify to be regarded as *mampu*. However, their income levels are not as high as RW *kader* husbands, with more than 60% of RT *kader* husbands at the income level between 750,000 and 1,000,000 rupiah. A majority of them are, then, only barely *mampu*.

Life course and participation

Community activities and *posyandu*

The disparity between *kader* and recipients concerning their participation becomes evident when we turn our eyes from *posyandu* to community activities in general. In *kampung* of Indonesia, various community activities such as *arisan* (rotating credit), *pengajian* (studying the Koran) and *senam* (aerobics and other types of exercise) are organized at RT, RW, *kelurahan* and *kecamatan* levels, or *dasawisma* (a lower level of RT), or across all these levels and conducted weekly, monthly or at other regular intervals. Many of these activities target married women. When I examined how many of these community activities my study subjects participated in, I found that the *kader* participated in more activities than did the recipients. Other than *posyandu*, a majority of recipients (nine people: 60.0%) participated in only one activity: mainly *arisan* at RT level. In contrast, over 90% of *kader* (twelve people, 92.3%) were involved in three or more activities. This result also seems to support the existence of class distinctions. However, we can prudently delay that conclusion until we examine this question from the perspective of life course.

What we must consider here is the relationship between life course and participation in community activities. As mentioned earlier, C Zone is a suburban *kampung* with the majority of its residents being newcomers. Those who are not originally from the area came to C Zone to live for various reasons. As far as *posyandu* participants are concerned, the main reasons are marriage and the purchase of a house. It is clear that they generally came to live in the zone after marriage, as married women.

Why do these married female newcomers participate in community activities? *Posyandu* participants (particularly recipients) have the clear purpose of 'improving and maintaining children's health.' Some of the other community activities also have direct purposes. For example, *arisan* is for saving money, *pengajian* is for religious training and *senam* is for the maintenance and promotion of physical strength. In addition, participation in community activities means exchange and communication with other residents. In fact, many of the recipients involved in my study participate in *arisan* at RT level for the reason of *bermasyarakat* (the word used by residents in the study area to mean 'to gather'). Of course there are some among recipients who do not participate in community activities, or limit the number of activities, because they want to concentrate on child-raising while their children are young or because they do not have enough money for savings to be collected at each *arisan* meeting. The issue of lack of money somewhat reflects class distinction factors in that quite a number of *kampung* residents are of lower income strata. Other than these women, married female newcomers participate in community activities, particularly *arisan* at RT level, which covers a smaller area and is closer to their own livelihood zone than RW, in order to get to know people, make friends and broaden their social network in the neighborhood.

There is of course a small difference between participation in community activities such as *arisan* and *pengajian* and participation in *posyandu* as *kader*. The primary purpose of the first two is to benefit oneself in the form of savings and religious training, while the latter is to provide support for other local residents. However, some *kader* volunteers consider their work as an opportunity for their own benefits by expanding a network of friends or acquiring more knowledge in healthcare. In this sense, participation as *kader* can be regarded as being of the same nature as participation in other community activities.

As stated earlier, many *kader* volunteers are women whose children no longer require hands-on care. At least, they are not burdened with caring for infants or children under the age of five. This is necessary because *kader* are required to not only spend half a day on *posyandu* activities every month (whereas *arisan* only takes a couple of hours), but also to support other supplementary activities in some cases. Such activities are a heavy burden on women with infants in particular and regarded as *repot* ('troublesome').

In terms of this study, it is therefore inappropriate to jump to the conclusion that inequality exists simply based on the fact that recipients, who are in the middle of child-raising, participate in fewer community activities than *kader*, who have almost finished child-raising (of children under five, at least). The difference in their pattern of participation stems from a difference in life stage rather than class differences as we saw earlier.[19] To recapitulate, recipients with children under five years of age participate in *posyandu* activities in order to receive health care for their children irrespective of their class positions. *Kader* volunteers, in contrast, do not do so out of need. RT *kader* in particular, many of whom are not very wealthy, volunteer to serve when they are no longer burdened with child-raising, and when they feel that they have at least sufficient income to be regarded as modestly *mampu*. In their decisions to take on responsible roles in the community, we may interpret a willingness for self-realization.

Pattern of participation

The correlation between the women's life stage and participation pattern can also be found in *kader's* pattern of participation in community activities. Let us try to classify the patterns of participation in community activities, including volunteer activities, according to the *kader* participants in this study. Beginning with the life history of the *kader* members, we find three main patterns of participation in community activities, particularly after they moved to the current area of residence (see Figure 7.1). Firstly, many *kader* follow the 'office-holder' pattern. In other words, they are 'forced' or compelled to participate in community activities because their husbands are office-holders (Kurasawa 1998). Almost regardless of the length of residency in the area, they become *kader* after their husbands assumed an important position in the community, or they themselves are appointed to official positions in some community programs at the same time. Or they begin to participate in several community activities such as *arisan* and *pengajian* immediately after (or at the time of) their appointment. Considering that one of the selection criteria for *kader* in this study was having a spouse in an official position at RT or RW level, as explained above, it is only natural that many women among the *kader* group follow the 'office-holder' pattern.

The second pattern is 'self-realization.' They participate in community activities for the purpose of self-realization relatively soon after moving into the area, although their husbands are not office-holders in the community. Similarly to the office-holder pattern, these *kader* tend to participate in several different activities almost at once, shortly after joining a certain activity. This is the second most common pattern, after the office-holder pattern, among the *kader* of my study.

The third pattern is 'staged/limited'. These women also participate in community activities independently of their spouse's position. After moving into the area, they tend to participate in community activities in a staged manner and limit their field of activity to a relatively small RT or RW. In one example of the staged/limited pattern, a *kader* first participated in *arisan* at RT level, and then gradually broadened her activity to RW level. She also took some time before participating in *posyandu* in stages after moving into the area. However, self-realization is also one of the objectives of the staged/limited pattern in terms of social networking and the development of ability or skills.

Based on this analysis, the staged/limited pattern is the most likely pattern to follow when a recipient, currently participating mainly in *arisan* and whose husband does not hold a RW or RT office, becomes a volunteer. In fact, some participants began as recipients, then accepted the invitation of *kader* members to become volunteers.

Conclusion

We have looked at the stratification of volunteers (*kader*) who participate in community healthcare activities, and recipients of the services in a *kampung* community in suburban Jakarta. Our primary aim was to discover any class differences in terms of occupation and income. We can summarize our findings in the following three points.

First, there appears to be ostensible class differences among RW *kader*, RT *kader*, and recipients in that order in that the proportion of white-collar workers with correspondingly higher income is highest among RW *kader* husbands, followed by RT *kader* husbands, and recipients showing the lowest proportion. This tempts us to the conclusion that recipients are poor in general and *kader* are wealthy.

Secondly, however, when we look beneath the surface appearance, we find that recipients consist of people of diverse class standings and it is not appropriate to classify them in terms of any one particular class. To be sure, one third of the recipient husbands have monthly income levels below 750,000 rupiah in contrast to *kader* husbands all of whom are in income levels above 750,000 rupiah. That the proportion of blue-collar workers with unstable income on daily payments or piecework rates is higher among recipient husbands indicates that many of the recipients are indeed poor whose lives are highly risky. At the same time, however, another one third of the recipients belong to income levels higher than 1,250,000 rupiah, clearly showing that wealthy residents are also among the recipients. It is clear that class standings of the recipients, both in terms of the amount of income as well as the kinds of occupation, are highly variable, reflecting the class diversity of *kampung* residents at large.

Thirdly, the difference between the recipients with diverse class standings on the one hand and *kader* restricted in relatively higher income levels on the other are related first to different life stages and second to different motivations that attract the two kinds of participants to *posyandu* activities. It has often been suggested that *posyandu* services are primarily for the poor: the wealthy people who can afford to pay higher costs choose to receive better health care provided by medical facilities and thus do not usually participate in community-level *posyandu* activities. At least in the community where I conducted my research, however, it has been ascertained that the wealthy also receive *posyandu* services. This does not mean that both the poor and the wealthy participate in the activities in the same way with the same regularity. Still, health-care interests for babies and infants are shared by parents at their child-raising stage: both wealthier and poorer parents come to receive *posyandu* services such as vitamin A pills provided twice a year or polio vaccinations.

As for motivations for serving as *kader* volunteers, we have identified certain differences between RW *kader* and RT *kader*: while a majority of the RW *kader* follow office-holder patterns without choice, many of the RT *kader* volunteers choose to serve for the purpose of self realization.

Let us now return to the two questions raised in the Introduction. The first question is whether *posyandu* activities are structured in such a way that the 'wealthy' support the 'non-wealthy'. Our answer is partially positive with important qualifications. The structure is not one in which the definitely wealthy support the definitely poor. As we have seen, *posyandu* activities are structured in such a way that *kader*, who belong to middle to upper levels of income among the residents of *kampung*, provide support to all the residents in need of such services including the poor as well as the wealthy.

The answer to the second question as to who are *mampu* and who are non-*mampu* is now clear. In the context of *posyandu* activities, those who are *mampu* are neither the absolutely wealthy nor the new middle class that appeared in Indonesia since 1980's. The term refers to those people who belong to the middle income level or above among the residents of *kampung*, many of whom have white-collar occupations, and who are aware that they have at least moderate and secure income. They are also past the stage of child-raising and thus have time to spare for community activities in which self-realization turn out to be a major motivation. The term non-*mampu* refers not to all the recipients of *posyandu* services but those belonging to lower income levels with blue-collar occupations who have no other access to health-care services.

I would like to close this paper by outlining the remaining issues. This study specifically looked at recipients in C Zone, particularly in C1 Zone. Firstly, there were two channels for recruiting *kader* volunteers in C Zone. The results of this study may not be applicable to other zones without these channels. Secondly, the study focused on recipients in C1 Zone, which was reported to have a higher proportion of newcomers than the other *posyandu* within C Zone. Similar studies must be conducted in other zones with different population characteristics. In this study, *posyandu* was treated as a community activity and *posyandu* participation was placed on the same level as participation in *arisan* or *pengajian* activities. Technically, however, *posyandu* cannot be put in the same category because it is primarily a healthcare activity for children under the age of five and different in kind from participation in *arisan* for the purposes of communication and savings or *pengajian* for religious training. Further analyses of participation in *arisan* and *pengajian* and women's life course in *kampung* are eagerly anticipated.

8 Local Security in Post-Suharto Bali: From Inequality to Equality of Participation

Kōsuke Hishiyama

Introduction

While the terrorist bomb attacks on the Indonesian island of Bali in October 2001 and October 2005 have provoked serious debates about issues of national security, they have also drawn attention to the question of how to ensure security at the local level. These debates are linked to the state of the world after the multiple terrorist attacks on the United States on 11 September 2001 as well as a series of decentralization moves after the collapse of the Suharto regime. While the domestic situation points to a path towards democratization that creates the scope for independent policymaking by each local community, it also means that the local community must share responsibility for local security, previously the exclusive realm of the national government. The local governments and residents are faced with the practical question of how to address various problems that have to be dealt with locally, including deterioration and confusion in the community environment due to the weakening of regulatory authorities caused by the frail central government and the influx of informal sectors into Bali from other islands.

Preceding studies have accumulated a substantial body of research on decentralization and democratization (for example Matsui (ed.) 2003), but few of these have specifically dealt with the local impact of these processes. In view of this situation, I examine in detail the current local control measures in the seaside resort area of Sanur and the process of establishing a local security strategy, and identify a link between the cohesive power of local residents, i.e., the process of developing common values for action, and local security activity. I focus particularly on a shift from inequality to equality of participation in local security organizations. Under the centralized administrative framework, administrative municipal units were uniformly superimposed on the areas of traditional custom-based collective living, and local security organizations were established in accordance with the central government's intentions under the municipal heads appointed by the central government. At the same time, the police and the military commands were set up to replace the neighborhood security operations formerly carried out by traditional communities, and the central government assumed authority over local security. In this process, the central government imposed restrictions on the capacity of local residents to participate in local security as well as the size and functions of their security organizations.

Opportunities to participate in local security used to be confined primarily to particular communities. In contrast, the disproportionate concentration in the central government of the power to approve the participation rights and determine the role of local security made the local security operation more centralized. As I shall discuss later, however, when problem solving action is called for at the local level, it appears that the implementation of local security depends largely on the establishment of equal participation rights as well as a shared perception that enhances the effectiveness of the local security systems.

'Effectiveness' here refers to the argument in Dahl and Tufte (1972). According to them, in an attempt to define an optimum unit for democracy, the effectiveness of the citizen is greatest when the unit is small and homogenous but conflicts with efforts to maximize the problem solving capacity of the system. Conversely, a larger, heterogeneous unit of democracy enhances this capacity. This viewpoint can be used as a guide in considering the size and heterogeneity of the units that support the effectiveness of equality of participation in local security in the post-Suharto era. On this basis, this paper examines the extent to which Indonesia's democratization and decentralization has spread to Balinese local communities and identifies how these communities are dealing with the impact of global-scale crises such as the Asian economic crisis and terrorist attacks as well as various associated problems.

Community structure in Bali

First, I shall briefly explain the characteristics of Balinese communities from the perspectives of the administrative and traditional functions on the one hand, and the two-layered structure of village and hamlet on the other.

Balinese society has developed around villages called *desa*, which symbolizes its cosmology.[1] There are two types of *desa*: *desa adat* which upholds tradition and custom and *desa dinas* which carries out administrative functions. The boundaries and population sizes of the two types of *desa* are slightly different but they overlap and coexist as constituent units of the society. The administrative village and the customary village both have their own caucus consisting of a village chief, secretary, treasurer, clerk and so on. The caucus of the administrative village mainly handles birth and marriage registration and address changes for residents while the caucus of the customary village deals with festivals and ceremonial services.

The administrative village (*desa dinas*) was created at the start of the twentieth century under Dutch rule for the purposes of population monitoring and taxation. Since the formal independence of Indonesia in 1949, and particularly since the Suharto era, it has been reinforced and used as a channel to convey the intentions of the government to local communities in order to incorporate Bali as part of the nation of Indonesia. However, the real Balinese society is said to exist in the customary village (*desa adat*). The village based on custom (*adat*) is comprised of several sub-units of different natures, including hamlets (*banjar*) that constitute the smallest community units, irrigation associations involved in paddy field operations, and also congregations in charge of ritual activities centering on temples.

As the nationally unified system of administration was developed under Suharto's increasingly centralized government, the *desa adat* in Bali was retained and autonomous activities were permitted as long as they were considered useful as tourism resources. Consequently, the *desa adat* was deprived of its administrative function and confined to its ceremonial role so that it was clearly distinguished legally and systematically from the *desa dinas*: only the latter was regarded as a tool to be used for national governance. After the collapse of the centralized government system makes way for decentralization, the *desa adat* attracted attention as a potential vehicle for self-government and its role was re-evaluated. In this connection, however, various questions emerged as to whether this re-recognition of *desa adat* meant recovery of its autonomy, or whether it was still part of the central government strategy. Some argued that it offered a potential foundation for nationalism (Suryawan 2005). In any case, the analytical focus on the institutional distinction of village functions between *adat* and *dinas* is still considered important for the study of Balinese society.

Another important characteristic of *desa* is its tiered structure. According to Geertz (1980: 47–53), there were several spheres of political forms below the level of the *desa*, with *banjar* (hamlet), *subak* (irrigation societies), and *pemaksan* (congregations), as mentioned above, constituting the three main village polities. These, along with various voluntary associations clustering around them, made up an entity of pluralistic collectivism. Although to a limited extent, what supported the rights of member residents was not an integrated village republic but a collection of separate groups with different functions, each of which partially contributed to the order of the village. Residents participating in such community organizations had equal rights to participation unrestricted by their origins or social status. Yet, the participation right did not lead to the organization of any other activities and did not spur residents to achieve self-government and autonomy.

Based on these community characteristics of Balinese society, it has been considered that broad characteristics of local resident organizations can be extracted by focusing on contrasting functions of custom (*adat*) and administration (*dinas*), as well as on village (*desa*) and its constituent polities such as hamlet (*banjar*) and so on. For example, Geertz (1980) stressed the significance of *desa adat* in the theatre state and Warren (1993) argued that *banjar adat* was the foundation of civic rights and freedoms. Arguably, what has been illustrated by Warren is the potential of pluralistic collectivism in modern times.

However, contemporary issues posed by globalization and urbanization can no longer be fully explained or resolved by the existing community frameworks or perspectives. As Yoshihara (2006) points out, there are opportunities to extend beyond such frameworks or strategically re-interpret the resident organizations from different perspectives. The operation of community security organizations, which is the subject of this paper, relates to this research trend and the current state of the community.

Nevertheless, organizations such as this, that are relatively free from the pre-existing community frameworks, do not always succeed. One example is the Agency of Coordination of Local Safety in Sanur (*Badan Koordinasi Keamanan Kawasan Sanur*: BK3S), which was an organization of various tourism operators for the purpose of alleviating tourism-related confusions arising after the Asian economic crisis in 1997. Therefore, the agency originally comprised mainly local hotel operators in the tourism precinct itself. Because the agency did not possess effective means of enforcing local safety on its own, however, it turned to state power, such as the military and police, for support. Eventually, state power supplanted the agency's control and thus became the enforcer of community control in general. It maintained its connection with the community by including the *desa dinas* officials while the participation of the representatives of various tourism sectors were gradually restricted. The structure of the agency was increasingly centralized before eventually becoming defunct.

The Special Safety Patrol Team in Sanur (*Tim Khusus Patroli Keamanan Sanur*: TimSus PKS) which emerged afterwards came to exert its influence over the whole community of Sanur by acting as the coordinator of various other organizations. This group secured participation of a variety of *banjar adat* groups, rather than the tourism industry alone, while taking on some functions of *desa dinas* and *desa adapt*.

The links between various forms of clustering in the community and the community security activities should become clearer as the formation and transformation of each organization are examined.

Study area

Having outlined the Balinese community composition, I now touch on the study area of Sanur. The description of Sanur outlined below is drawn from Warren (1998) and Picard (1996) as well as my own survey.[2] The area of Sanur discussed here is part of South Denpasar District within Bali's provincial capital and the Ordinance-Designated City of Denpasar. It is a seaside tourist area about six kilometers southeast of the center of Denpasar. There are three *desa dinas* and three *desa adat* encompassing different populations and areas within the area, containing twenty seven *banjar* hamlets. The number of residents was 23,127 in 2000, which accounted for only 0.7% of Bali's total population of 3 million.[3] However, the daytime non-resident population is much larger, since many tourism industry workers come from neighboring districts. Among registered residents, 60% of the employed work for private enterprises, including those in the tourism sectors, followed by all types of shops and restaurants (12%), skilled jobs (7%, of which 8% are in tailoring), transport (7%) and hotels (4%). The high proportion of tourism and hospitality employment is notable. Similarly, the commercial and industrial sector accounts for a large portion (26.53%) of the gross production of the area, second only to the public service industry. Transport and telecommunications are mainly for tourism operation and property rental entails holiday rental accommodations for foreigners. A large part of the day-to-day work of banks is currency exchange for tourists. It is obvious that Sanur has developed as a tourism area that is far removed from Bali's traditional image of a rural community.

Sanur's famous main street (*jalan*), Jalan Danau Tamblingan, runs North/South and is lined with many souvenir shops. Many fashionable Balinese-owned hotels stand side-by-side on the beachfront, and their guests enjoy lazing on the beach or shopping along the street. Although Sanur has been described as quiet, relaxed and retaining the atmosphere of old Bali, such adjectives were not applicable to this main street until very recently. At the end of the 1990s, it was crowded with all types of informal sector workers and plagued by traffic jams and fights and squabbles between operators scrambling for customers. Several factors were responsible for the transformation of Sanur, including the local regulations of the Bali Provincial Government and the Ordinance-Designated City of Denpasar which were formulated as a result of government decentralization. Another factor in this change was the establishment of the Special Safety Patrol Team in Sanur (*Tim Khusus Patroli Keamanan Sanur*: TimSus PKS) and local control activity by the Sanur Development Foundation (*Yayasan Pembangunan Sanur*: YPS). I now look at the process of transformation culminating in the birth of local security organizations and the present condition of Sanur by examining various initiatives implemented during the Suharto era, the post-Suharto era and by the YPS.

Local security in the Suharto era

In this section I discuss local security under the Suharto regime, and then consider the impact of its collapse and local changes on the subsequent formation of local security organizations.

A distinctive feature of the security system under the Suharto regime was the Neighborhood Security System (*Sistem Keamanan Lingkungan*), generally known as Siskamling, which was set up in 1980 and carried out security at the community end of the centralized system. This local security system has been discussed in detail in preceding studies (for example Barker 1999; Dwianto 1999; Mizuno 2006); however the following two points need to be emphasized. First, the system was comprised of the Security Guard (*Satuan Pengamanan*: Satpam) for corporations and government offices and the Civilian Defense Unit (*Pertahanan Sipil*: Hansip) at the community level. Second, apart from the name given to the newly established security system by the state, the term Siskamling also means 'night watch' in everyday language. The latter referred to informal night watch by residents and the resultant mutual surveillance was widely carried out in the community. What was called *jaga bahaya* (someone who prevents danger) in and around Java was an example of an informal night watch activity.

I shall refer to the community end of the centralized system as the Neighborhood Security System and the informal night watch activity by residents as the Night-Watch.

The counterpart in Bali of Javanese *jaga bahaya* as Night-Watch is *ronda* as they were generally called before 1980. We should also take note of another one called *pecalang* which refers to the guards in traditional Balinese dress who have controlled traffic and crowds at religious festivals in recent years. The members are elected from each customary hamlet (*banjar adat*) to form *pecalang* at the *desa adat* level. According to Widnyani and Widia (2002), *pecalang* historically refers to resident associations organized in various areas for the purpose of providing mutual community support when Hinduism was introduced. However, *pecalang* was used for guarding temples in the era of multiple kingdoms from the latter half of the seventeenth century to the end of the nineteenth century, and then for guarding merchants under colonial rule. Subsequently, under the Suharto regime, its role was limited to traffic control at festivals, and the scale and number of *pecalang* were reduced. In most cases, their activities were limited to new-year patrols. Thus, its function and form have not been constant throughout its history. *Pecalang* have been drawing attention in recent years because they were summoned to guard the Indonesian Democratic Party-Struggle (*Partai Demokrasi Indonesia-Perjuangan*: PDI-P) of former president Megawati when it staged a political campaign in Bali in 1998. Since then, the *pecalang* was organized in various districts and became more influential to the extent that the Bali Provincial Government included a provision in its 2001 regulation that the *pecalang* should carry out part of local security operations in the *desa adat*.

However, opinions are divided on this resurgence of the *pecalang*, even within Balinese society. The argument in support of the *pecalang* claims it is the product of decentralization and democratization and presents an opportunity to achieve self-reliance for the *desa adat*, which embodies the spirit of Bali, as opposed to the *desa dinas*, which has gained power with the support of the central government

(Widnyani and Widia 2002). The argument against the *pecalang* raises serious questions regarding its out-of-control actions in some districts (Suryawan 2005). For example, the *pecalang* has reportedly been involved in illegally checking residency records, in cases of forceful eviction, in the demolition of homes and in attacks on informal sector workers from other islands. Skeptics of the *pecalang* find signs of ethnocentrism or fascism in its activities and in the state of the local community that demands them. It is important to consider the relevance of the present situation surrounding the *pecalang* when we discuss local security organizations in Bali today. I shall revisit this point in my discussion of the role and activities of TimSus PKS below.

Under the Suharto regime, *pecalang* was restricted and discouraged. Instead, Siskamling as Night-Watch was already active as an autonomous local security organization and was engaged in night watch and neighbourhood security activities. On rare occasions, Night-Watch unofficially cooperated with the officially established Neighbourhood Security System in forcefully removing outsiders, but its main role was contained within its own *banjar*. Night-Watch was not connected or involved in community development or tourism-related activities either. Hence, the autonomous local security found during the Suharto era was totally different in nature from *pecalang* that came to power in the post-Suharto era.

When the Suharto regime unraveled in the aftermath of the Asian economic crisis, the Neighborhood Security System controlled by the central government became much weaker. Conversely, the economic crisis triggered a massive influx of immigrants from other islands into Bali in pursuit of tourist dollars. The decreasing number of tourists and the corresponding drop in jobs in the tourism industry led to the emergence of many informal sectors on the street and a rising crime rate. Individual shops hired private security guards in response to this situation. Many shops that could not afford their own guards were forced to share a single security guard with several other shops. Some of the unemployed became thugs (*preman*) who attacked security guards and put pressure on shops to hire them instead. Tourist precincts were crowded with various informal sector operators, including peddlers, pushcart stalls, newspaper sellers and beggars. Persistent hustling of tourists, conflicts over customers, increased littering and traffic congestion became noticeable. At the same time, unscrupulous businesses, pickpockets and robbers also became active. The local community was forced to take prompt measures.

New local security organization: BK3S

Under such circumstances, a group consisting mainly of hotel operators in Sanur petitioned to the Denpasar City Tourism Office for the establishment of a local security organization. The City took the lead in setting up the Agency of Local Safety Coordination in Sanur (*Badan Koordinasi Keamanan Kawasan Sanur*: BK3S) in 1997. The mayor of Denpasar City and the police superintendent of Badun regency (its jurisdiction included Sanur) were appointed as co-supervisors (*pelindung*) and the head of the ward of South Denpasar and the police superintendent of South Denpasar precinct were appointed as advisers (*penasehat*). Hotels, the tourism association, banks and the Sanur Development Foundation (YPS) formed the caucus (*panitia pelaksana*). The representation (*perwakilan*) consisted of officials from each of six grades of hotels, restaurants, banks, retail shops, rent-a-car shops and travel agencies (Walikota Denpasar 1997). The BK3S exercised a certain level of effort as a community-based organization by adopting rationality of purpose to concentrate firstly on security measures for the tourism precinct separately from community security problems and by including a wide variety of personnel in order to identify and resolve various issues.

In 1999, only two years after it was founded, BK3S underwent major changes. The head of Badun army area (*Komandan Distrik Militer*: DANDIM) was added to the co-supervisors. The number of advisors was increased to nine and three *desa dinas* chiefs, the director of the tourism office and the head of the army station (*Komandan Rayon Militer*: DANRAMIL) were added to the lineup. At the same time, the number of caucus officials was reduced and the tourism industry was represented by only one official, representing a hotel. The rest were representatives of the *desa dinas* and the tourism office. The representation was replaced by four new sections, namely the economy section (*bidang dana*), the organization section (*bidang organisasi*), the equipment section (*bidang perlengkapan*) and the general affairs section (*bidang umum*). Only three hotels and one travel agency represented the tourism industry; the rest were representatives of the *desa dinas* and the South Denpasar branch police station (Walikota Denpasar 1999).

Obvious changes to the BK3S included the expansion of the upper echelons and inclusion of a military official, the substantial reduction of tourism industry representation and the addition of the *desa dinas* chiefs and representatives. The meeting of BK3S officials in 1998 draws our attention as the turning point in this change of direction. Decisions were made at this meeting concerning the need 'to support safety in Sanur area in order to improve the image of Bali in general and particularly Sanur as a tourist destination' and 'to call on tourism businesses for cooperation in order to create an atmosphere of safety and security' (Dinas Pariwisata 1998a). To this end, it was argued that a leadership coordination council called the Conference of Provincial Leaders (*Musyawarah Pimpinan Kecamatan*: Muspika), consisting of the head of each ward, the head of each army station and the chief of each branch police station, and local officials (*pejabat setempat*) such as *desa dinas* chiefs should be added to the 1997 lineup of executives.

The stipulations concerning local security officers also saw some changes (Dinas Priwisata 1998b). Some of the prerequisites for officers followed the patterns of police and military practices from the start, including a three week training program with the police, conformity with the training and education programs of the Indonesian national forces, and medical certification by a police doctor. There were forty-five field officers, including fifteen from each of the *desa dinas* in 1997, then an eight-member (paid) tourism police unit was added in 1998. Furthermore, the South Denpasar branch police station was used as a temporary office for the field officers, suggesting the team's increasingly stronger ties with the police and the military. The main duty of the field officers was a patrol, which was limited in terms of time (from 8 am to 8 pm), place (the main street only) and method (on motorcycle). They targeted the informal sector operators such as parking attendants and peddlers, in addition to criminals such as pickpockets. With the former, the officers intervened only if they were bothering tourists and did not question their existence or forms of business.

As described above, ties with the police and military as well as the *desa dinas* for administrative population control were pursued for the purpose of strengthening local security operations. This process was undertaken by internalizing state authority and led to a more centralized organizational structure and the exclusion of the original tourism operator members from the agency. In addition to its top-heavy structure, its community ties stopped at the *desa dinas* level and the Agency never formed links to other community organizations. It also aborted its initial endeavor to include a wide range of participants so that it could reflect the wishes of the tourism precinct and gather information from the tourism industry. The implementation of the field team operation could be ensured only by its association with the police and the military and it fell far short of being an organization tailored to local conditions. As a result, this organization failed to cope with the rapidly changing local situation and quickly lost its momentum.

In December 1999, YPS and BK3S had a meeting, with the help of the mayor of Denpasar. It was decided that the head of the YPS would assume the position of the head of BK3S and provide monthly funds as well as collecting contributions from hotels, tourism businesses and Denpasar City.

After assuming this management role, YPS decided to adopt a resolution concerning BK3S at its quinquennial Service Conference (*Musyawara Kerja*: Muker) for board election and service reporting. It stated, 'BK3S is the embodiment of cooperation among YPS, business operators in Sanur, the City of Denpasar and the tourism police and its board consists of local men of Sanur. Its members are also local young men from Sanur and neighboring districts' (Yayasan Pembangunan Sanur 2000a). This statement emphasized that it was a form of cooperation among various organizations rather than a unilateral effort by BK3S and that its members had ties with the local Sanur community because YPS realized that BK3S alone could not bring the whole Sanur area under control. As far as its ties with the local community were concerend, YPS was aiming to steer the organization and its operational environment toward the creation of a 'unified Sanur' with broad participation based on the *banjar adat* rather than the *desa dinas*.

Following the handover of the management authority of BK3S to YPS, the number of field officers was thirty-three, down from forty-five, as of November 2000. Their salary was also reduced from 350,000 rupiah to 252,500 rupiah. An official document of Denpasar City clearly declared collaboration with other local organizations by stating that BK3S was 'to facilitate coordination among formal and informal bodies, organizations and relevant authorities that are addressing the issue of peace and safety in the tourism precinct of Sanur' (Walikota Denpasar 2000a).

BK3S was scaled back over time and it had only nine field officers effectively headed by one director as of October 2005. Instead, the Special Patrol Team for Safety in Sanur (*Tim Khusus Patroli Keamanan Sanur*: TimSus PKS) emerged at the forefront of local security efforts in Sanur. The local control program conducted at the end of 2000 under the direction of YPS gave rise to the formation of this organization. How did YPS bring the area under control and put the new local security organization on the right track to the extent that it was praised by the police as a 'successful example of Balinese local security'?

Local control program and success of TimSus PKS

I begin with an overview of the nature of YPS which organized TimSus PKS (from Warren 1994, chapter 7; Yayasan Pembangunan Sanur 2005b). In 1965, President Suharto embarked on the construction of the ten-story high Bali Beach Hotel, due to be completed in the following year, as the first symbol of Balinese resort development using wartime reparation funds from Japan. Sanur community was faced with the threat of exploitation and ruination by the government and tourism industry at the expense of other sectors and residents who had been accustomed to the quiet rural environment. In response, Ida Bagus Brata, a Brahmana (Hindu priest) who was trusted by the community, initiated a grass-roots establishment of an organization for the purpose of protecting the future lives of Sanur residents. The move resulted in the Foundation for the Fund of Village Development (*Yayasan Dana Bantuan Pembina Desa*), which is the predecessor of YPS. This foundation established a bank and a community development fund, set up a volunteer-operated junior high school, promoted industries and supported steady local community development.

Around the time of Brata's passing in 1986, the corporations and enterprises established under the auspices of the Foundation began to pursue their own profits amid Indonesia's economic recession caused by an oil shock. The flow of funds back into the community became stagnant and it became difficult to reach a consensus of opinion. At the same time, it became likely that one of the *desa* in Sanur was going to be reclassified as a *kelurahan* (town) and removed from the decision making process of the local community. The *kelurahan* did not have its own council or financial authority and had to follow the government's development policy. The issue of local security was raised at YPS against the backdrop of economic recession and government interferences which were threatening to transform the local community.

The Foundation was originally set up for the benefit of local residents, but the resolution at the second Service Conference (*Musyawra kerja II*: Muker II) in 1988 redefined its role to include the provision of support for *desa dinas* activities and the Civilian Defense Unit

(*Hansip*), or security within the village development, to complement the centralized government system (Yayasan Pembangunan Sanur 1988). Here, YPS was expected to act like a subcontractor of the *desa* government.

It was not until its reorganization in 1992 that the Foundation abandoned this quasi-governmental role and began to work for local autonomy to benefit the community (Yayasan Pembangunan Sanur 2000a). There were two matters of particular importance in this respect: the inclusion of the *desa adat* in the membership of YPS and giving a double function to the head of each *banjar adat*, entailing supervision of both the religious/cultural aspect of the *banjar* and the business aspect of enterprises of YPS and PT (joint stock companies operated by the *desa*). Consequently, the heads of the *banjar adat* were able to acquire a certain level of authority based on their membership in YPS.

After the reorganization, the third Service Conference (*Musyawara kerja III*: Muker III) was convened in June 2000. The meeting adopted a plan for its services from 2000 to 2005, incorporating specific provisions for the local security division (Yayasan Pembangunan Sanur 2000a, 2000b). The pre-conference documentation included a provision for the promotion of the activities of the *pecalang* and BK3S, but the final decision designated the Night-Watch as the local control entity. It is clear that YPS still did not have a control entity of its own at the time and there was uncertainty as to what (or who) should be the basis for the delivery of local security. However, YPS differed from BK3S in that it targeted the entire Sanur tourism precinct for its local security activities and aimed to create a more integrated environment that was 'beautiful and harmonious.' Similarly, the targets of its control were clearer and more extensive. The pre-conference documentation listed specific targets, including peddlers, beggars, robbers, pickpockets and pushcart stalls (*kakilima*). In the final decision, 'enforcement of the local government regulation of Denpasar City' was added.

The local government regulation referred to was approved by the City of Denpasar on 10 May 2000 (Law 2000 No.3), prior to Muker III. The regulation was adopted as a result of the Local Administration Act proclaimed by the Indonesian government in 1999 and contained provisions about the local environment, beautification, rules and safety (Walikota Denpasar 2000b). More specifically, it included, among others, the following stipulations: garbage and wastewater should be properly disposed of in appropriate places; vehicles and motorbikes should be parked in garages; the selling of goods at public facilities is not allowed unless a proper authority is notified; trading from a pushcart or similar setup is not permitted on the street or public facilities; and the mayor has the power to delegate authority to villages and hamlets in relation to support, operation or regulation for the order, discipline and safety of the community.

YPS used this local regulation to legitimize its activities and began to expand its local security program rapidly in cooperation with the local community. One of the outcomes was a series of local control activities conducted over the period of one month from the end of November 2000. At the beginning of this initiative, YPS considered it necessary to organize a new control entity and attract community interest. Until then, it was understood that the *Hansip* existed for the *desa* and the *pecalang* related to community religion and rituals under the jurisdiction of the head of *desa adat*. Similarly, BK3S was regarded to be still dependent on Denpasar City and the police, even though its supervision had been transferred to YPS. Each of these entities recruited its members from its assigned district only, had limited functions and did not interact with each other (Yayasan Pembangunan Sanur 2005b).

This situation gave rise to the question of who was going to be responsible for the security of Sanur and its surrounding communities as a whole, and who was actually going to deliver the service. As a result, YPS held a large-scale panel discussion and decided that community issues should be regarded as issues of the Sanur area in general and as issues immediately affecting all individuals (Yayasan Pembangunan Sanur 2000f). YPS assembled not only BK3S but also youth associations, seaside tourism workers, the *Hansip* and the Night-Watch, including the *pecalang*, as volunteer members. We must note that all of these associations had in common being representatives of the *banjar adat*. Under the initiative of YPS, representatives from these groups formed a unit that YPS called the Special Team.

Members of the Special Team were assigned to particular areas or times for a one month period to observe and record information on the informal sector workers (peddlers, newspaper vendors and *kakilima*) operating in Sanur, how they dealt with tourists and whether they obeyed the local regulations of Denpasar City. This volunteer team was taken over by TimSus PKS, which was formed at the Board meeting in early December 2000. Two members from each *banjar* were recruited (Yayasan Pembangunan Sanur 2000c). Subsequently, TimSus PKS played a central role in distributing letters advising of trade regulations in Sanur to the informal sector operators and visiting them to explain the contents of the letter, the requirement of permission and the penalties associated with non-compliance (Yayasan Pembangunan Sanur 2000d). The letter advised that all sectors of the tourism industry in Sanur should take responsibility for the 'restoration' of the image of Bali and Sanur in accordance with the decision under the local regulation of Denpasar City and the decision of YPS (Yayasan Pembangunan Sanur 2000e). At the end of December, TimSus PKS handed over the tasks of directing, supervising and addressing informal sector problems to Trantib[4] and most of the informal sectors were subsequently banned from the Sanur area.

This local control program achieved success by securing participation of a wide range of people and helping them to confront issues in the area and work in cooperation with one another. It not only transformed the landscape of the area but also created an image and sense of values about Sanur and gave the participants a sense of effectiveness through their involvement in these efforts. Starting from this program, TimSus PKS gradually increased the legitimacy of local security and strengthened its influence and ability to deliver.

TimSus PKS continued to work not only in the tourism precinct but also controlled illegal waste dumping along the bypass road passing through the Sanur area, managed informal sector activities, rescued people and vehicles involved in accidents and played the role of security coordinator in relation to festivals and various social activities (Yayasan Pembangunan Sanur 2005b). Thus, TimSus PKS increased its presence in day-to-day living. In response to this development, discussions on security issues at the fourth Service Conference (Muker IV) were dominated by topics concerning TimSus PKS.

TimSus PKS' relationships with the existing local security organizations were clarified at the fourth Service Conference where it was established that TimSus PKS should take over the role of BK3S, eventually absorb its members, and that it should work in cooperation with the *pecalang* and the *Hansip*. It was also confirmed that TimSus PKS should be comprised of representatives from the *banjar adat* and remain a volunteer organization (Yayasan Pembangunan Sanur 2005a, 2005c).

Although the basic feature as a voluntary association continues to be emphasized, at the fourth Service Conference it was decided that YPS should employ several full-time staff to work for TimSus

PKS. They were to be paid a monthly salary of about 550,000 rupiah, which was based on the minimum wage in Bali at the time. Other members continued to participate purely as volunteers. As of October 2005, twenty of the twenty-nine members were volunteers. A sum of 10,000 rupiah was offered to the volunteer members as symbolic appreciation for their participation—twelve hours at a time. As an informal measure to secure the participation of these volunteers, YPS recommended them as security guards upon request from hotels and shops in the Sanur area. In this way, TimSus PKS was able to exert its influence in terms of opportunities for paid work for its members with local networks and knowledge and latent control of the tourism sector. Further, TimSus PKS provides assistance for registration and checking of residency, which is a function of the *desa dinas*. At the *desa adat* level, members of the Special Team are entitled to participate in religious festivals in the *desa adat* as the *pecalang* anytime. TimSus PKS has taken on many roles and functions in this way.

Conclusion

As far as members of TimSus PKS are concerned, their role is similar to that of the police, but they are not legally the police. They play the role of the *pecalang* but their existence is not formally defined by their *banjar*. In their minds, their role should not be one or the other. They implement local control and at the same time they must act as coordinators or advisors mediating between various security organizations and between them and the community. It is important to uphold custom and tradition but it does not mean that members place more importance on the role of the *pecalang*. Similarly, they are not trying to use the religious authority of *adat* as the absolute basis for their legitimacy. It is a reflection of their thinking that their activities should be evaluated on the basis of Sanur social standards above everything else. This is underpinned by the idea that TimSus PKS members should not confine themselves within the boundaries of particular communities as other organizations did in the past, but must treat the Sanur area as the aggregate of all such communities. When it comes to the diversity of their roles and the equality of participation, members are reminded of the local control program in 2000, which led to the formation of the Team. While they share the trait of being the representatives of the *banjar adat*, the diversity of participating organizations and people continued to be the basis for local security activities to date.

If these control activities were confined within the framework of particular communities, a sense of effectiveness among participants might have been heightened, but the control activity in the Sanur area as a whole would not have succeeded and might have led to an intervention by other organizations or the state in order to achieve more effective control. Even if the diversity of participants was ensured, Sanur would not have succeeded if there was no mutual understanding of who was in charge of which area, or if there were conflicts over the issue of legitimacy, as was the case in Desa Kuta which was targeted by terrorist bombs. In its various roles and local control activities, TimSus PKS has been able to effectively expand the territory of its concern beyond the bounds of the *desa*, which has been the unit of development in the past, to include the residential and tourism precincts, while attracting more diverse participation. The point lies in the fact that, throughout this process, TimSus PKS has succeeded in retaining the basic sense of effectiveness among participants at the neighborhood level of the *banjar adat*. This has ensured equality of participation while flexibly setting the territorial extension of identification depending on the issues concerned.

On these accounts, the case of Sanur can be assessed as a successful case of a grass-root level response to changing circumstances accompanying the expansion of tourism. Although we must carefully examine whether such movements can be expanded further in scale, we may discern in such activities a possible basis for decentralization and democratization in the tourism area of Bali.

9 Employment Structure of the Urban Informal Sector: The Formation of Porter Commitment Relationships in Hanoi
Erika Obara

Introduction

The migration of agricultural laborers to the cities of developing countries is, generally speaking, not a new phenomenon. This holds true for Vietnam where marketization has been promoted since the implementation of the Doi Moi policy. For example, many vendors can be seen selling bread or fruit on the streets of Hanoi. Apart from street vending, the types of work taken on by those who have moved from farms to the cities seem endless, including collecting trash, washing clothes, and shining shoes. While these types of economic activities are not clearly defined, they form part of a sector that encompasses small informal economic activities that are not guaranteed to last and are not officially recognized. They are typically referred to as the 'urban informal sector' (hereinafter referred to as 'urban IS').[1]

In this paper I examine the working relationship among porters and the employment relations between porters[2] and their employers based on surveys conducted in September 2005 and March 2006 in the markets of Hanoi, Vietnam. My aim is to reveal the internal structure of the porter labor market and develop some insights regarding the mechanisms by which the urban IS absorbs the influx of laborers who work as porters.

The porter labor examined in this paper is primarily carried out by women. The women travel to the city to work as porters either in-between their farm work, or by asking their spouse or a relative to take care of the children and home in order to make the time. The frequency of their returns home may vary anywhere between weekly and monthly, and in exceptional cases only once every six months or so. No clear patterns are found in the length of their stay in the city or the frequency of their return home. Yet, the livelihoods of these women are primarily based on the farm and they do not intend to make the city their permanent place of residence, hence they tend to share low-priced accommodation with many others while in the city.

Although there are no statistics regarding migrant workers who frequently travel from the countryside to the city in this manner, the following data confirms that Hanoi is the destination of migrant workers from the rural areas surrounding Hanoi. First, the Vietnamese population census indicates that few migrate from the Vietnamese Red River Delta region to the South-Central region, and that there is a comparatively high number of intra-regional migrants (refer to Table 9.1). Second, previous research conducted using sample surveys has revealed that the labor market in the Red River Delta region is a principal employment destination (Li 1996; Dang 2000; Ha and Ha 2001; Jensen and Donald 2000; Cu 2005; General Statistics Office 2005, 2006).[3] Third, there are many articles in the online newspapers describing the lives and employment of migrant workers that indicate that many of the migrant workers in Hanoi are farmers from the areas surrounding Hanoi, and are seasonal workers who frequently return home. The homepages of online newspapers such as Laodong and Ngoisao carry many articles on such topics (http://www.laodong.com.vn, http://srv.ngoisao.net/news/thoi-cuoc/).

These migrant workers exhibit work behavior that cannot be fully accounted for by the existing analytical framework of urban IS research. According to previous research, employment is generally found in the urban IS through acquaintances known through hometown connections and blood relations. The employment relationships gained through these acquaintances sometimes develop into patron-client relationships. For those working in the urban IS, hometown and kinship networks perform the important function of providing continuous employment opportunities, and opportunities to switch to jobs that are higher paying or have better conditions (Banerjee 1983; Jaganathan 1988; Nakanishi 1991; Wang 1990; Zhou 1994; Yamaguchi 2001).

Particularly in regions of Asia where it is assumed that kinship forms the foundation of society, it seems natural to conclude that those with hometown connections and blood relations would strengthen their bond with each other through their work in the urban IS. However, how these connections develop or among which occupational groups these bonds are likely to develop has not yet been established through proper research.

Porters employed in the markets of Vietnam are faced with a different situation than that suggested in the prevailing assumption

Table 9.1: Population migration by region: 1994–1999 (%)

	Place of Residence in 1999									
	Red River Delta		North-east	North-west	Northern Central	South Coast	Central Highlands	Southeast		Mekong Delta	Total
		Hanoi							Ho Chi Minh		
Place of Residence in 1994											
Red River Delta	7.98	4.76	3.27	-	-	1.35	2.36	6.63	2.60	-	23.67
Northeast	4.11	2.55	3.85	-	-	-	2.39	2.44	2.55	-	13.78
Northwest	-	-	-	-	-	-	-	-	-	-	1.54
Northern Central	1.90	1.28	-	-	1.44	1.02	3.47	6.46	2.29	-	15.13
South Coast	-	-	-	-	-	1.88	2.04	4.45	2.86	-	9.28
Central Highlands	-	-	-	-	-	-	-	-	-	-	2.74
Southeast	-	-	-	-	-	-	1.24	10.16	4.47	2.08	16.05
Mekong Delta	-	-	-	-	-	-	-	10.27	7.29	7.29	18.19
Total	16.32	9.35	8.14	1.39	4.06	5.93	12.41	41.16	22.43	10.59	100.00
Net influx	-7.35	-	-5.64	-0.16	-11.07	-3.35	9.67	25.11	-	-7.60	-

Note: Numbers are displayed as a percentage of all migrants. A dash (-) indicates a value of less than 1%.
Source: UNDP, 2001. *Population and Housing Census Vietnam 1999.*

above. These porters generally do not mark out their territory to monopolize the jobs there, and are not introduced to work through hometown or kinship connections. Also, few porters form patron-client relationships with their employers. It seems as though each porter is competing with every other. If this is the case, then what type of employment structure do these porters operate under?

In this paper I focus on the fact that the relationship between porters and their employers is nothing more than mere acquaintanceship. The purpose of having such relationships—which are, in fact, merely acquaintances—is for both the porters and employers simply to minimize the risks that arise while the porting work is carried out in an informal labor market. Although this is similar to a patron-client relationship, there is no fixed relationship as in a patron-client bond, which is based on the assumption that the patron will provide protection to the client or that the client will support the patron. I therefore aim to analyze the employment behavior of these porters by incorporating the concept of 'commitment,' as well as to elucidate the mechanisms of the labor market in general.[4]

The field research carried out for this paper remains exploratory and provisional. This is in part because there is no nominal register of porters, and in part due to the lack of a framework for accessing the porters who frequently travel to and from Hanoi, making it difficult to find respondents for the survey. Therefore, a genuinely random sampling method has not been possible. Furthermore, due to the small sample size, it is not possible to ascertain the extent to which the data collected is representative of porters in Hanoi. Though the data, where inadequate, has been supplemented using results from interviews, it is impossible to completely eliminate doubt regarding the representative nature and credibility of the study. Consequently, the analytical results of this study are presented here as hypotheses that require verification through more extensive research.

The topics covered in this paper can be broadly split into three categories. First, I aim to determine what types of people are engaged in porting by examining the attributes of the porters and their reasons for working away from home. Second, I discuss whether or not the network between the porters is serving any function by analyzing the route taken by the porters to gain entry into the porter market, the gathering places of the porters, and the hometown connections and blood relations that may exist among the porters. Third, I construct a model for the various hiring and employment strategies used by analyzing the risks and costs incurred by the employers, as well as the costs incurred by the porters, even though the factors are rather simplified. This study will elucidate the mechanisms through which porters are assimilated into the labor market. The results of questionnaires and interviews conducted with porters and their employers in the wholesale market of Hanoi in 2005 and 2006 will be used to this end.

Outline of survey regions and methodology

While motorcycles are widely used in the urban areas of Hanoi, the admission of these vehicles into the market area is restricted to some degree, resulting in the employment of many porters within the market places. The demand for porters who carry goods using a single bamboo pole is particularly high in wholesale markets, where there is a volume of goods involved in each transaction.

Two wholesale markets were surveyed for the purpose of this paper: the Dong Xuan market, the largest wholesale market in Hanoi primarily selling daily commodities, miscellaneous goods, clothing, and so forth; and the Long Bien market, an area approximately ten minutes walk away from Dong Xuan, in which fruit is the main commodity sold. The Dong Xuan market has a history that extends back more than a century, so it attracts not only local buyers but also a fair number of foreign tourists as well. This market place occupies a space of approximately 6500m^2 of land where a three-story building stands, containing approximately 1500 shops. The Long Bien market was established in 1992 and is operated by Long Bien District. About 500 shops occupy its approximately 2000m^2 space.[5]

Because the Dong Xuan and Long Bien markets are in close proximity to one another, many porters work at both. The porters are not managed by the markets, and they seem to have free access to the markets. However, the office of the Hoan Kim district, in which Dong Xuan market is located, often, but not on any regular schedule, takes these porters into custody and transports them back to their rural homes.[6]

I conducted a survey based on a written questionnaire with fifty-one porters who worked at both markets in August 2005, and conducted interviews with several porters, porter employers, and market managers in March and October 2006 as a supplementary study. The results of the questionnaire provide the primary data used in this analysis. The results obtained through the interviews provide supplementary data in cases where there is some doubt over the representative nature of the data due to the small sample size, or when there is a qualitative question that the questionnaire does not adequately elucidate.

The questionnaire method was as follows. First, several 'interview points' in the Dong Xuan and Long Bien markets were selected and interview assistants were positioned at these locations. 'Informants' were then selected by calling out to porters walking near these interview points approximately every half an hour. The interview assistants then asked the informants the questions listed on the interview sheet, and recorded their responses. These interviews were conducted between 2:00 pm and 5:00 pm, as the porters do not have much work during this period of time. As a supplementary study, thirty porters and fifteen shop owners in the Dong Xuan and Long Bien markets were interviewed in March 2006, and six porters and managers of the Dong Xuan and Long Bien markets were interviewed in October 2006.[7]

Economic activities of porters

Socioeconomic characteristics of porters

A summary of the data collected at both markets is shown in Table 9.2. It is generally accepted in Vietnam that 'petty trade is women's work' and that 'the market is a woman's workplace,'[8] and all the porters at these markets are female. Their average age is thirty-nine, the youngest porter being twenty years old and the oldest fifty-five. Women in their forties comprise approximately fifty percent. Eighty percent of the women are married, and at least sixty percent have two or three children. At least half completed middle school.[9] About half of the porters come from villages or rural districts located in Hung Yen Province, which is approximately sixty km from Hanoi, while the hometowns of the other half are scattered throughout various other provinces surrounding Hanoi. A relatively high number of the porters surveyed work at the markets between six and nine months a year. It appears that their annual working hours are divided between farm work, domestic duties, childcare, and migrant labor.

Those with previous experience outside of the agricultural sector comprise only approximately thirty percent of the sample, which suggests that porting is an occupation that those without experience in migrant work can easily enter. Peddling fruit and vegetables, shop keeping, arranging goods, dishwashing, cleaning and laundry are the main types of work that these women would have engaged in prior to, or in addition to, porting. In the interviews, many of the women indicated that there are certain places near the markets where prospective employers come to find workers, thus attracting workers looking for jobs. These places are not formally designated as such, but the women workers say they obtained dishwashing, cleaning, laundry and other odd jobs mainly in these informal but *de facto* centers for employment. The porters are not engaged in micro-enterprise management, which requires managerial skills, or factory work, which has relatively fixed working hours. They seem to wander and hop from one simple, manual labor job that does not require any special skills to another.

At least seventy percent of the porters move to the city with relatives and/or friends. They stay with these relatives or friends in low-priced accommodation that costs them about 3500 Vietnam Dong (approximately US$0.25) per day. Their monthly income is approximately 600,000 Dong (about US$40),[10] but this may increase or decrease depending on the time of year. During the month of the lunar New Year, when there is a high demand for their work, they may earn around US$60–70 per month.

One characteristic of the porters' behavior that was not revealed by the written questionnaire but became apparent through the interviews is the irregularity of their returns home. Being the women of the household, they need to be flexible about how they go about their migrant work depending upon their circumstances at home. They

Table 9.2: Attributes and basic employment characteristics of porters

Item	Number of porters	%	Item	Number of porters
Gender			*Means of entering the market*	
Female	51	100.0	Family/relative	12
Marital status			Friend/acquaintance from hometown	27
Married	45	88.2	By oneself	8
Single	5	9.8	Not sure	4
Divorced	1	2.0	*Prior job*	
Age			Farm work	36
19 or younger	0	0.0	Peddling fruit and vegetables	6
20 to 29	7	13.7	Tailor	2
30 to 39	16	31.4	Serving at food stands	2
40 to 49	26	51.0	Selling clothes	1
50 or older	2	3.9	Ice cream seller	1
Education			Helper	1
No education	1	2.0	Brick carrier	1
Primary school	13	26.0	Other	1
Middle school	29	58.0	*Side work*	
High School	8	16.0	No	23
Home province			Yes	28
Hung Yen	25	49.0	Sales assistant	8
Thanh Hoa	12	23.5	Odd hand	
Ha Tay	6	11.8	Selling fruit	5
Vinh Phuc	4	7.8	Serving at food stands	3
Tuyen Quang	1	2.0	Brick carrier	3
Bac Ninh	1	2.0	Lunch delivery	1
Lang Son	1	2.0	Laundress	1
Ly Nhan, Ha Noi	1	2.0	Garbage collecting	1
Number of children			???	1
1	0	0.0	*Spouse's job*	
2	19	37.3	Farm work (full time)	28
3	13	25.5	Farm work + sideline work	13
4	8	15.7	Construction work	4
5	4	7.8	Selling fruit	2
0	7	13.7	Cargo work	3
Number of months worked in one year			Other	4
Less than 3 months	4	7.8	None (due to illness)	1
3–5 months	11	21.6	Not sure	3
6–8 months	23	45.1		
9–11 months	7	13.7		
12 months	1	2.0		
Not sure	5	9.8		

return home up to three times per month,[11] but the timing and length of these stays is uncertain.[12]

Amongst the forty-two porters interviewed who are married, twenty-eight, or more than half, have spouses who work full-time on the farm. Thirteen of the spouses do sideline work in addition to farm labor, including construction work, selling fruit and vegetables and cargo work. Judging from the fact that they temporarily earn their income through construction work only during the agricultural off-season, it can be assumed that the nonagricultural industries in the hometowns of the porters are not developed. Amongst the interviewees, all owned at least some agricultural land, with one exception—a divorced porter. The average area of land owned is 0.4ha and the main cultivated crop is paddy rice.

Overview of job activities

The porters begin working early in the morning, when the shopkeepers start to stock merchandise at the market. Starting at midnight, the market shopkeepers travel to the market parking lot to purchase merchandise. Product samples are lined up in front of trucks packed with goods, and shopkeepers assess these products before purchasing them. At this time, a porter is employed to transport the products from the parking lot back to the shop. Most of the work for the porters is in the early morning. At 6:00 am, the porters return to where they are staying, and rest until around noon. They go back to the market in the afternoon to transport the goods that customers have purchased from the shops to destinations specified by the customers (often the parking lot where the customer's motorbike is parked), as well as cleaning the interiors of the shops, organizing products, tending shops, and doing other odd jobs as requested by the shopkeepers. They may also have a few hours to work in the market's cafeteria washing dishes and doing laundry as previously mentioned.

Let us now examine the exchange between the market customers and porters from the customers' point of view. I will use the Long Bien market as an example here. Customers who shop at the Long Bien market are primarily brokers, so a large amount of shopping is done here. Many brokers come to the market as male/female couples on motorbikes. A couple parks their bike in a parking lot and the woman goes to the market alone to shop while the man waits at the bike. After the woman buys a large enough amount of goods, she employs a nearby porter. The porter ties a rope around the customer's pack, and

Photo 9.1: Porter and market customer carrying goods purchased

then suspends the pack from her bamboo pole for carrying. At this time, if the customer/employer is acquainted with the porter, she will simply tell the porter where the motorbike is parked while continuing to shop. If they do not know each other, then the woman will either tell the porter where the parking lot is, as well as the motorbike's number plate, and have the porter deliver the products there,[13] or accompany the porter to the motorbike as a cautionary measure. After the porter finishes transporting the customer's pack back to the bike, the man waiting at the bike pays her for the work. Costs are not negotiated beforehand; rather, the customer/employer offers payment according to an approximate market rate. However, if the payment is lower than the porter was expecting, she may request additional money. However, the customer/employer generally has upper-hand in the negotiations, so the porter's requests are not necessarily fulfilled. The porters ultimately have no choice but to accept the amount they are offered.

Relationships between porters

Hometown and kinship relationships

As mentioned, the porters primarily come to Hanoi with acquaintances known through hometown connections and blood relations. The advantage of being accompanied by such acquaintances is probably to help avoid various risks that can arise due to lack of information. However, according to the interviews conducted with the porters, despite the fact that the porters travel back and forth in large groups with relatives and friends, these relationships do not necessarily provide positive advantages for their work. Let us consider the following case studies.

Case study 1
A porter works at the Long Bien market. She is forty years old, has two children, and is from a village in Hung Yen Province. There are approximately fifteen porters from this area. Although they come to the city from the farmland together, they disperse when work begins. Although they may call upon a friend from the same hometown if there are too many packs to port, or if the packs are too heavy and the job must be done quickly, they will undertake the work alone by making several trips if time allows. If a job request for a single individual arises while the porters are waiting for customers together with their friends, each will try to run to the customer faster than the others to get the job (October 2006).

Many porters indicated in the interviews that they are involved in competitive relationships even with those from the same hometown. Let us consider the presence or absence of employer acquaintanceship by focusing on individuals from Hung Yen, the region from which the highest number of porters come. Data regarding the presence or absence of employer acquaintanceship with individuals from Hung Yen is shown in Table 9.3.

As Table 9.3 shows, more than sixty percent of porters from Hung Yen Province do not have employers with whom they have any degree of acquaintanceship. In contrast, approximately half of all porters from regions other than Hung Yen Province do have employers with whom they have some degree of acquaintanceship. It seems that porters from Hung Yen Province do not introduce employers with whom they are acquainted to one another, although this cannot be claimed with absolute certainty due to the small sample size. There were also many porters who indicated during the interviews that the people they know through hometown and blood relationships do not make work compromises for them. For example, if an opportunity for a single porter arises at a gathering place where the porters chat with each other, all start running toward the person looking for a porter, and the one who reaches the employer first wins the opportunity for the job.[14] This type of competition proves that elements such as age,

Table 9.3: Presence or absence of employers with whom the porters have a degree of acquaintanceship, by hometown

Hometown	Have an employer with whom they have a degree of acquaintanceship	Do not have an employer with whom they have a degree of acquaintanceship	Total
Hung Yen	9 (34.6%)	16 (61.5%)	25 (100%)
Any other location	13 (52.0%)	13 (44.8%)	26 (100%)

hometown and kin relationships are not reflected in the procurement of job opportunities.[15]

Porters' gathering places

In both the Dong Xuan and Long Bien markets, many porters can be seen gathering together to chat with each other, either standing or sitting, in locations such as underneath stairs or in spaces where shops have closed early. Gathering in such places, the porters exchange information about jobs, such as the personality of shopkeepers and their personal experiences of being poorly treated by employers. These gathering spots have three characteristics, as determined through participant observation and interviews.

First, there are no separate places for relatives and individuals from the same hometown to gather. Porters from various hometowns join the gathering spots either alone, or with some others. The relationships found at the gathering places are not only those between relatives and individuals from the same hometown, but also those between friends established through working at the market or acquaintances whose hometowns are unknown. The porters do not show any effort to monopolize information in order to carve out turf for their work.

Second, participants at the gathering places are always coming and going. Many porters can be seen strolling into a gathering spot, and heading back to wander around the market again as soon as they have arrived.

Third, the locations where porters gather vary. They tend to gather in relatively inconspicuous areas, such as beside the rear entrance to the market, underneath stairs, or inside vacant shops. They may disperse after several minutes, or congregate for several hours.

Let us now examine the functions performed by these gathering places by looking at some case studies drawn from the interviews.

Case study 2
One porter who works at the Dong Xuan market is forty years old, has three children, and is from the Yen My district in Hung Yen Province. Her husband is a farmer, and is also engaged in construction work. She has been working as a porter for five years. She has approximately ten friends from the same area who also work as porters. At first sight, the porters seem free to work at the Dong Xuan market. However, considering that people from the public safety office occasionally clamp down on them, there would seem to be some regulations against such workers (but see note 6 above). If the porters are caught during the crackdown, they will be detained for several months, and then returned to their hometowns. The employers with whom the porters are acquainted tell them when a crackdown is coming. This information is shared between all porters regardless of their hometown, and the porters work only at nighttime during these crackdown periods (October 2006).

Case study 3
A porter at the Long Bien market is forty years old, has two children, and is from a village in Hung Yen Province. Her husband stopped working as a migrant laborer (factory work) due to health problems, and now works on the farm. She once had a promised job cancelled one-sidedly by the employer. She protested against this treatment and was supported by other porters from her hometown who were present and had witnessed the development. Yet, that was a very rare case of united protest. In most cases, the porters will accept jobs even if the conditions are not favorable to them because there are not enough jobs. When she started porting, she learned from other porters from the same hometown how to tie things using a rope and methods of transporting that are not physically strenuous. Although she has given this same advice to other new porters from other hometowns, it did not lead to lasting relationships with them: she is no longer in contact with them (October 2006).

The porters are in competitive relationships with each other, even those who are relatives or from the same hometown. Each aims to maximize her own income. However, behaving selfishly and uncooperatively tends to not be the best way of achieving this goal. In the face of various uncertainties in the market, the porters must pick up information at the gathering spots to protect themselves from malicious employers, and to be prepared for crackdowns. Competition remains, though, even after they have developed loose-knit relationships with one another that extend beyond hometown and kin relationships and use these relationships as a minimal safety net.

Employment relations between porters and employers

Why are the relationships between porters competitive? To address this question, let us first outline the relationships between porters and their employers, as depicted by the leading research concerning economic transactions in unstable environments.

Commitment relationships

How do people minimize risks in the urban IS when making economic transactions, such as purchasing and selling goods and hiring people, considering that the urban IS, by definition, is not institutionalized and is thus fraught with uncertainties?

Kollock's (1994) discussion of commitment relationships is useful when considering this question. Commitment relationships are ongoing business relationships established in order to avoid the risks that can arise due to lack of information and mutual distrust.[16] Kollock conducted a comparative analysis of the forms of transactions used for crude rubber and rice in Southeast Asia, and discovered that the presence or absence of a commitment relationship depends on the nature of the good being transacted. That is, ongoing business relationships maintained over several generations between producers and brokers are present for crude rubber trading, whose quality cannot be determined until it is processed into final products, and thus mutual trust is an essential part of the transaction. In contrast, the relationships between parties trading rice are temporary, as the quality of rice can be determined immediately. Transactions are made with the parties who offer the most lucrative conditions in markets where a large number of parties are selling their goods.

Let us now examine the state of the relationships between porters and their employers. An application of Kollock's analytical framework reveals the relationships between the porters and employers to be as follows. First, other than transporting goods, the services that the porters provide include packaging goods, packing boxes, shop cleaning, arranging goods and shop tending.[17] Labor that can be traded on the spot, like that observed in Kollock's example of rice trading, involves transporting the employer's goods to a nearby location under the supervision of the employer. For this type of work, the employer does not require information such as whether or not the porter is hard working. Conversely, crude rubber trading corresponds to porters transporting goods over long distances without being escorted by their employers, as well as shop tending and packaging goods. Because risks such as loss of and damage to the goods accompany such work, the employer requires information about the porter's work ethic and so forth. As a result, the employers hire porters with whom they have developed commitment relationships in order to avoid such risks.

One form the employer-employee relationship can take is that of a patron-client relationship. The patron-client relationship has received the attention of many researchers as it ultimately causes a vicious cycle of poverty by stifling competition and contributing to the inefficient allocation of resources (Nakanishi 1991: 166). Patron-client relationships are such that the patron, who has wealth and power, provides protection for the client who has neither. In return, the client supports the patron. More specifically, the client receives aid from the patron during emergencies in the form of interest-free or low-interest loans, in exchange for the client not betraying the patron. This type of relationship continues based on the existence of 'laborers living at the subsistence level who have little spare time because they have to work long hours just to obtain their daily food provisions, and are thus forced to rely upon their relatives and friends who have limited information, as well as employers who rely on hiring people through personal connections via guarantors because they need highly reliable information' (Nakanishi 1991: 170). In other words, patron-client relationships represent one type of commitment relationship, and can be understood as hierarchical commitment relationships.

Patron-client relationships can quite plausibly allow both parties to avoid risks associated with economic transactions in the highly unstable urban IS. However, in the porter interviews, such relationships were limited to only a few cases found in the second-floor textile shops in the Dong Xuan market and a few of the fruit shops in the Long Bien market. As mentioned, the porters are essentially in competition with one another. If the patron-client relationship hinders competition, then the relationship between porters and their employers must be defined by something other than the patron-client relationship.

Let us hypothesize that what may be called a 'weak commitment relationship' exists between the porters and their employers. This is not a rigid or solid relationship like a patron-client relationship, but a relationship of mere acquaintanceship.

How commitment relationships are forged

How then do the porters forge these commitment relationships? Methods by which they are forged are shown in Table 9.4. There are few porters who forged commitment relationships through hometown connections, relatives, and friends, while more than seventy percent indicated that relationships were forged by working diligently and gaining the trust of employers.

Consequently, it appears that the generally accepted notion in the research conducted on the urban IS—that workers are introduced to work opportunities by friends and relatives—is not applicable to porters. This is indicated by the testimonies of several porters who reported that 'other porters who are known through hometown connections are only called upon when there is too much for one individual to carry; if the load only requires a single individual, then it is never handed over to another porter,' as indicated in Case study 1.

Analysis of employment relationships

The following case studies of relationships between porters and their employers are classified into three types according to their level of commitment: (1) strong commitment relationship; (2) weak commitment relationship; and (3) no commitment relationship.

Case study 4: Strong commitment relationships

A forty-two year old porter has been working on verbal agreements for eight years at a textile shop located on the second floor of the Dong Xuan market. She earns 1,000,000 dong per month. She tends the shop, ports goods, arranges goods, and cleans the shop from the time the

Table 9.4: How commitment relationships are forged

Method (Multiple selection)	Number of people
Working diligently and gaining the trust of their employers	22
From the same hometown as their employer	2
Introduced by a porter from the same hometown	2
Introduced by their own relative	1
Introduced by a friend the porter met at the market	1
Other	3
Total	31

shop opens until it closes. She does the same work for another shop run by her employer's relative located a few doors down, because she cannot refuse the request from her employer. Although it is difficult for her to return home frequently, she continues to work as it provides her with a stable income.

The textile shop owner who employs this porter is forty-five years old. Eight years earlier, this porter was waiting for customers/employers in the square in the centre of the first floor of the Dong Xuan market, so the textile shop owner called her over to do some work for her. After employing her a few times, she saw that the porter was a diligent worker, and decided to hire her on a monthly salary basis. This same employer says that, if she finds that she does not like the porter, she will stop employing her. When searching for a new porter, she says she simply goes to the hall on the first floor and finds someone appropriate from the porters waiting for customers there. She assesses the porter's performance herself, and does not employ porters who someone else has introduced to her (March 2006).

Although no monthly agreements were observed in the Long Bien market, a wholesale fruit market, there were a few shops where the owners would always employ the same porters. The porters do not wait at the shops as is the case under a monthly agreement; rather, these specific porters are sought when a job arises, and are paid hourly for their work. Work in which such strong commitment relationships are desirable often requires manual dexterity on the part of the laborers, for duties such as carefully wrapping fruit in paper without bruising it and then neatly placing it in cardboard boxes and so forth.

It seems that there are very few porters who are in strong commitment relationships. This is because not all shop owners place a high value on strong commitment relationships; further, once they enter a strong commitment relationship with a porter, the relationship tends to continue for a long time. Although it appears that many porters would like to forge strong commitment relationships with employers, porters testified that employers who value strong commitment relationships have already forged such relationships with other porters, so there are no openings left for late-comers.

Case study 5: Weak commitment relationship
A thirty-six year old porter is acquainted with approximately ten employers at the Long Bien market. It is very important that she become acquainted with employers, as they will then give her work. She therefore always does her jobs carefully. It is also important for

her to memorize the locations where she will be transporting her customers' goods. Competition is still fierce though, as there are many other porters with whom her employers are acquainted (October 2006).

An undergarments wholesale shop owner who is thirty-eight years old has had bad experiences with porters' losing goods in the past. She therefore searches for porters she is acquainted with and has entrusted work to before, who have completed jobs satisfactorily. There are many such porters, so when she goes to the hall on the first floor someone she knows will usually be there waiting for customers. She will not give work to porters she has never employed in the past (October 2006).

'No commitment relationship' refers, as expected, to a relationship in which no acquaintance or trust relationship has been forged between employer and porter. Employers who do not feel that commitment relationships are necessary simply yell out 'Porter!'[18] when a job arises, and whoever can get to the employer the fastest gets the job.

Case study 6: No commitment relationship

A forty-two year old porter has been working for six years. She has two children aged six and eight, and a mother-in-law living on the farm. Her husband fell ill and passed away a year ago. She works at the market for ten days, then returns to the farm for two weeks due to her concern for her mother-in-law who she entrusts with the care of her children. Because she must frequently return home, she cannot become really acquainted with any employers. As a result, she has less work than other porters, and does not get any information about crackdowns from shop owners either. Although she is warned about crackdowns by other porters from her hometown, they do not concede any work to her (October 2006).

Conceptual diagrams of these three types of relationship are shown in Table 9.5. The squares represent the employers, and the circles represent the porters. A solid line indicates a strong commitment relationship, while a dotted line indicates a weak commitment relationship. The arrow indicates the direction of the commitment. Because the incentive to forge a commitment relationship can lie with both the employer and the porter, the arrows are bi-directional. As described above, the porters work independently, and are fundamentally in competitive relationships with each other. As a result, there are no arrows joining the circles (porters), but only between the porters and the employers. Porters in weak commitment relationships and no

Table 9.5: Diagrams of the relationships between porters and their employers by type

Conceptual diagram	■ ↕ ●	■ ↙↓↘ ● ● ●	■ ● ● ●
Type	Strong commitment	Weak commitment	No commitment relationship
Number of porters involved in the relationship	One porter for every employer	Several porters for every employer	None
Number surveyed and survey method	2 (interview)	22 (written questionnaire)	29 (written questionnaire)

Note: The circles are porters, and the squares are the employers.

commitment relationships were the focus of the questionnaires given in August 2005. The number of samples for each type was twenty-two and twenty-nine, respectively.

Thus far I have attempted to classify the relationships between the porters and their employers. In order to clarify the structures underlying the porter market, I continue the analysis by focusing on one-on-one business relationships between porters and employers.

Examining risk avoidance and cost reduction strategies

As mentioned, the relationships between porters and customers/employers are not uniform, but can be broken down into three types based on the strength of the relationship. It is clear that there is a determining factor behind the type of behavior selected by both employers and porters. I will now attempt to explain this determining factor by analyzing the risks and costs borne by employers and porters.

Hiring practices of the employers

How do employers choose which porters to employ? Fifteen employers in the market were interviewed in the supplementary study regarding this question. Let us consider the hiring practices of the employers based on two factors: first, the presence or absence of porters with whom employers are acquainted and who they prefer to employ; and second, the number of porters who are preferentially employed. Employers who responded that there are no porters who they prefer to employ are classified under 'no commitment relationships;' those who responded that there are several porters they prefer to employ are classified under 'weak commitment relationships;' and employers who responded that there is only one porter they prefer to employ are classified under 'strong commitment relationships.' Of the fifteen employers, three were in strong commitment relationships, eight were in weak commitment relationships, and four were in no commitment relationships.

Next, I will examine the associated risks and costs for the employer as the factor determining whether the employers choose to be in a strong commitment relationship, weak commitment relationship, or no commitment relationship (refer to Table 9.6).

The risks for the employer include loss of or damage to goods. If the employer wishes to avoid these risks to the greatest extent possible, he or she will search the market for a porter who has proven to be trustworthy through previous employment experiences, and hire her again. Since the porter does not have any means of communication such as a mobile phone, the employer must bear search costs for locating her in the market. Thus, an employer who will locate a specific porter, even if it means high search costs, is in a strong commitment relationship with the latter.

However, if an employer wishes to minimize risks, and yet also wishes to minimize search costs, he or she will keep a pool of acquainted porters and employ one of them when need arises. If the pool contains ten or twenty porters, the chance of encountering one of them in the market without much searching is enhanced. We may

Table 9.6: Risks and costs for the employer when hiring a porter

	Employer with a strong commitment relationship with a porter	Employer with a weak commitment relationship with porters	Employer with no commitment relationships with porters
Risk of loss of or damage to baggage	Low	Low	High
Search costs	High	Low	Low

Note: Costs for bribes and gifts in order to maintain relationships were not observed in any of the three types.

call such relationships weak commitment. Many employers indicated in the interviews that they have weak commitment relationships with at least ten porters.[19] Employers who are not so concerned about risks simply call any nearby porter when a job arises, regardless of whether or not they have a relationship with them.

Porter work behavior

Work behavior

What latent factors affect the formation of commitment relationships on the part of porters? Let us posit that these factors include the energy expended by porters in order to find work (hereafter 'costs of searching for work') and the costs of maintaining relationships with their employers (hereafter 'relationship maintenance costs').

Relationship maintenance costs are generally monetary or material costs for gifts and so forth. However, the porters do not have a custom of offering gifts to their employers. Of course, language and behavior that offends the employer works against relationship maintenance, so porters pay strict attention to these behavioral aspects around their employers. In this sense, the relationship maintenance costs are psychologically based. Table 9.7 provides an analysis of the work behavior of porters in the context of the costs of searching for work and relationship maintenance costs.

Work for porters who do not have commitment relationships with employers is sporadic. The porters walk around the market looking for job opportunities while keeping a close eye on the shops. If an opportunity arises and they are forced to compete with other porters, whoever rushes to the employer first generally gets the job. As a result, close attention and agility are required for finding work. Consequently, porters who do not have commitment relationships

Table 9.7: Work costs borne by porters

	Porters who have a strong commitment relationship with their employer	Porters who have weak commitment relationships with their employers	Porters who have no commitment relationships with their employers
Costs searching for work	Low	Medium (high)	High
Relationship maintenance costs	High	Medium	Low

with their employers have to expend high levels of energy in order to find work. These are rated as 'high' costs of searching for work in Table 9.7.

If porters forge weak commitment relationships with employers, they will be given priority over porters with no commitment relationships for a job if they meet one of these employers in the market. These are rated as 'medium' costs of searching for work in Table 9.7. In comparison, porters who have strong commitment relationships with their employers and are sought out by these employers without having to expend any energy have even lower costs of searching for work. Such porters' costs for finding work are rated 'low' in Table 9.7.

As mentioned, porters also bear costs for maintaining relationships with their employers. Porters who have strong commitment relationships with their employers must work hard to ensure that their employers do not terminate the relationship. These porters' relationship maintenance costs are rated 'high' in Table 9.7. Porters in this category indicated in the interviews that they endeavor to return home less frequently and accept work even when they are feeling somewhat unwell.

It seems that porters in weak commitment relationships also feel that they may lose these relationships if they return home too frequently. These porters' relationship maintenance costs are labeled 'medium' in Table 9.7. Porters who have no commitment relationships do not bear any relationship maintenance costs, and accordingly, their relationship maintenance costs are rated 'low' in Table 9.7.

It is possible in theory to assume that the distribution of costs is as shown in Table 9.7. However, consider the costs of searching for work for porters in weak commitment relationships. Although the cost distribution is ranked 'medium,' it is more likely to be 'high' in the actual labor market. This is because the mechanism at work means that the employers' search costs are lowered as the number of weak commitment relationships they forge with porters' increases. If the employers have weak commitment relationships with many porters, then competition between porters in weak commitment relationships automatically escalates. As a result, the advantage of a reduction in search costs for porters in weak commitment relationships is lost. As mentioned above, many employers indicated in the interviews that they have weak commitment relationships with at least ten porters, so the competition between porters in weak commitment relationships is likely to be quite intense.

Porter comparison: Weak versus no commitment relationships

Let us now consider what type of porters forge weak commitment relationships. An analysis of the characteristics of weak commitment relationships and no commitment relationships is shown in Table 9.8.

Porters in weak commitment relationships have worked for an average of 4.7 years, while porters in no commitment relationships have worked for only 2.7 years. A certain amount of time is necessary to establish a commitment relationship, so these data confirm what intuition would suggest.

Interestingly, no great difference in pay based on the presence or absence of a weak commitment relationship could be confirmed. This suggests that competition between porters in weak commitment relationships is extremely fierce and that even though they have invested a certain degree of human capital in the form of commitment relationships, this is not reflected in their pay.

Conclusion

To conclude, I will summarize the findings elucidated in this paper and their implications.

Basic porter profile

Those who pursue porting work are middle-aged women from the farmlands surrounding Hanoi. They are primarily native small-holder farmers who cultivate paddy rice, and work as porters in the markets of Hanoi to earn cash during the agricultural off-season. When in Hanoi, they stay at low-priced hotels with friends and relatives, and return home roughly two to three times per month. Although they earn 600,000 dong (approximately US$40) on average per month, this income is unstable. The porters travel to the city with friends and relatives, but do not carve out turf with them. This is because their employers do not hire porters through introductions made to them via family and friends. As a result, a competitive market with a low entry barrier is formed.

Porters' employment strategies

Although much attention is focused on patron-client relationships in the discussion of employment relationships in the urban IS in developing countries, most porters do not have patrons. It seems that

Table 9.8: Characteristics of porters in weak and no commitment relationships

	Total	Weak commitment relationships	No commitment relationships
Number of porters	51 (100%)	22 (43.1%)	29 (56.9%)
Individual characteristics			
Birthplace			
Hung Yen	26 (100%)	9 (34.6%)	16 (61.5%)
Other locations	25 (100%)	13 (52.0%)	13 (44.8%)
Average age	38.7	37.5	39.7
Education			
High school or higher	37 (100%)	17 (45.9%)	20 (54.1%)
Middle school or lower	14 (100%)	5 (35.7%)	9 (64.3%)
Number of children	2.5	2.4	2.6
Work characteristics			
Income (dong)	585,588.2	589,318.2	582,758.6
Years worked	3.6	4.6	2.7
Previous job			
Non-farm work	25 (100%)	11 (44.0%)	14 (56.0%)
Farm work	24 (100%)	11 (45.8%)	15 (62.5%)
Sideline work			
Yes	23 (100%)	12 (52.2%)	11 (47.8%)
No	28 (100%)	10 (35.7%)	18 (64.3%)
Number of months porter works per year			
6–8	23 (100%)	11 (47.8%)	12 (52.2%)
Other	28 (100%)	11 (39.2%)	17 (60.7%)
How they started porting			
With a friend or relative	41 (100%)	19 (46.3%)	22 (53.4%)
By themselves	10 (100%)	3 (30.0%)	7 (70.0%)

Source: Created by the author based on survey results.
Note: 'Income' includes income from sideline work. Refer to Table 9.1 for a list of the sideline work.

forging an acquaintance with employers, or a so-called commitment relationship, is connected to job stability. Commitment relationships allow employers to avoid risks like the loss of entrusted goods, and save porters the trouble of searching for work.

The relationships between porters and employers have been classified into three types, emphasizing the strength of the relationship: strong commitment relationships, weak commitment relationships, and no commitment relationships. Few porters have strong commitment relationships. Several employers always employ specific porters, and will bear the search costs to find them, depending on the details of the job. In return, porters can also obtain work without incurring costs searching for it. Once a strong commitment relationship is formed, it is likely to last a long time.

Weak commitment relationships are those in which the porters and employers are merely acquainted with each other through work. The risks to the employers of damage to or loss of goods are reduced by these relationships. Search costs are also decreased as the number of porters with whom they are in weak commitment relationships increases. As a result, there is an incentive for employers to forge many weak commitment relationships.

Commitment relationships are determined by the employer after assessing the work ethic of the porter. They are not forged through the introduction of a porter by acquaintances known through hometown connections and kin relations. As a result, the porters seem to believe that commitment relationships can only be forged by working diligently and gaining the trust of their employer.

Porters who frequently return home tend to not form commitment relationships with employers. The livelihood of porters who also play the role of homemaker is essentially based on the farm. The length of time these porters stay in the city and the time spent at the farm are uncertain due to their duty of care for children and other urgent tasks. Such attributes affect the formation of commitment relationships between porters and employers.

Porter employment mechanism

A focus on the qualitative differences of porter employment shows that the porter employment mechanism can be depicted in a schematic way, as shown in Figure 9.1.[20] First, porters entering the porter market enter into Type C in which competition is severe. They then forge weak commitment relationships with employers after working for several years, and ascend from Type C to Type B. It is quite easy to make this ascension. This is because the costs of searching for work are reduced for the porters by having commitment relationships with employers. At the same time, employers can better avoid the risks of loss of and damage to goods without paying search costs as the number of weak commitment relationships they forge increases. This is attractive for both parties, making the ascension from Type C to Type B easy for porters.

What many of the employers need are weak commitment relationships. There are only a limited number of employers who need strong commitment relationships that incur high search costs. Furthermore, once porters and employers enter into a strong commitment relationship, the relationship lasts for many years, thus new openings are rarely available. As a result, it is difficult to ascend from Type B to Type A, and many porters remain in Type B.

Additionally, if a Type B porter returns home to the farm and stays there for a long period of time, they will lose their weak commitment relationships. If that happens, they will have to re-enter the market at Type C. Consequently, many porters repeat the pattern: from Farm → to Type C → to Type B → to Farm.

Porters also exchange necessary work information, for example information about irregular crackdowns and bad employers, with each other at spontaneously formed gathering places not based on hometown or kinship connections. These gathering spots fulfill the important function of helping to prevent various risks for the porters who work in an unstable work environment with no safety nets.

The information presented in this paper highlights merely one aspect of the urban IS. Although it is clear that the porters' returns

Figure 9.1: Porter employment structure

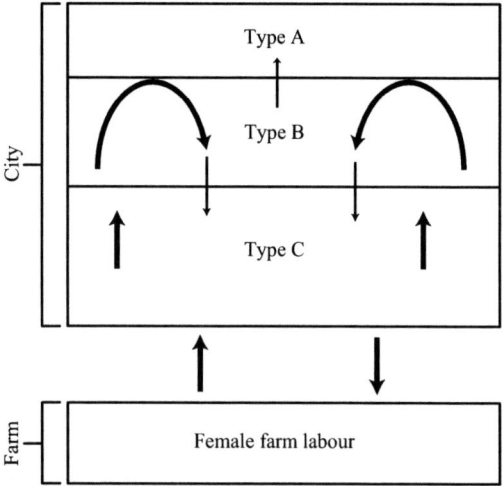

home, their land ownership, and farmer employment strategies regulate labor supply patterns in the urban IS, a detailed analysis of how conditions on the farm push these women to begin porting was not conducted. Analyses of such topics must await further research.

Acknowledgement

This research was conducted with the support of the Tohoku University 21st Century COE Program's Center for the Study of Social Stratification and Inequality.

Notes

Chapter 1

1 *Onmyōji* refers to artists who engaged in fortune-telling, exorcisms and similar activities using black arts based on Yin, Yang and the five elements. Visitors to *Onmyōji* were said to be entertained with baths and feasts. When visiting *hōgi*, people played ball games called *kemari*.
2 The head of the *bakufu* as a samurai government. Formal name is *seii-tai-shōgun*.
3 Samurais who were granted a fief worth at least 10,000 *koku* of rice. *Koku* describes the yield of land in terms of the amount of rice produced. One *koku* is approximately 180 liters.
4 An audience with the *Shōgun* upon entering a master-servant relationship with him or paying him formal respects.
5 In this context, *osaji* refers to a chief doctor, although it was usually an honorific title for a personal physician to the *shōgun* or *daimyō*.
6 Maids who worked for the Great Interior.
7 Kushimoto (1974) provides detailed descriptions of other types of *bakufu* doctors.
8 People who were engaged in commerce and industry were distinguished from samurais and farmers in terms of class and were called *chōnin* (literally: townspeople). *Machi-i* referred to doctors from the *chōnin* class.
9 The priestly ranks granted to doctors were of three kinds, *Hōin*, *Hōgen*, *Hokkyo*, in that descending order.
10 The head of a *kachigumi*, or a household guard, which provided security services to the *shōgun*.
11 *Hara-kiri*, or *seppuku*, was a method taken by samurai in committing suicide by cutting his own abdomen with a sword that began to be practiced towards the end of Heian period (794–1185). During the Edo period, it was one of the punishments imposed on convicted samurai.
12 '*Azuke*' refers to a type of criminal punishment, in which an unconvicted prisoner was confined in the care of a private individual, including *daimyō*, or an organization or, in the case of a convicted prisoner, he served a sentence of imprisonment under the same condition, instead of being directly imprisoned by the *bakufu*.
13 The director of the Ten'yaku-ryō (Pharmaceutical Bureau), which was in charge of medical care for public servants and training of medical doctors under an ancient system of centralized government based on the *ritsuryō* codes. The *bakufu* had the same organization during the Edo Period.
14 Officers who were in charge of administrative, judicial, police and related community services.
15 Some argue that specific spaces for *bakufu* doctors on ceremonial occasions were designated in September 1658 (Fujinami 1942: 69; Sinmura (ed.) 2006: 106), but no grounds for this have been shown.

16 For example: Version 1659-1 shows fifteen different titles and personal names under the palace seating rank number two, while Version 1659-2 shows sixteen titles under the same rank; the name of the third seating rank sounds similar in both versions but is expressed in different Chinese characters; and the sixth and tenth ranked seats in Version 1659-1 are ranked numbers nine and eight, respectively, in Version 1659-2.
17 It is unknown what *tozama-no-ishi* doctors were in charge of. Their rank is the lowest among the *bakufu* doctors in Version 1659-1 and is not high in Version 1659-2. *Tozama-no-ishi* may be another name for *yoriai-ishi*, the lowest ranked *bakufu* doctor class in the 1744 regulation.
18 The name of the twenty-third ranked seating room is *ishi-no-ma* (literally: doctors' room). It is unknown exactly when this room was established, but it can be found in an article for 29 April 1711, in *Tokugawa jikki* (True chronicle of the Tokugawa) compiled by the *bakufu*.
19 Performers in priest's attire who engaged in the business of *sarugaku* (traditional ceremonial performing arts).
20 *Sentō* means the residence of an ex-emperor. *Sentō-tsuki* was an official title for officers attending to an ex-emperor.
21 A type of position allowance paid by the *bakufu* to the holders of certain offices.
22 A position that supervised the administrative affairs conducted by the *bakufu*.
23 *Kengyō* was the highest title given to a blind person. In this context, *kengyō* means *bakufu* doctors who had the title of *kengyō*.
24 The calculation was based on the historical materials presented by Suzuki (1971, Table 7: pp. 210–11): *Kokuji wake bukan*; *Buke ryakkei*; and *Meiyo burui*. The total numbers of *hatamoto* as per these three documents are 5205, 5176 and 5159 persons, respectively.
25 As of 1712. See Table 3 of Suzuki (1984: 30).
26 See Table 1.14. To be detailed later.
27 *Ashigaru* is a class whose members were engaged in miscellaneous services in times of peace and served as foot soldiers in times of war. *Chūgen* is a class below *ashigaru*. *Chūgen* members were servants of samurai families and were engaged in miscellaneous services.
28 The following are among the *han* that created positions of low-ranking doctors: (16) Shōnai, (22) Matsushiro, (23) Numazu, (26) Toba (ii), (27) Hamada, (30) Sonobe, (36) Kumamoto, and (38) Shibata.
29 It has been argued that in the Muromachi Period (1392–1573), doctors were given higher and higher ranks because doctors retained by the authorities started to seek traditional authority in the competition against private doctors and because Court nobles gave official ranks to doctors as fees for treatment (Shinmura (ed.) 2006: 55–6).
30 Umihara (2007) argues that different sizes and different political and economic environments of different *han* resulted in significant disparities in the conditions of *han* doctors and in the roles they were expected to play. This paper has described some of the specifics of their conditions. Umihara does not mention the concept of *hōgi*, but we must also pay attention to this issue as well as the historical experiences undergone by different *han* domains.

Chapter 2

1 The author acknowledges the sensitive nature of the subject material presented within this study. But he also wishes to assure the reader that the stated objective of this research does not extend beyond trying to grasp how Japanese people participate in and respond to conflictual situations. In an effort to protect the privacy of residents in the subject village, the names of people and places have been changed to provide anonymity.
2 Some recent examples: in 2001 a fire engulfed seventy-four acres of woodlands. Perhaps more destructive was a flood in 1999 that caused over sixty recorded landslides and forced the evacuation of 120 households.
3 *Honke* is the central or parent household in a lineage to which branch households (*bunke*) trace their origin.
4 The two clans are also known as the Genji and Heike respectively.
5 For a more detailed account of the conflict between the Minamoto and the Taira see Sansom (1964).
6 The statue measures only twenty centimeters.
7 Similar to other rural areas in Japan, the village population has been battered by a decreasing birth rate and an exodus of younger generations to urban areas.
8 Seemingly unrelated deaths are to the villagers aligned in an often unforeseen pattern of supernatural causation.
9 Likely candidates are the ill and the elderly. Most traumatic to the community are unexpected deaths, that is, accidents, suicides, and young deaths. Talk of possible victims waylays fears over unexpected death. Conversely, the deaths of the elderly, those over eighty years of age, are greeted with congratulations for a long life.
10 As curses are more commonly attributed to a lack of worship, this is a noteworthy case.
11 The shrine constructed in the mid-18th century enshrines a deity worshipped to protect against fire.
12 House names (*yagō*) have been used to distinguish between households, which was particularly beneficial in areas where households shared the same surname.
13 All told, these neighborhoods have been depicted as the bastions of conservative adherence to tradition in Kogata. This tendency toward conservatism has been noted by Sugano (1980) in her study of an *Ochiudo* community in Akita prefecture.
14 The community is said to have become divided over loyalties to either of two *Ochiudo* 'bosses' who, being unable to make peace, resettled further apart from each other. One boss, Tamura, took with him the majority of the *Ochiudo* households.
15 In a similar vein, while explaining that the villagers of one Japanese community exhibit their wealth via their graves, Ronald Dore points out that 'the older generation, are very susceptible to pride of ancestry' (1994: 287).
16 Dore similarly reports the difficulty of having an altercation with people with whom you come into contact daily (1994: 48).

17 Concerns over supernatural contamination determine the social relations entered into for households in the community (Yoshida 1967, 1984).

Chapter 3

1 The *Nikkan Supōtsu* was launched as a sports newspaper in 1946, the *Daily Supōtsu* in 1948, and the *Supōtsu Nippon* and the *Supōtsu Hōchi* in 1949.
2 Ichirō (Ichirō Suzuki, 1973–) is one of the most respected athletes in Japan who, after his success in the Japanese baseball league from 1992 to 2000, moved to Major League Baseball in 2001 and broke the season batting record in 2004.
3 This lengthy description, 'sporting celebrities' and 'players, managers, coaches, etc.,' may be substituted with 'athletes' in some places of this paper for simplicity.
4 I say 'purport to be self-penned' because this type of book is often ghost-written even if the writer is not credited, or the original text may be substantially altered by the editor in some cases. This would be a serious obstacle if I was trying to discover the 'real view' of the athlete-author but it is rather more interesting to find out how these 'filters' work when I am trying to study the contents of sports books in relation to the role they play in society. This is because these books are typically edited in such a way as to correspond to the dominant values of society with a strong awareness of readers as consumers. This paper, however, does assume that the books published as autobiographies would not contain alterations that are unacceptable to the authors.
5 It is almost impossible to select 'representative samples' from sports books because the boundaries of the genre are ambiguous and the contents are diverse. With regard to the 300 books I have used for this study, I do not claim rigorous proof of their representative nature or theoretical saturation but I believe the sample is sufficient for a valid content analysis.
6 It is necessary to add a brief explanation of the terminology 'value patterns'. Components of a text that are generally called values, notions, ideas or subjects have cultural connotations which are embedded in the language and are therefore, technically speaking, untranslatable or incommensurable in themselves. Value patterns are derived by separating and extracting these components of a text according to specific criteria for the consequential behavior they can produce, or their relationship with behavior. The introduction of this term is intended for clarification of analysis criteria which is an essential aspect of comparative cultural research.
7 The stories of athletes and the values presented in these narratives that circulate in society are continually 'filtered' and transformed during the social communication process. The same applies to stories about historical figures. See for example Sakurai's discussion (2003) on the historical formation process of the story of legendary master swordsman Musashi Miyamoto (1584?–1645), who is commonly cited in the sports community.
8 There actually are two different Japanese words pronounced '*shugyō.*' They are written in different Chinese characters, one originally refers to Buddhist practices and the other is a more general word for learning or training in an

apprentice system. Because their meanings are overlapping, they are now often regarded as synonyms.
9 Classical studies that discuss this point and are highly relevant to this study include Benedict (1946), Bellah (1957) and Yasumaru (1974).
10 Although Oh has a Chinese father and is of Chinese (The Republic of China) nationality, he has grown up in the Japanese education system and does not speak Chinese. Anyway, his origins are not an issue in this study, since our focus is on his influence on Japanese society.
11 When Bourdieu and Passeron (1991) use the term 'reproduction' in their discussion of France's education system, it implies the continuation of disparities or asymmetry in a social structure as well as the process of maintaining the concealed value patterns and the 'symbolic violence' it exercises. In this paper, the word reproduction does not refer to the former, due to the nature of the subject matter, but focuses on the latter.

Chapter 4

1 Late Imperial China refers to the period approximately from the middle of the Ming Dynasty in the fifteenth century until the end of the Qing Dynasty in 1912, as per common usage among recent researchers.
2 In this paper Romanization in Mandarin follows the Pinyin system, while that in Cantonese follows *Cantonese Dictionary* by Rao et al, 1997. In the glossary at the end of this paper M or C following Chinese characters indicate whether the characters are read in Mandarin or Cantonese.
3 A *lingsheng* referred to the status awarded to an applicant who achieved an excellent result in an exam sat by *shengyuans*. The government provided him with a scholarship. It also made him eligible to study at a national institute in the capital so that he could advance his career beyond the position of *shengyuan* (Miyazaki 1993: 83).
4 In the latter half of the seventeenth century, following the Coastal Evacuation Order enforced by the Qing administration to drive off the remnants of the Ming forces, new settlers flooded into the Pearl River Delta to push the vested rights in the area to the brink of disarray. The relative time of settlement continued to be of vital significance in the struggle for survival in a village community. One had to find a way to assert one's legitimate background.
5 Huang Zuo, for example, was a bureaucrat during the reign of Jiajing in the Ming Period (sixteenth century). After his retirement from the civil service, he went home to Guangzhou and wrote a book titled *Taiquanxiangli*, in which he encouraged all people to construct an ancestral hall and practice the *zongfa* to bring about social order. Confucians in Guangdong in the sixteenth century promoted the book, distributing copies to the prefectures and counties where they lived in an attempt to popularize the practice that Huang Zuo preached (Inoue 2000: 379–88). Huo Tao was from Foshan, which shared a border with Guangzhou. He was a bureaucrat involved in the central government's reform of the *Li* system in the early sixteenth century, while at home he set an example by actually compiling a genealogy, building an ancestral hall and living with his extended family (Inoue 2001,

2004a: 38–45). Ex-bureaucrats such as Li Yizhuang of Panyu, Luo Yuchen of Shunde, Yuang Changzuo of Dongguang and other members of the Delta elite initiated action to advocate the establishment of the *zongfa* as early as the sixteenth century (Inoue 2000: 378–9).
6 For the details of He lineage in Shawan, see Liu (1995).

Chapter 5

1 On the first day of my long-term study, Zhang Moxiong, the father-in-law of my friend at university, kindly helped me find a room to rent. After having a long talk with Liao Yingjiu, the manager of an apartment building, Zhang Moxiong said to me, 'That person is my relative and you can talk to him if you have any problem.' I was intrigued because I knew those two gentlemen had never met before. At a later date, I asked Zhang Moxiong what the nature of his relationship was. He explained, 'About one thousand years ago, three brothers under the surname of Zhang lost a war. When fleeing south, the second brother and the third brother changed their surname to Liao and Jian respectively just in case they were caught by the enemy.' He said that was why he and Liao Yingjiu were relatives. This episode demonstrates a sense of togetherness which stems from the historical fact that the three surnames could be traced back to one common surname.

2 Common-surname linkage has been analyzed from two different perspectives: one regards it as quasi-kinship and the other regards it as genuine kinship. The former interprets it as a device to impose the kinship norm of mutual assistance on total strangers (Horie 1988: 61). The latter considers that relationships formed through a 'common surname' are part of the relationships of common descent. Suzuki (1979) regards the common-surname association as one type of patrilineal kin group by arguing that the 'distinction between genuine blood relations and quasi-kin relations is very fluid depending on various social environments' and 'it is unwise to exclude [the common-surname association] from "kinship organizations" without careful consideration' (Suzuki 1979: 294).

I am skeptical about the quasi-kinship perspective. Considering that even an established lineage contains some elements of fiction (Segawa 1996), we would lose sight of the flexibility inherent in the Han-Chinese kinship system if we should regard 'common surname' as fictitious and separate it from other types of kinship. Also, such a fiction should involve some act of imitation that is not found with 'common surname' associations. Unlike fictive kinship relations that are sometimes set up between total strangers in imitation of genuine kinship relations, there is nothing in common-surname linkage to imitate. They consider a person with the common surname as their relative because of the common surname and not because they feel they must imitate a certain behavioral pattern between relatives.

3 Although the Taiwanese regard people with a common surname as their relatives, they treat such relationships differently from relationships with parents, children or siblings. The parent-child relationship is qualitatively different from the common-surname relationship. There is a concept called '*renqingzai*' in Taiwan. It signifies a feeling of indebtedness arising when

someone has done something for another person, who must then reciprocate in some form in order to resolve this feeling. It is a psychological debt in personal relations. For example, when A provides financial assistance to B who is in financial trouble, B owes a *renqingzai* to A.

This *renqingzai* does not arise in the parent-child relationship (or in the husband-wife relationship). The common-surname relationship is qualitatively different from the parent-child relationship in this regard since *renqingzai* develops in the common-surname relationships.

The *renqingzai* also arises in the relationship between siblings, but the level of obligation to assist is very different from that of the common-surname relationship. As discussed in this paper, people do not help their siblings unconditionally just because they are their siblings. It is not uncommon for siblings with vastly different financial standings to have little contact with each other. However, it is generally considered that they should assist each other with weddings, funerals and other special occasions. Unlike the case of the common-surname relationship, they have no discretion to decide whether to help or not depending on the nature of the relationship. The norm concerning the obligation to provide assistance is considerably different for the common-surname relationship and the sibling relationship.

4 Taiwan is a multiethnic country which consists of the Han, as well as aboriginal groups such as the Amis, the Atayals. This study concentrates on kinship among the Han-Chinese who account for about 98% of the population.

5 However, an executive of the Liu Surname Association told me that the members of the Korean Liu common-surname association claim that they were Koreans.

6 According to Makino (1985b: 274–5), it is disrespectful to have a rite of ancestor worship conducted by someone whose genealogical relationship with the subject of the rite is unclear. However, members of the Association did not see this as a problem at all.

7 Please note that all personal names in the following cases are fictitious.

8 The genealogical records issued by surname associations make it a place for information exchange. Many of the genealogical records published by surname associations, whether Liu or others, contain family photographs of interested members in addition to their genealogical charts (not all are connected). They are usually accompanied by personal details such as family composition, the names of employers and (children's) schools and a brief personal history. Such information is made available so that the common-surname relatives can get to know and feel familiar with them. The information also enables other members to discern their economic standing, social status and education levels.

9 It is said that siblings tend to drift apart if their economic standings are different. Yan Binkun, a medical doctor, has three younger brothers but he rarely has contact with them except on special occasions such as weddings and funerals. He says that they feel uncomfortable with each other when they meet. Yan Binkun has very close relationships with other doctors of his age group in central Taiwan rather than his own brothers.

10 The year 2006 was very difficult for President Chen Shuibian. In summer, nearly 100,000 demonstrators gathered to demand his resignation because of an insider trading scandal involving his son-in-law. This was triggered by the son-in-law's profiteering from his position as a member of the President's family. In Taiwan, preferential treatment based on family connections is harshly criticized these days due to revulsion and a backlash against the KMT era when corruption was rife.
11 Some people not only put the interests of their own branch before that of the whole kin group but also act dishonestly. Suenari (1983) reports that those who manage the assets of their kin group sometimes add to their own wealth by pilfering rice and other property from the group.
12 There is a well-known proverb in China which says, 'When the master is promoted to a high position, even his chickens and dogs rise to the heavens.' This means that when one family member attains an important position, his entire family also becomes important. It suggests the strength of connections in Chinese society. However, this is not the case in Taiwan. As entrenched income disparities have become an issue in Taiwan, wealthy siblings do not extend their support beyond their own family unit to poor siblings in order to bring them up to their standard of living or resolve income disparities.
13 Sonoda (2000) argues that the use and transformation of kinship should be analyzed in the context of its response to the external environment rather than its 'cultural genes.' Similarly, Segawa expresses strong criticism: 'A stereotyped theory that views Chinese society as a familism- and kinship-based society only provides a biased image of Chinese society. If it merely sets Chinese society against modern Western society as an intrinsically different society according to the dualistic patterns of tradition versus modern, East versus West, kinship-based society versus civic society and so on, it is an extremely crude typology' (2004: 216–17).

Chapter 6

1 Here I use the term 'provincial' as opposed to the capital or the center of the dynastic state in the pre-modern context (so-called '*hyangch'on*' or '*chaeji*' in Korean) and to the urban in modern context. Basically, I will not use the term here without any note as an adjective form of Korean province (*do*) which is the uppermost local administrative unit.
2 '*Yangban*,' also referred to as '*sajok*,' was the most prestigious status group in the Chosŏn era (1392–1910), consisting of dynastic bureaucrats, their families and descendants, who, if qualified, were thus eligible for high bureaucratic offices. At the county level, the local gentry of *yangban* origin played a subsidiary role in the local administration and are often referred to as '*chaeji-yangban*' or '*chaeji-sajok*' in the literature.
3 '*Ŭmnae*' was the administrative township in which a local bureaucratic office was located during the Chosŏn era.
4 The Korean civil service examination of Chinese origin was introduced at the beginning of the Koryŏ era in the mid-tenth century. It had four different divisions during the Chosŏn era: *munkwa* for the recruitment of

high-grade officers or bureaucrats; *saengwŏnsi* and *chinsasi* (recognized and advancing scholars' examination for knowledge of classics and literary composition skills) to gain eligibility to study at the highest seat of dynastic education, Sŏnggyungwan, and to take the *munkwa* examination; *mugwa* for the recruitment of military officers; and *chapkwa* for the recruitment of technical officers such as foreign language specialists (*yakkwan*), medical specialists (*ŭigwan*) and astrologists (*ŭmyangsa*) (Han 2003: 255–6).

5 In the Korean naming system, patri-clan is identified as the combination of *pongwan* (or clan seat, which is the name of place associated with the patri-clan's forebear (*sijo*)) and surname (*sŏng*) succeeded agnatically. For example, the royal family of Chosŏn dynasty was from Chŏnju I clan in which Chŏnju (one of the major counties of Chŏlla Province) is *pongwan* and I is surname. Clan and family names are expressed according to this system in this paper.

6 The name and function of each *yukpang* office is as follows: *ibang* was in charge of personnel matters of functionaries; *hobang* was in charge of household and land registration and taxation; *yebang* was in charge of ceremonial music, rituals, civil examination and Confucian education; *pyŏngbang* was in charge of military and police affairs; *hyŏngbang* was in charge of legal affairs and slaves; *kongbang* was in charge of building and repairs.

7 A *hyanggyo* was an institution for Confucian education and indoctrination set up in each county under a royal mandate during the early Chosŏn period. It always had shrines for Confucius and other Confucian sages on its campus. Its educational function was lost over time, but rituals at the shrines continued to be conducted by the local *yangban* and *yurim* (Confucian intellectuals) even after the modern reforms at the end of Chosŏn era. A *yangsajae* was a training institution for dynastic officers and taught literature and proper manners of behavior. At Namwŏn Yangsajae, a hall was built at the end of the 19th century with funds contributed by the *yurim* at the recommendation of the Namwŏn county head in order to enshrine the portraits of Lü Dajun, who reportedly had drafted the local *hyangyak*, and Zhu Xi, who had compiled works of New Confucianism.

8 However, according to the literature concerning Kyŏnghagwŏn, which succeeded the dynastic university of Sŏnggyungwan, 'Since the annexation, the Government-General has been treating the *yangban* in the capital well but ignoring the *yangban* and Confucian intellectuals in the provinces and not giving them proper treatment'; 'Functionaries and young people have become rampant and they do not hesitate to insult not only the *yangban* and Confucian intellectuals but also the elders in order to break down old customs and destroy the hierarchy' (Ryu 2005: 178 n.51). It appears that the authority of the provincial *yangban*, Confucian intellectuals and older generations was shaken under pressure from the *rijok* and younger generations. However, it is certain that the *yangban* and Confucian intellectuals were in a more advantageous position in maintaining their status in comparison to the descendants of the *rijok* and other old status groups which did not have any social networks beyond their pre-modern county.

9 The lowest was 59.7% for Sandong District, followed by 67.6% for Wangch'i District. Sandong District had a high proportion of women in manufacturing, perhaps due to the inclusion of weaving; a secondary job for many women in farming. The highest was 94.4% for Ibaek District, followed by 90.9% for Hŭksong District.
10 The family line of the second mayor I Chŏnggŭn is unknown. The office of the mayor was briefly taken up by prominent Japanese residents under the war regime.
11 According to the 1930 census, 79.6% of men in Namwŏn County were born in their local district while only 66.2% of men in Namwŏn District were born there.
12 According to the 1930 census, mainland Japanese migrants accounted for 5.2% of the population of Namwŏn Township. They accounted for 0.8% of the county population and 77.8% of them lived in Namwŏn District. According to the 1935 census, they accounted for 5.3% of the population of Namwŏn District, 0.9% of the county population and 83.5% of them lived in Namwŏn Township.
13 The population growth in Namwŏn District over a period of fifteen years (1910–1925) was 34.7%. While the growth rate for five years (1925–1930) in Namwŏn County was 3.85%, it was 17.31% in Namwŏn District. From 1930 to 1935, it was 4.01% for the county and 18.21% for Namwŏn Township.
14 For reference, the direct tax amount for 1935 in Namwŏn County was 0.883 *yen* for a Korean resident and 19.26 *yen* for a Japanese migrant; over twenty times more than the amount for a Korean (*Tong-a Ilbo*, 25 June 1936).
15 The *tosŏwŏn* was a chief functionary at a local tax office which handled agricultural taxes.
16 Namwŏn District (Namwŏn-myŏn) became Namwŏn Township (Namwŏn-ŭp) under the Government-General Ordinance No. 132 issued on 20 October 1931 and enforced on 1 November 1931 (*Chōsen Sōtokufu Kanpō*, 20 October 1931).
17 It had seven other members, including Namwŏn County Head, Pak T'aeyŏng, Chief Officer of the Office of Financial Affairs, Nagata, and Yang Ch'unmo of Namwŏn Ŭmnae.
18 *P'ansori* is a form of opera in which one singer performs a long epic story to the accompaniment of a drum. The style was reportedly established in the southwestern part of the Korean peninsula in the 17th and early 18th centuries. *Ch'unhyangga* is one of the most widely performed and best loved *p'ansori* pieces.

Chapter 7

1 I stayed in Indonesia in February and March 2006 to conduct this study. I would like to acknowledge the support given to me by the Center for East Asian Cooperation Studies, Faculty of Political and Social Sciences, University of Indonesia which hosted me, the Center for the Study of Social Stratification and Inequality, The 21st Century Center of Excellence Program, Tohoku University which provided a study grant, and Reza Anggara and Muhamad Azhar who were students of the Faculty of Political

and Social Sciences, University of Indonesia who acted as my field study assistants, as well as residents of C Zone. This paper is an expanded and revised version of my report presented at the Tohoku Sociology Society Conference held on 29 and 30 July 2006 (at Iwate Prefectural University).

2 '*Posyandu* is short for *pos pelayanan terpadu* (integrated health post), which provides a comprehensive range of basic health services' (Saito 2006c: 90).

3 Medical officers are supplied by the regional healthcare center (*puskesmas*), but volunteers are selected from among local residents.

4 Volunteers do not have to be female. The existence of male volunteers has been pointed out by earlier studies. I was able to confirm one male volunteer in one of my survey areas in Jakarta. However, almost 100% of volunteers were female in my survey areas in Jakarta (Saito 2006a).

5 See the section under '*mampu*' in *Kamus Indonesia Inggris*.

6 The main focus of Konno's discussion is the new middle class. While acknowledging studies that use the consumption pattern as the *merkmal*, Konno adopts occupation-based stratification because of limitations associated with the former (Konno 1999: 322).

7 J. Sullivan (1992) also argued on stratification in urban communities (particularly RK (*rukun kampung*) which is said to be the predecessor of RW) although they were situated in the Javanese city of Jogjakarta rather than Jakarta. According to Sullivan, RW leaders belong to the white-collar middle class and have higher status jobs (administrators, managers and professionals) and higher educational qualifications than the average *kampung* resident. Conversely, RT leaders and officials belong to a lower hierarchy (J. Sullivan 1992: 119).

8 According to suggestions from *kader* in C1 Zone.

9 I also conducted a similar survey in one RT area (C2 Zone) which reportedly had a higher proportion of homegrown residents, but will not comment on the result in this paper.

10 Based on internal information of C Zone RW. The area size is unknown. Other fragmented data I have obtained shows six self-employed workers (*wiraswasta*) and twelve public servants (August 2002) among working residents of C1 Zone, which means a majority are private sector employees.

11 I gathered the data in my interviews with C Zone *posyandu* leaders from January to May 2003. However, it became clear at a later date that the occupation-based data classification was less than clear-cut as mentioned above.

12 Between my surveys in 2003 and 2006, I conducted an additional survey of thirteen *kader* volunteers in August 2004. The survey samples for 2006 was different from those for 2004 as three people declined to be interviewed and had to be replaced by three new samples. Ages used in this paper have been simply calculated by subtracting their birth years from 2006.

13 Although women have been appointed as RW executives occasionally in other districts, there has been no female RW executive in C Zone since 2002.

14 The treasurer declined to be interviewed in detail.

15 According to interviews, such *kader* volunteers are recruited by *posyandu* leaders in some cases.

16 Some of the women under study do have occupations. However, very few of the working women work full-time. In the sense that they are not involved in wage-earning activities, six *kader* (46.2%) and all fifteen recipients are 'housewives.' Among the seven *kader* involved in wage-earning activities, only two do so every weekday (a laundrywoman and a small stall of school cafeteria's operator), and even they are not full-time workers. The remaining five are involved in dressmaking/homemade cake-making, their husband's business, homemade cake-making/canned milk sales, money lending and catering, but they only work for several days a month.

17 Recently in the analysis of Japanese society, eight new major categories are often used which reflect occupational status and the size of company. In this research the eight new major categories are not used. This is because during interviews significant answers were not collected. When I asked husband's company size, most informants said "I do not know". Therefore in this paper the eight old major categories are adopted which do not consider the size of company (Naoi and Seiyama 190: 188–92). This is a method to categorize occupation into eight categories: Professional, Managerial, Clerical, Sales, Skilled, Semi-skilled, Unskilled, and Farmer. In addition I regarded Professional, Managerial, Clerical and Sales workers as white-collar and Skilled, Semi-skilled and Unskilled workers as blue-collar. In this research, no respondents answered as farmer.

18 Twenty-five percent of RW husbands and 33.3% of RT husbands had no job or have died and 20.0% of recipient husbands did not answer the question. Therefore those who could not be classified are excluded from the total number.

19 Another obstacle to the conclusion of inequality of participation is the 'attitude' of recipients towards participation. It is of course just an attitude, but 66.7% (ten out of fifteen) of the recipients in this study replied that they 'want to participate' in community activities and many of them were willing to participate as *kader* volunteers if such opportunities arose in the future.

Chapter 8

1 See Geertz and Geertz (1975), Geertz (1980), Kagami (2000) Warren (1993) and Yamashita (1999) for community structure.
2 This survey was conducted jointly with the Center for Japanese Language Studies, Faculty of Letters, Udayama University, in March and August–October 2005 and March and August 2006.
3 See Desa Sanur Kaja (2000), Desa Sanur Kauh (2000) and Kelurahan Sanur (2000) for quantitative data for the area.
4 Trantib: *Ketertiban dan Satuan Polisi Pamong Praja Kota Denpasar*, a public body in charge of local security, order and discipline in Denpasar City.

Chapter 9

1 According to the ILO's definition, the informal sector is characterized by: (1) low entry barriers; (2) utilization of local resources; (3) family-run

and other small-scale production units; and (4) labor-intensive with low technical standards. However, it is difficult to provide a strict definition due to its diversity in terms of region, industry sectors, and types of work. See Torii (1981) and Nakanishi (1991) for a more detailed definition.

2 Although the work covered in this paper is primarily porting, the workers may also organize goods, package fruit, or clean the shops for hourly wages, at the request of their employers. As detailed in this paper, there are many opportunities to do such non-porting work, but these opportunities only arise after the workers have become acquainted with their employers. Until then, they only perform physically demanding porting work. Furthermore, even the individuals who organize baggage and package fruit generally always bring along a bamboo pole for porting work. This paper studies workers who carry bamboo poles, including those who also do non-porting work for hourly wages. Although the term should be written as 'porter,' in this paper the quotation marks shall be omitted for the sake of simplicity.

3 According to a survey carried out by the General Statistics Office of Vietnam with the assistance of the UNFPA in 2004, domestic labor migration in Vietnam has two characteristics. First, at least 70% of the individuals in the survey sample were either from the Red River Delta region or the Northwestern region of Vietnam and 70% of those from the Red River Delta region and Northwestern region migrate to Hanoi. Second, migrants in the Central Highlands, Ho Chi Minh, and the South-Central region come in equal numbers from throughout Vietnam.

4 A vast amount of research has been carried out in fields such as social psychology regarding the debate concerning commitment. The aim of this paper is to explain the porter labor market and employment behavior of porters by incorporating this concept of 'commitment.' A discussion of the concept of 'commitment' itself must be left for future research.

5 The information is based on an interview with the Assistant Administrator of the Long Bien market.

6 The legal grounds for this transportation are not clear. For additional information, Dong Xuan market, which used to be under the control of the district office, was turned into a stock corporation in 1996. In contrast, at Long Bien market, which is operated by the district office, the assistant director of the market remarked that there is as yet no regulation specifically concerning the porters. The porters testify that there have been no cases of custody or deportation in this market.

7 The interview assistants used in this study were three individuals who were either Vietnamese exchange students at the Tokyo University of Agriculture or students at the Vietnam National University. Students at the Hanoi University of Foreign Studies and Vietnamese exchange students at Tohoku University participated in the supplementary study.

8 Misaki Iwai 1995: 274. A similar situation seems to prevail in other parts of Southeast Asia. For example, in Indonesia, small commerce in markets in which only small amounts of money are handled is historically thought of as menial, and is thus considered women's work (Wolf 1992: 63–4). However, in the case of the markets where I did my research, at least during

the night time, there were many male laborers as well as female laborers who were engaged in porting. This topic needs further research.
9 Children normally start to attend primary schools at the age of six. Education at this level lasts for 5 years. Middle schools teach students from grade 6 to 9. Primary and middle school education is compulsory for all children.
10 As of March 2006, one dollar equals 15,800 dong.
11 According to a study conducted by Rolf Jensen in 2000 involving interviews with 379 street vendors in Hanoi there are four types of migrant labor, based on whether or not the labor is considered migrant work and the length of the migrant worker's stay: (1) Commuting street vending (returning to home villages every day); (2) Cyclical street vending (staying in Hanoi for at least one night); (3) Permanent street vending (not born in Hanoi, but live in Hanoi); and (4) Non-migratory street vending (born in Hanoi, and live in Hanoi). The largest group is the cyclical street vending category, comprising 44.3% of migrant labor.
12 The porters were interviewed during the supplementary study to determine the details of their returns home. Amongst thirteen interviewees, one returned home once per week, five returned home once every ten to fourteen days, six returned home once per month, and one returned home once every half year.
13 In the interviews I conducted, many porters stressed the importance of memorizing the location where they are to take the goods and the motorbike number.
14 I frequently observed such situations during the interviews.
15 However, porters confirmed that if a job cannot be handled by one individual due to the porter being in poor physical condition or the weight of the parcel, they will call upon a friend or relative to assist them. I observed many situations in which a friend would call upon a porter during the interviews. Each porter is essentially in a competitive relationship with every other, but they do not completely ignore their hometown, kinship and friendship relationships.
16 Let us consider, for example, a situation in which a customer has just moved to the area. This individual has no idea which of the greengrocers in the market sells cheap, fresh produce. They will usually pick one shop and purchase their produce from there, and if they are satisfied with the price and freshness of this produce, they will continue to shop there in the future. They may find another greengrocer that sells cheaper and fresher produce, and yet continue to go to the first shop, on the assumption that, 'As long as this greengrocer doesn't sell rotten produce, it's fine to continue shopping here.' The trust relationship developed with the shopkeeper on this basis is called a 'commitment relationship.' Refer to Yamagishi (1998) for a more extensive discussion of commitment in this sense.
17 As indicated in Note 2 above, the porters do a variety of jobs at hourly rates at the request of employers. In this paper, all individuals who carry the required bamboo pole with them for porting, including those who also do non-portering work, are considered to be porters.
18 'Gánh ơi' or 'này gánh' in Vietnamese. The employer will also often call out the name of a porter if they know it.

19 A breakdown of the interviews is as follows:

Number of porters in weak commitment relationships per employer	Number of employers
0	4
1 to 3	5
4 to 6	2
7 or more	2
Not sure	1
Total	14

20 As the central data used in this paper was based on data from fifty-one individuals collected from a written survey, it cannot support any analysis of quantitative differences. A composition ratio of the porters in strong commitment relationships, weak commitment relationships, and no commitment relationships will be a topic of future research.

References

Historical Reference Materials used in Chapter 1

Gokenin bungen chō『御家人分限帳』(A book of *gokenin* ranks), edited by Suzuki, Hisashi 鈴木寿, 1984, 東京：近藤出版社 (Tokyo: Kondō Shuppansha).

Hen-nen Edo bukan: Bunka bukan 2『編年江戸武鑑　文化武鑑2』 (A chronological directory of *daimyō* and *hatamoto* in the Edo period: Bunka directory vol. 2), edited by Ishii, Ryōsuke 石井良介, 1981, 東京：柏書房 (Tokyo: Kashiwa Shobō).

Ofuregaki Kanpō shūsei『御触書寛保集成』 (A *Kanpō* collection of governmental notifications), edited by Takayanagi, Sinzō 高柳真三 and Ryōsuke Ishii 石井良助, 1934, 東京：岩波書店 (Tokyo: Iwanami Shoten).

Ofuregaki Tenmei shūsei『御触書天明集成』 (A *Tenmei* collection of governmental notifications), edited by Takayanagi, Sinzō 高柳真三 and Ryōsuke Ishii 石井良助, 1936, 東京：岩波書店 (Tokyo: Iwanami Shoten).

Tokugawa kinrei kō: zenshū dai-2『徳川禁令考　前集第二』 (A study of Tokugawa prohibitory decrees: part I, volume 2), edited by Ishii, Ryōsuke 石井良助, 1959, 東京：創文社 (Tokyo: Sōbunsha).

Original Sources in Indonesian cited in Chapters 7 and 8

Desa Sanur Kaja (The North Sanur Village), 2000, *Profil Desa/Kelurahan: Daftar Isian Data Dasar Profil Desa/Kelurahan* (Village/Town Profile: Data list of village/town profile).

Desa Sanur Kauh (The West Sanur Village), 2000, *Profil Desa/Kelurahan: Daftar Isian Data Dasar Profil Desa/Kelurahan* (Village/Town Profile: Data list of village/town profile).

Dinas Pariwisata (Tourism Office), 1998a, *Laporan Bahan Rapat BK3S pada tanggal 5 Mei 1998* (Report of the meeting material of BK3S, May 5 1998).

Dinas Pariwisata (Tourism Office), 1998b, *Laporan Hasil Rapat BK3S Tanggal 6 Mei 1998 di Hotel The Grand Bali Beach* (Report of the meeting result of BK3S, May 6 1998.at the Grand Bali Beach Hotel).

Dinas Pariwisata (Tourism Office), 2000, *Laporan Perihal Peranan Polisi Pariwisata.* (Report about the role of tourism police).

Kelurahan Sanur (The Sanur town), 2000, *Profil Desa/Kelurahan: Daftar Isian Data Dasar Profil Desa/Kelurahan* (Village/Town Profile: Data list of village/town profile).

Perpres (Peraturan Presiden Republik Indonesia) Nomor 1 Tahun 2006 tentang Penyesuaian Gaji Pokok Pegawai Negeri Sipil menurut Peraturan Pemerintah Nomor 11 Tahun 2003 tentang Perubahan atas Peraturan Pemerintah Nomor 7 Tahun 1977 tentang Peraturan Gaji Pegawai Negeri

Sipil sebagaimana telah beberapa Kali Diubah Terakhir dengan Peraturan Pemerintahan Nomor 26 Tahun 2001 ke dalam Gaji Pokok Pegawai Negeri Sipil menurut Peraturan Pemerintah Nomor 6 Tahun 2005 tentang Perubahan Ketujuh atas Peraturan Pemetintah Nomor 7 Tahun 1977 tentang Peraturan Gaji Pegawai Negeri Sipil (Presidential Regulations of the Republic of Indonesia Number 1 Year 2006 on Reconciliation of Regular Wage for Public Servant based on the Government Regulation Number 11 Year 2003 on the Change based on the Government Regulation Number 7 Year 1977 on Wage Regulation of Public Servant as had been changed several times and changed for the last time by the Government Regulation Number 26 Year 2001 on Regular Wage of Public Servant, based on the Government Regulation Number 6 Year 2005 on 7th Revision based on the Government Regulation Number 7 Year 1977 on Public Servant's Regular Wage).

Propinsi Bali (The Province of Bali), 2001, *Peraturan Daerah Propinsi Bali Nomor 3 Tahun 2001 Tentang Desa Pakraman* (The Local Regulation of the Province of Bali, Number 3, 2001, about Traditional Village).

Suryawan, I Ngurah (2005), Bali, *Narasi Dalam Kuasa: Politik & Kekerasan di Bali* (Bali, narration in the power: Politics and violence in Bali), Yogyakarta: Ombak.

Walikota Denpasar (The Mayor of Denpasar), 1997, *Rencana Pembiayaan Operasional Badan Koordinasi Keamanan Kawasan Sanur (BK3S)* (The Financial Program of the Agency of coordination of the local safety in Sanur).

Walikota Denpasar (The Mayor of Denpasar), 1999, *Keputusan Walikotamadya Kepala Daerah Tingkat II Denpasar tentang Susunan Keanggotaan Pengurus Badan Koordinasi Keamanan Kawasan Pariwisata Sanur di Wilayah Kotamadya Daerah Tingkat II Denpasar* (The Decision of The Mayor of Local Level II Denpasar about the Composition of the Membership of the Board of the Agency of coordination of the local safety in Sanur in the Level II of the Ordinance-Designated City of Denpasar).

Walikota Denpasar (The Mayor of Denpasar), 2000a, *Keputusan Walikota Denpasar Nomor 579 Tahun 2000 Tentang Pemberian Honorarium Kepada Tenaga Satpam Badan Koordinasi Keamanan Kawasan Sanur (BK3S) Kota Denpasar Tahun 2000* (The Decision of the Mayor of Denpasar Number 579, 2000, about the Awarding of Honorarium of the Agency of coordination of the local safety in Sanur).

Walikota Denpasar (The Mayor of Denpasar), 2000b, *Peraturan Daerah Kota Denpasar Nomor 3 Tahun 2000* (The Local Regulation of the Ordinance-Designated City of Depnasar, Number 3, 2000).

Widnyani, Nyoman dan I Ketut Widia (2002), *Ajeg Bali Pecalang dan Pendidikan Budi Pekerti* (Consistency of Bali: Traditional guard and education of morals): SIC.

Yayasan Pembangunan Sanur (Sanur Development Foundation), 1988, *Keputusan Musyawarah Kerja II Yayasan Pembangunan Sanur* (The Decision of the Second Service Conference of Sanur Development Foundation).

Yayasan Pembangunan Sanur (Sanur Development Foundation), 1999, *Surat Keputusan Yayasan Pembangunan Sanur Tentang: Bantuan Kepada Badan Koordinasi Keamanan Kawasan Sanur (BK3S)* (The Document of the

Decision of Sanur Development Foundation about the Help for the Agency of coordination of the local safety in Sanur).

Yayasan Pembangunan Sanur (Sanur Development Foundation), 2000a, *Materi Musyawarah Kerja III Yayasan Pembangunan Sanur Tahun 2000* (The Material of the Third Service Conference of Sanur Development Foundation 2000).

Yayasan Pembangunan Sanur (Sanur Development Foundation), 2000b, *Keputusan Musyawarah Kerja III Yayasan Pembangunan Sanur Nomor: 05/Muker.III/YPS/VI/2000 Tentang Pengesahan Pertanggungjawaban Ketua Umum YPS Periode 1988–2000* (The Decision of the Third Service Conference of Sanur Development Foundation, Number 05/Muker.III/YPS/VI/2000, about the Confirmation of the Responsibility of the Leader of Sanur Development Foundation among 1988–2000).

Yayasan Pembangunan Sanur (Sanur Development Foundation), 2000c, *Laporan Perihal Mohon Bantuan Tenaga, Nomor:03/TK-YPS/XII/2000* (The Report about the Request of the Help of Staff, Number 03/TK-YPS/XII/2000).

Yayasan Pembangunan Sanur (Sanur Development Foundation), 2000d, *Laporan Perihal Sosialisasi, Nomor:07/TK-YPS/XII/2000* (The Report about the Socialization).

Yayasan Pembangunan Sanur (Sanur Development Foundation), 2000e, *Seruan kepada Pedagang Acung dan Asongan di Kawasan Sanur, Nomor:1.a/YPS/XII/2000* (The Announcement for the Peddlers and Vendors in Sanur Area, Number 1a/YPS/XII/2000).

Yayasan Pembangunan Sanur (Sanur Development Foundation), 2000f, *Proposal Diskusi Panel 2000: Sanur Kami, Sanur Kita: Mengembalikan Citra Pariwisata Sanur* (The Proposal of the Panel Discussion 2000: We Sanur, Our Sanur: The Restoration of the Image of Tourism of Sanur).

Yayasan Pembangunan Sanur (Sanur Development Foundation), 2005a, *Materi Musyawarah Kerja IV Yayasan Pembangunan Sanur Tahun 2005* (The Material of the Fourth Service Conference of Sanur Development Foundation 2005).

Yayasan Pembangunan Sanur (Sanur Development Foundation), 2005b, *Keputusan Musyawarah Kerja IV Yayasan Pembangunan Sanur Nomor: 05/Muker.IV/YPS/IV/2005 Tentang Pengesahan Pertanggung Jawaban Pengurus Yayasan Pembangunan Sanur Periode 2000–2005* (The Decision of the Fourth Service Conference of Sanur Development Foundation, Number 05/Muker/IV/YPS/2005, about the Confirmation of the Responsibility of the Leader of Sanur Development Foundation among 2000–2005).

Yayasan Pembangunan Sanur (Sanur Development Foundation), 2005c, *Keputusan Musyawarah Kerja IV Yayasan Pembangunan Sanur Nomor: 04/Muker.IV/YPS/IV/2005 Tentang Program Kerja Yayasan Pembangunan Sanur Periode 2005–2010* (The Decision of the Fourth Service Conference of Sanur Development Foundation, Number 04/Muker.IV/YPS/IV/2005, about Service Program of Sanur Development Foundation among 2005–2010).

Consolidated Bibliography

Baker, Hugh D. R. (1968), *Chinese Lineage Village: Sheung Shui*, Stanford: Stanford University Press.

Banerjee, B. (1983), 'The Role of the Informal Sector in the Migration Process: A test of Probabilistic Migration Models and Labour Market Segmentation for India,' *Oxford Economic Papers*, 35: 399–422.

Barker, Joshua (1999), 'Surveillance and territoriality in Bandung', in Vincente Rafael (ed.), *Figures of Criminality in Indonesia, the Philippines, and Colonial Vietnam*, New York: Cornell Southeast Asia Program Publications, pp. 95–127.

Bellah, Robert (1957), *Tokugawa Religion*, New York: Free Press.

Benedict, Ruth (1946), *The Chrysanthemum and the Sword*, Boston: Houghton Mifflin.

Bourdieu, Pierre and Jean-Claude Passeron (1970), *La reproduction*, translated by Miyajima, Takashi 宮島喬 as 『再生産: 教育・社会・文化』, 1991, 東京: 藤原書店 (Tokyo: Fujiwara Shoten).

Bruner, Edward M. (1986), 'Ethnography as Narrative', Victor W. Turner and Edward M. Bruner (eds), *The Anthropology of Experience*, Urbana: University of Illinois Press, pp. 139–55.

Caillois, Roger (1958), *Les jeux et les hommes*, translated by Tada, Michitarō 多田道太郎 and Mikio Tsuskazaki 塚崎幹夫 as 『遊びと人間』, 1990, 東京: 講談社 (Tokyo: Kōdansha).

Chi, Sŭngjong 池承鐘 (1991), 「身分観念과 身分構造」 (The concept of status and the status structure), 서울大学校 社会学研究会編 (Society for Sociological Research at Seoul National University (ed.)), 『善丁 金彩潤 教授 回甲記念論文集 社会階層—理論과 実際』 (Social stratification—Theory and reality: Collected papers in celebration of Professor Kim Ch'aeyun's 60th birthday), 서울: 茶山出版社 (Seoul: T'asan Ch'ulp'ansa).

Chi, Sŭngjong 池承鐘, Kim Chunhyŏng 金俊亨, Hŏ Kwŏnsu 許捲洙, Chŏng Chinsang 鄭震相 and Pak Chaehŭng 朴再興 (2000), 『근대사회변동과 양반』 (Modern social change and *yangban*), 서울: 아세아문화사 (Seoul: Aseamunhwasa).

Chōsen Sōtokufu (Government-General of Korea) 朝鮮総督府 (1921), 『朝鮮総督府統計年報』大正10年版 (Statistical yearbook, Government-General of Korea, 1921 edition), 京城: 朝鮮総督府 (Keijō: Chōsen Sōtokufu).

Chōsen Sōtokufu (Government-General of Korea) 朝鮮総督府 (1933), 『昭和5年朝鮮国勢調査報告道編』第4巻全羅北道 (Census of Korea 1931, Province Section, vol. 4: North Chŏlla Province), 京城: 朝鮮総督府 (Keijō: Chōsen Sōtokufu).

Chōsen Sōtokufu (Government-General of Korea) 朝鮮総督府 (1936), 『朝鮮総督府統計年報』昭和11年版 (Statistical yearbook, Government-General of Korea, 1936 edition), 京城: 朝鮮総督府 (Keijō: Chōsen Sōtokufu).

Cohen, M. (1968), 'The Hakka or "Guest people": Dialects as a sociocultural variable in Southeastern China,' *Ethnohistory*, 15: 237–92.

Cu, Chi Loi (2005), 'Rural to urban migration in Vietnam,' in Ha, Huy Thanh and Shozo Sakata (eds), *Impact of socio-economic changes on the livelihoods of people living in poverty in Vietnam*, Institute of Developing Economies, Chiba: Japan External Trade Organization, pp. 115–43.

Cukier, Judie and Geoffrey Wall (1994), 'Informal tourism employment: Vendors in Bali, Indonesia', *Tourism Management*, 15(6): 464–76.

Dahl, Robert A. and Edward R. Tufte (1973), *Size and Democracy*, Stanford, California: Stanford University Press.

Dang, Nguyen Anh (2000), 'Women's Migration and Urban Integration in the Context of Doi Moi,' *Vietnam's Socio-Economic Development*, 23: 66–80.

Dore, Ronald (1994), *Shinohata: A Portrait of a Japanese Village*, Berkeley: University of California Press.

Dwianto, Raphaella D. ラファエラ D. ドウィアント (1999), 「都市暴動と自警団」 (Urban riots and vigilante groups), 『東北都市学会研究年報』 (*Annual report of the Tōhoku Society for Urbanology*), 1: 34–51.

Echols, John M. and Hassan Shadily (1989), *Kamus Indonesia–Inggris* (*Indonesian–English dictionary*) 3rd ed., Jakarta: Gramedia.

Eckert, Carter J. (1991), *Offspring of Empire: The Koch'ang Kims and the Colonial Origins of Korean Capitalism 1876–1945*, Seattle: University of Washington Press.

Elias, Norbert and John L. Scotson (1994), *The Established and the Outsiders: A Sociological Enquiry into Community Problems* (2nd ed.) London: Sage Publications Ltd.

Faure, David (1986), *The Structure of Chinese Rural Society: Lineage and Village in the Eastern New Territories*, Hong Kong: Oxford University Press.

Faure, David (1989), 'The Lineage as a Cultural Invention: The Case of the Pearl River Delta,' *Modern China*, 15(1): 4–36.

Fei, Xiaotong 費孝通 (1991), 『鄉土社会』 (Rural China), 香港: 三聯書店 (Hong Kong: Salian Press).

Freedman, Maurice (1958), *Lineage Organization in Southeastern China*, London: The Athlone Press.

Freedman, Maurice (1966), *Chinese Lineage and Society*, London: The Athlone Press.

Freedman, Maurice (1979), 'Immigrants and associations: Chinese in nineteenth-century Singapore' in M. Freedman (ed.), *The Study of Chinese Society*. Stanford: Stanford University Press, pp. 61–83.

Fried, M. H. (1962), 'Kinship and Friendship in Chinese Society,' Unpublished paper presented at the seminar on Micro-Social Organization on China, Ithaca, New York, 11–13 October.

Fujinami, Gōichi 藤浪剛一 (1942a), 「江戸幕府医官制度」 (System of medical officers in the Edo *bakufu*). 『日本医史学雑誌』 (Journal of the Japan Society of Medical History), 1300: 61–70.

Fujinami, Gōichi 藤浪剛一 (1942b), 「江戸幕府医官の序列」 (Ranks of medical officers in the Edo *bakufu*), 『日本医史学雑誌』 (Journal of the Japan Society of Medical History), 1302: 129–32.

Funo, Shūji 布野修司 (1991), 『カンポンの世界―ジャワの庶民住居誌』 (The world of kampung: An ethnography of people's housing in Java), 東京: パルコ出版 (Tokyo: Parco Shuppan).

Furuhashi, Hironoshin 古橋廣之進 (1997), 『力泳三十年』 (Swimming hard for thirty years), 東京: 日本図書センター (Tokyo: Nihontosho Sentā).

Fuse, Shōichi 布施昌一 (1979), 『医師の歴史 その日本的特長』 (History of doctors: Their Japanese characteristics), 東京: 中央公論社 (Tokyo: Chūōkōron-sha).

Futagoyama, Katsuji 二子山勝治 (1978), 『心・技・体』 (Spirit, technique and physical condition), 東京: 日本文芸社 (Tokyo: Nihonbungeisha).

Geertz, Clifford (1980), *Negara: The Theatre State in Nineteenth-Century Bali*, Princeton, N.J.: Princeton University Press.

Geertz, Hildred and Clifford Geertz (1975), *Kinship in Bali*, Chicago: The University of Chicago Press.
General Statistics Office (2005), *The 2004 Vietnam Migration Survey: Major Findings*, Hanoi: Statistical Publishing House.
General Statistics Office (2006), *The Quality of Life of Migrants in Vietnam*, Hanoi: Statistical Publishing House.
Goldberg, C. N. (1973), 「양반, 상놈과 인류학자—人類学的理論과 cross-cultural studies를 비추어본 韓国社会階級과 同族集団의 調査」 (Gentry, commoners and an anthropologist: Research on Korean social classes and kin groups in light of anthropological theories and cross-cultural studies), 『文化人類学』 (*Munhwa Inryuhak*), 6: 161–7, 서울: 韓国文化人類学会 (Seoul: Korean Society for Cultural Anthropology).
Gupta, Akhil, and James Ferguson (1997), 'Culture, Power, Place: Ethnography at the End of an Era', in Gupta, Akhil and James Ferguson (eds), *Culture, Power, Place: Explorations in Critical Anthropology*. Durham: Duke University Press, pp. 1–29.
Ha, T. P. T. and Ha, Q. N. (2001), *Female Labour Migration: Rural–Urban*, Hanoi: Women's Publishing House.
Hamashima, Atsutoshi 濱島敦俊 (1990), 「明清時代、江南農村の「社」と土地廟」 (Communal villages (*she*) and *tudi miao* in Rural Jiangnan during the Ming and Qing periods,' 明代史研究会明代史論叢編集委員会編 (Society for Ming history study, editorial committee of essays on Ming history (ed.)), 『山根幸夫教授退休記念 明代史論叢 下巻』 (Essays on Ming history in honor of professor Yamane Yukio's retirement, vol.2), pp. 1325–57, 東京: 汲古書院 (Tokyo: Kyūko SHōin).
Han, Yŏng-u 韓永愚 (2003), 『韓国社会の歴史』 (History of Korean society), 吉田光男訳 (translated by Mitsuo Yoshida), 東京: 明石書店 (Tokyo: Akashi Shoten).
Hashimoto, Seiko 橋本聖子 (1994), 『聖火に恋して』 (Falling in love with the Olympic torch), 東京: 日刊スポーツ出版社 (Tokyo: Nikkan Supōtsu Shuppansha).
Honda, Hiroshi 本田洋 (1999), 「韓国の地方邑における「郷紳」集団と文化伝統—植民地期南原邑の都市化と在地勢力の動向」 ("Gentry" of *ŭpch'i* and their cultural traditions in a Korean local town: A case study of Namwŏn District during the colonial period), 『アジア・アフリカ言語文化研究』 (*Journal of Asian and African studies*), 58: 119–202.
Honda, Hiroshi 本田洋 (2004), 「吏族と身分伝統の形成—南原地域の事例から」 (Families of local functionaries and formation of their status traditions: Case of Namwŏn), 『韓国朝鮮の文化と社会』 (*Korean culture and society*), 3: 23–72, 東京: 韓国・朝鮮文化研究会 (Tokyo: Association for the Study of Korean Culture and Society).
Honda, Hiroshi 本田洋 (2006), 「邑治の儀礼空間と近代—韓国南西部南原地域の吏族と関王廟の事例」 (Reformation of the ritual space of *ŭpch'i* in the modern period: The families of local functionaries and the shrine for Guan Yu in Namwŏn, Southwestern Korea), in Tanabe, Shigeharu 田辺繁治 and Nishii Ryoko 西井凉子 (eds), 『社会空間の人類学』 (*The anthropology of social space*), 京都: 世界思想社 (Kyoto: Sekaishisōsha), pp. 329–48.
Honda, Hiroshi 本田洋 (2007), 「地域開発と媒介者に関する試論—韓国南原地域の事例」 (Community development and mediators: Case study in Namwŏn,

Korea), in Itō, Abito 伊藤亞人 and Kyŏnggu Han 韓敬九 (eds), 『中心と周縁からみた日韓社会の諸相』 (*Aspects of Japan and Korean societies in terms of centrality versus periphery*), 東京：慶應義塾大学出版会 (Tokyo: Keio University Press), pp. 87–130.

Hong, Sŏngch'an 洪性讚 (1992), 『韓国近代農村社会의 変動과 地主層—20세기 前半期 全南 和順郡 同福面 일대의 事例』 (*Modern change of Korean peasant society and landowners: Case of Tongbok District, Hwasun County, South Chŏlla Province*), 서울: 지식산업사 (Seoul: Chisiksanŏpsa).

Horie, Shun'ichi 堀江俊一 (1988), 「親しい他人と見知らぬ親族—台湾漢族における二つの擬制的親族」 (Good friends and unacquainted relatives: Two kinds of quasi-kinship in the Han Chinese in Taiwan), 『文化人類学』 (*Cultural anthropology*) 5: 50–63, アカデミア出版会 (Tokyo: Akademia Shuppankai).

I, Hunsang (Lee, Hoon-sang) 李勛相 (1990), 『朝鮮後期의 郷吏』 (*The local government functionaries in late Chosŏn Dynasty*), 서울: 一潮閣 (Seoul: Ilchogak).

Imura, Masayo 井村雅代 (2001), 『愛があるなら叱りなさい』 (Scold them if you love them), 東京：幻冬舎 (Tokyo: Gentōsha).

Inoue, Tōru 井上徹 (2000), 『中国の宗族と国家の礼制』 (*The Chinese lineage and the Li system of the state*), 東京: 研文出版 (Tokyo: Kenbun Shuppan).

Inoue, Tōru 井上徹 (2002), 「魏校の淫祠破壊令–広東における民間信仰と儒教–」 (The Destruction of Unauthorized Temples by Wei Xiao: Heathenism and Confucianism in Guangdong), 『東方宗教』 (*The journal of Eastern religions*), 99: 1–17.

Inoue, Tōru 井上徹 (2004a), 「霍韜による宗法システムの構築–商業化・都市化・儒教化の潮流と宗族–」 (The *zongfa* system made by Huo Tao : The lineage association in Confucian culture under the influence of commercialization and urbanization.), 『都市文化研究』 (*Studies in urban cultures*), 3: 34–51.

Inoue, Tōru 井上徹 (2004b), 「珠璣巷伝説の成立と霍氏」 (Formation of the Zhujihang legend and the Huo clan), 『アジア遊学』 (*Intriguing Asia*), 67: 8–21.

International Labor Organization (ILO) (1972), *Employment Income and Equality: A Strategy for Increasing Productive Employment in Kenya*, Geneva: ILO.

Ishida, Hiroshi 石田浩 (1996), 『中国同族村落の社会経済構造研究–福建伝統農村と同族ネットワーク』 (*A study of socio-economic structure of single lineage villages: Traditional villages and the surname network in Fujian*), 大阪: 関西大学出版部 (Osaka: Kansai University Press).

Ishii, Ryōsuke 石井良助 (ed.) (1959), 『徳川禁令考　前集第二』 (*A study of Tokugawa prohibitory decrees: part 1, volume 2*), 東京: 創文社 (Tokyo: Sōbunsha).

Ishii, Takashi 石井孝 (1984), 「江戸幕府御目見医師について」 (An Essay on *Omemie-ishi* of the Edo *bakufu*), 『史報』 (*Shihō*), 6: 16–31.

Ishizuki, Hiroko 石附啓子 (2004), 「湖南画壇の形成と展開」 (Formation and development of Honam painting circle), 『韓国朝鮮の文化と社会』 (*Korean culture and society*), 3: 73–96, 東京：韓国・朝鮮文化研究会 (Tokyo: Association for the Study of Korean Culture and Society).

Itō, Abito 伊藤亜人 (1986), 「朝鮮半島」 (Korean Peninsula), in 日本民族学会編 Japanese Society of Ethnology (ed.), 『日本の民族学1964〜1983』 (*Ethnology in Japan 1964–1983*), pp. 186–8, 東京：弘文堂 (Tokyo: Kōbundō).

Ivy, Marilyn (1995), *Discourses of the Vanishing: Modernity, Phantasm, Japan.* Chicago: University of Chicago Press.
Iwai, Misaki 岩井美佐紀 (1995), 「家族と社会主義」 (Family and Socialism), Sakurai, Yumio 桜井由躬雄 (ed.), 『もっと知りたいベトナム(第2版)』 (More to know about Vietnam, 2nd edition), pp. 264–78, 東京：弘文堂 (Tokyo: Kōbundō).
Iwashita, Tetsunori 岩下哲典 (2000a), 「尾張藩『御医師』の基礎的研究(上)」 (Basic research on "*on-ishi*" of Owari *han*, part 1), 『徳川林政史研究所研究紀要』 (*Bulletin of the Tokugawa Institute for the History of Forestry*), 34: 123–45.
Iwashita, Tetsunori 岩下哲典 (2000b), 「尾張藩『御医師』の基礎的研究(中)」 (Basic research on "*on-ishi*" of Owari *han*, part 2), 『徳川林政史研究所研究紀要』 (*Bulletin of the Tokugawa Institute for the History of Forestry*), 35: 147–65.
Iwashita, Tetsunori 岩下哲典 (2000c), 「尾張藩『御医師』の基礎的研究(下)」 (Basic research on "*on-ishi*" of Owari *han*, part 3), 『徳川林政史研究所研究紀要』 (*Bulletin of the Tokugawa Institute for the History of Forestry*), 36: 115–24.
Jagannathan, N.V. and Animesh H. (1988), 'A Case Study of Pavement Dwellers in Calcutta: Occupation, Mobility and Rural–Urban Linkages,' *Economic and Political Weekly*, 39(4): 2602–5.
Janelli, Roger L. and Dawnhee Yim Janelli (1982), *Ancestor Worship and Korean Society*, Stanford, California: Stanford University Press.
Jensen, R. and Donald, M. P. Jr. (2000), 'Roving Street Sellers in Hanoi: A Look at the Urban Informal Sector,' *Vietnam's Socio-Economic Development*, 24: 35–43.
Kagami, Haruya 鏡味治也 (2000), 『政策文化の人類学−せめぎあうインドネシア国家とバリ地域住民』 (*Anthropology of the culture of politics: The state of Indonesia and the local habitants of Bali in negotiation*), 京都：世界思想社 (Kyoto: Sekaishisōsha).
Kamizuru, Hisahiko 上水流久彦 (2004), 『台湾漢民族のネットワーク構築の原理—台湾の都市人類学的研究』 (*Principals behind networks in the Han Chinese society in Taiwan: An urban anthropological study of Taiwan*), 広島：渓水社 (Hiroshima: Keisuisha).
Katayama, Tsuyoshi 片山剛 (2004), 「"広東人"誕生・成立史の謎をめぐって−言説と史実のはざまから−」 (The mystery of historical genesis of the '"Cantonese people": Some inferences from discourse and historical evidence about them), 『大阪大学大学院文学研究科紀要』 (*Memoirs of the Graduate School of Letters, Osaka University*), 44: 1–32.
Kawakami, Tetsuharu, 川上哲治 (1992), 『川上哲治の坐禅入門』 (*An introduction to Zen meditation by Tetsuharu Kawakami*), 東京：ごま書房 (Tokyo: Goma Shobō).
Ke, Dawei 科大衛 and Zhiwei Liu 劉志偉 (2000), 「宗族与地方社会的国家認同−明清華南地区宗族発展的意識形態基礎−」 (Clans and state representation in local society: The ideological foundation of the development of clans in south China during the Ming and Qing periods), 『歴史研究』 (*Historical Research*), 265: 3–14.
Kim, Hyŏnyŏng (Kim, Hyun-young) 金炫榮 (1993), 「朝鮮後期 南原地方 士族의 鄕村支配에 관한 硏究」 (A study of the sajok/local gentry's local

autonomy system of Chŏlla-do Namwŏn County in the later Chosŏn period), 서울대학교대학원 国史学科 文学博士論文 (PhD dissertation, Department of National History, Graduate School of Seoul National University).

Kim, Ikhan 金翼漢 (1996), 「植民地期朝鮮における地方支配体制の構築過程と農村社会変動」 (The process of establishment of local administration system and social changes in peasant society in colonial Korea), 東京大学大学院人文社会系研究科東アジア歴史社会専門分野文学博士学位論文 (PhD dissertation for doctor of literature, Graduate School of Humanities and Sociology, The University of Tokyo).

Kim, Kwangŏk (Kim, Kwang-ok), 金光億 (2000), 「지방연구 방법론 개발을 위한 시론」 (Preliminary study on the methodology of research on local society), 『지방사와 지방문화』 (Journal of local history and culture), 2: 9–41, 전남: 역사문화학회 (Chŏllanamdo: Korean Society for Local History and Culture).

Kim, P'ildong 金弼東 (1991), 「身分構成理論을 위한 예비적 고찰」 (Preliminary discussion on the construction of a theory of status). 서울대학교 사회학연구회 (Society for Sociological Research at Seoul National University) (ed.), 『善丁 金彩潤 教授 回甲記念論文集 社会階層—理論과 実際』 (Social stratification: Theory and reality—Collected papers in celebration of Professor Kim Ch'aeyun's 60th birthday), pp. 447–65, 서울: 茶山出版社 (Seoul: T'asanch'ulp'ansa).

Kimura, Kōji, 木村幸治 (1984), 『瀬古利彦』 (Toshihiko Seko), 東京: 徳間書店。 (Tokyo: Tokuma Shoten).

Kimura, Motoi 木村礎, Tamotsu Fujino 藤野保 and Tadashi Murakami 村上直 (eds) (1988–1990), 『藩史大事典』 (The encyclopedia of han history, 8 volumes), 東京: 雄山閣 (Tokyo: Yūzankaku).

Kinugasa, Sachio 衣笠祥雄 (1985), 『自分とどう闘いつづけるか』 (How to keep challenging yourself), 東京: PHP 研究所 (Tokyo: PHP Kenkyūjo).

Kobayashi, Kimiko 小林公子 (1990a), 『遙かなりウィンブルドン』 (A long road to Wimbledon), 東京: 河出書房 (Tokyo: Kawaide Shobō).

Koide, Yoshio, 小出義雄 (2000), 『君ならできる』 (You can do it), 東京: 幻冬舎 (Tokyo: Gentōsha).

Kojima, Tsuyosi 小島毅 (1989), 「正祠と淫祠–福建の地方志における記述と論理–」 (Orthodox and heterodox temples: The discourse in the local histories of Fujian), 『東洋文化研究所紀要』 (The memoirs of the institute of oriental culture), 114: 87–213.

Kollock, P. (1994), 'The Emergence of Exchange Structures: An Experimental Study of Uncertainty, Commitment, and Trust,' American Journal of Sociology, 100: 313–45.

Komatsu, Kazuhiko 小松和彦 (1997), 『悪霊論　異界からのメッセージ』 (Discourse on evil spirits: A message from the spirit world), 東京: 筑摩書房 (Tokyo: Chikuma Shobō).

Konno, Hiroaki 今野裕昭 (1999), 「社会階級・階層の変動」 (Changes in social stratification), Miyamoto, Kensuke 宮本謙介 and Kazuyuki Konagaya 小長谷一之 (eds), 『アジアの大都市(2)–ジャカルタ』 (Asian mega-cities, vol.2. Jakarta), 東京: 日本評論社 (Tokyo: Nihon Hyōronsha).

Krausse, Gerald Hans (1975), The Kampungs of Jakarta, Indonesia: A Study on Spatial Patterns in Urban Poverty, (PhD thesis, University of Pittsburgh).

Kuksap'yŏnch'anwiwŏnhoe, Taehanminguk Mungyobu (National Institute of Korean History, Ministry of Culture and Education, Republic of Korea) 大韓

民国文教部国史編纂委員会 (1990), 『韓国社会史資料1(南原)』 (*Materials of Korean social history 1: Namwŏn*), 韓国史料叢書第34 (Series of Korean historical materials, no. 34), 서울: 大韓民国文教部国史編纂委員会 (Seoul: National Institute of Korean History, Ministry of Culture and Education, Republic of Korea).

Kurasawa, Aiko 倉沢愛子 (1998), 「女性にとっての開発―インドネシアの家族福祉育成運動の場合」 (Development for women: A case of the family welfare movement in Indonesia). Kawada, Junzō 川田順三, Katsuhito Iwai 岩井克人, Takehiko Kamo 鴨武彦, Keiichi Tsunekawa 恒川惠市, Yōnosuke Hara 原洋之介 and Masayuki Yamauchi 山内昌之 (eds), 『開発と政治』 (*Development and politics*), 東京: 岩波書店 (Tokyo: Iwanami Shoten).

Kushimoto, Tsunetaka 久志本常孝 (1974), 「(特別講演)徳川幕府における医師の身分と職制について」 (On the Staff Organization and the Social Position of Physicians in the Tokugawa Shogunate), 『東京慈恵会医科大学雑誌』 (*Tokyo Jikeikai Medical Journal*), 89(3): 329–41.

Lewis, Michael (1978), *The Culture of Inequality*, Amherst: University of Massachusetts Press.

Li, Futai 李福泰 (editor in chief) (1998), 『番禺県志・同治版』 (*Panyu xianzhi: Tongzhiban, or 1871 edition*), with annotations by Deng Guangli 鄧光礼 and Jia Yongkang 賈永康, 广州, 广東人民出版社 (Guangzhou: Guangdong renmin chubanshe).

Li, Tana (1996), *Peasants on the Move*, Singapore: Institute of Southeast Asian Studies.

Liu, Zhiwei 劉志偉 (1995), 'Lineage on the Sands: The Case of Shawan,' Faure, David & Helen F. Siu (eds), *Down to Earth: The Territorial Bond in South China*, Stanford, California: Stanford University Press, pp. 21–43.

Liu, Zhiwei 劉志偉 (1999), 地域空間中的国家秩序―珠江三角洲 "沙田–民田" 格序的形成」 (The state order in a regional space: The formation of the *satian-mintian* hierarchy in the Pearl River Delta), 『清史研究』 (*Studies in Qing history*), 2nd quarter: 15–24.

Logsdon, Martha Gay (1974), 'Neighborhood organization in Jakarta,' *Indonesia*, 18: 53–70.

Makino, Tatsumi 牧野巽 (1985a), 『牧野巽著作集 第五巻 中国の移住伝説 広東原住民族考』 (*Collected works of Makino Tatsumi, vol. 5: Chinese migration legends, Research on indigenous people of Guangdong*), 東京: 御茶の水書房 (Tokyo: Ochanomizu Shobō).

Makino, Tatsumi 牧野巽 (1985b), 『牧野巽著作集 六巻 中国社会史の諸問題』 (*Collected works of Makino Tatsumi, vol. 6, Issues on Chinese social history*), 東京: 御茶の水書房 (Tokyo: Ochanomizu Shobō).

Matsuda, Yoshirō 松田吉郎 (1981), 「明末清初広東珠江デルタの沙田開発と郷紳支配の形成過程」 (The cultivation of *sha-t'ien* and the process of *hsiang-shen* control at Chu-Chiang Delta in Kuang-tung during the late Ming and the early Ch'ing period), 『社会経済史学』 (*Socio-economic history*), 46(5): 55–81.

Matsudaira, Yasutaka 松平康隆 (1972), 『負けてたまるか』 (*I will never lose*), 東京: 柴田書店 (Tokyo: Shibata Shoten).

Matsudaira, Yasutaka 松平康隆, (1977), 『負け犬になるな』 (*Don't be a loser*), 京都: PHP 研究所 (Kyoto: PHP Kenkyūjo).

Matsui, Kazuhisa 松井和久, Yasuo Fukao 深尾康夫, Motoko Shimagami 島上

宗子 and Kazuko Oguni 小國和子 (2003), 『インドネシアの地方分権化–分権化をめぐる中央・地方のダイナミクスとリアリティ』 (*Decentralization in Indonesia: Central-local dynamics and the realities*), 東京：アジア経済研究所 (Tokyo: Ajia Keizai Kenkyūjo).

Matsumoto, Takenori 松本武祝 (1998), 『植民地権力と朝鮮農民』 (*Colonial power and Korean peasants*), 東京：社会評論社 (Tokyo: Shakai Hyōron-sha).

Matsuo, Mieko 松尾美恵子 (1981), 「大名の殿席と家格」 (Palace seating order and family status of daimyō), 『徳川林政史研究所研究紀要　昭和55年度』 (*Bulletin of the Tokugawa Institute for the History of Forestry, for the 1980 academic year*), pp. 301–28.

McCutcheon, Russell T. (2001), *Critics Not Caretakers: Redescribing the Public Study of Religion*. Albany: State University of New York Press.

Miyajima, Hiroshi 宮嶋博史 (1995), 『両班(ヤンバン)』 (*Yangban*), 東京：中央公論社 (Tokyo: Chūōkōron-sha).

Miyajima, Takashi 宮島喬 (1999), 『文化と不平等』 (*Culture and inequality*), 東京：有斐閣 (Tokyo: Yūhikaku).

Miyazaki, Ichisada 宮崎市定 (1993), 『宮崎市定全集　15　科挙』 (*The complete works of Ichisada Miyazaki, vol.15: Civil service examination*), 東京：岩波書店 (Tokyo: Iwanami Shoten).

Mizuno, Kōsuke 水野広祐 (2006), 「夜警と夜回り—ジャカルタにおける住民による安全確保とコミュニティ」 (Night-watch and night-patrol: Assurance of security and community by habitants in Jakarta), 『アジア遊学』 (*Intriguing Asia*), 90: 106–16.

Nakamura, Takeshi 中村豪 (2001), 『イチローに教えたこと、教えられたこと』 (*The things I taught Ichirō and the things he taught me*), 東京：日本文芸社 (Tokyo: Nihonbungeisha).

Nakane, Chie (1967), *Kinship and Economic Organization in Rural Japan*, London: The Athlone Press.

Nakanishi, Tōru 中西徹 (1991), 『スラムの経済学–フィリピンにおける都市インフォーマル部門』 (*The economical analysis of the Sulms: The case of urban informal sector in Philippines*), 東京：東京大学出版会 (Tokyo Daigalou Shuppankai).

Naoi, Yū 直井優 and Seiyama Kazuo 盛山和夫編 (eds) (1990), 『現代日本の階層構造(1)社会階層の構造と過程』 (*Stratification of Modern Japan, vol. 1, Structure and process of social stratification*), 東京：東京大学出版会 (Tokyo: Tokyo Daigaku Shuppankai).

Narita, Mayumi 成田真由美 (1976), 「半田地域にみる幕末の村方医師—亀崎村医師願達留を中心として—」 (Village doctors in the closing days of the Tokugawa shogunate as seen in the Handa community: An analysis focusing on the Kamezaki Village Book of Requests from and Notices to Doctors), in Gorō Chatani 茶谷悟郎 (ed.), 『半田地域にみる幕末の村方医師—亀崎村医師願達留を中心として—』 (*Village doctors in the closing days of the Tokugawa shogunate as seen in the Handa community: An analysis focusing on the Kamezaki Village Book of Requests from and Notices to Doctors*), pp. 1–24, 半田：出版社不詳 (Handa: publisher not identified).

Nishikawa, Kikuko 西川喜久子 (1981), 「清代珠江下流域の沙田について」 (The *sha-t'ien* in the Pearl River Delta during the Ch'ing dynasty), 『東洋学報』 (*The journal of the research department of the Tōyō Bunko*), 63(1 & 2): 93–135.

Odauchi, Michitoshi 小田内通敏 (1923), 『朝鮮部落調査予察報告 第一冊』 (*Preliminary report on Korean village research, vol. 1*), 京城: 朝鮮総督府 (Keijō: Government-General of Korea).
Oh, Sadaharu 王貞治 (2000), 『回想』 (*Memoir*), 東京: 日本図書センター (Tokyo: Nihontosho Sentā).
Okada, Hiroki 岡田浩樹 (2001), 『両班—変容する韓国社会の文化人類学的研究』 (*Yangban: Cultural anthropology of changing Korean society*), 東京: 風響社 (Tokyo: Fūkyōsha).
Pan, Hongli 潘宏立 (2002a), 『現代東南中国の漢族社会』 (*Han Society in Modern Southeast China*), 東京: 風響社 (Tokyo: Fūkyōsha).
Pan, Hongli 潘宏立 (2002b), 「福建省南部農村の同姓結合と華僑」 (Surname ties in farm villages of Fujian province and overseas Chinese), Yoshihara, Kazuo 吉原和男 and Masataka Suzuki 鈴木正崇 (eds), 『拡大する中国世界と文化創造』 (*Expansion of Chinese Society and Cultural Invention*), 東京: 弘文堂 (Tokyo: Kōbundō).
Panyushi difangzhi bangongshi (The office of the committee of Panyu city gazetteer) 番禺市地方志辦公室 (1995), 『番禺県志』 (*Panyu county gazetteer*), 広州: 広東人民出版社 (Guangzhou: Guangdong renmin chubanshe).
Panyushi difangzhi bianzuan weiyuanhui bangongshi (The office of the editorial committee of gazetteer in Panyu city) 番禺市地方志編纂委員会辦公室 (1996), 『番禺県鎮村誌』 (*Gazetteer of the townships and villages in Panyu county*), 広州: 広東人民出版社 (Guangzhou: Guangdong renmin chubanshe).
Parsons, Talcott (1964), *The Social System*, New York: Free Press.
Pasternak, Barton (1972), *Kinship and Community in Two Chinese Villages*, Stanford: Stanford University Press.
Picard, Michel (1996), *BALI: Cultural Tourism and Touristic Culture*, Singapore: Archipelago Press.
Potter, Jack M. (1966), *Capitalism and the Chinese Peasant: Social and Economic Change in a Hong Kong Village*, Berkeley: University of California Press.
Potter, Jack M. (1970), 'Land and Lineage in Traditional China,' in M. Freedman (ed.), *Family and Kinship in Chinese Society*. Stanford: Stanford University Press, pp. 121–38.
Rao, Bingcai 饒秉才, Jueya Ouyang 欧陽覚亞 and Wuji Zhou 周無忌 (eds) (1997), 『広州話詞典』 (*Cantonese Dictionary*), 広州: 広東人民出版社 (Guangzhou: Guangdong Renmin Chubanshe).
Ryu, Mina 류미나 (2005), 「식민지권력에의 '협력'과 좌절—経学院과 향교 및 문묘와의 관계를 중심으로」 ("Collaboration" with the colonial power and its collapse: Relations among Kyŏnghagwŏn, local Confucian academies and shrines for Confucius), 『韓国文化』 (*Korean culture*), 36: 157–91.
Ryu, Mina 柳美那 (류미나) (2004), 「植民地期朝鮮における経学院—儒教教化機関と儒教イデオロギーの再編」 (Kyŏnghagwŏn in colonial Korea: An institution for the promotion of Confucianism and reformation of Confucian ideology), 『朝鮮史研究会論文集』 (*Journal of Japanese society for Korean history*), 42: 105–32.
Saitō, Ayami 齊藤綾美 (2005a), 「ポスヤンドゥ活動の歴史的展開—チキニの場合」 (Historical development of *posyandu*: The case of Cikini), Yoshihara,

Naoki 吉原直樹 (ed.), 『アジア・メガシティと地域コミュニティの動態—ジャカルタのRT/RWを中心にして』 (*An Asian mega-city and the dynamics of local community: Around RT/RW DKI Jakarta*), 東京：御茶の水書房 (Tokyo: Ochanomizu Shobō).

Saitō, Ayami 齊藤綾美 (2005b), 「ポスト・スハルト期のポスヤンドゥ活動—ソーシャル・セーフティネット・プログラムの実施をめぐって」 (The activities of *posyandu* in the post-Suharto period: on the enforcement of the Social Safety Net Program), Yoshihara, Naoki 吉原直樹 (ed.), 『アジア・メガシティと地域コミュニティの動態—ジャカルタのRT/RWを中心にして』 (*An Asian mega-city and the dynamics of local community: Around RT/RW DKI Jakarta*), 東京：御茶の水書房 (Tokyo: Ochanomizu Shobō).

Saitō, Ayami 齊藤綾美 (2006a), 『インドネシアの地域保健活動の成立と展開—地域社会からみた「開発の時代」』 (Establishment and development of community health activity in Indonesia: 'Era of development' for local community), 博士論文 (Ph.D. Dissertation), 東北大学大学院文学研究科 (Graduate School of Arts and Letters, Tohoku University).

Saitō, Ayami 齊藤綾美 (2006b), 「『実践コミュニティ』としての地域保健活動—メガシティ・ジャカルタ郊外地域の事例」 (Community health activities as a "community of practice": A case study of a suburban community of mega-city Jakarta), 『日本都市学会年報』 (*Annual Report of Japan Society for Urban Studies*), 39: 81–90.

Saitō, Ayami 齊藤綾美 (2006c), 「地域保健活動とカンポンの女性の生活」 (Community health activities and women's life in a *kampung*), 『アジア遊学』 (*Intriguing Asia*), 90: 88–105.

Saitō, Yuriko 斎藤友里子 and Toshio Yamagishi 山岸俊男 (2000), 「日本人の不公平感は特殊か?」 (Is the Japanese sense of inequality peculiar?), in Umino, Michio 海野道郎 ed. 『日本の階層システム2』 (Japan's stratification system 2), 東京：東京大学出版会 (Tokyo: Tokyo Daigaku Shuppankai), pp.127–149.

Sakurai, Yoshiki 櫻井良樹 (2003), 『宮本武蔵の読まれ方』 (*How Musashi Miyamoto is read*), 東京：吉川弘文館 (Tokyo: Yoshikawa Kōbunkan).

Sansom, George (1964), *A History of Japan, vol. 1. To 1334* (2nd ed), London: The Cresset Press.

Sasaki, Mamoru 佐々木衞 (1993), 『中国民衆の社会と秩序』 (*Society and Order among Chinese people*), 東京：東方書店 (Tokyo: Tōhōshoten).

Sasaki, Masaya 佐々木正哉 (1959), 「順德縣郷紳と東海十六沙」 (The gentry of *Shun-te hsien* and the *Tung-hai* district), The seminar on Modern China 近代中国研究委員会 (ed.), 『近代中国研究　第三輯』 (*Studies on Modern China, No.3*), pp. 163–232, 東京：東京大学出版会 (Tokyo: Tokyo Daigaku Shuppankai).

Sasama, Yoshihiko 笹間良彦 (1972), 『江戸幕府役職集成(改訂増補版)』 (*The collection of posts and occupations of Edo bakufu, revised and enlarged edition*), 東京：雄山閣 (Tokyo: Yūzankaku).

Schnell, Scott (1995), 'Ritual as an Instrument of Political Resistance in Rural Japan,' *Journal of Anthropological Research*, 51(4): 301–28.

Schnell, Scott (1997), 'Sanctity and Sanction in Communal Ritual: A Reconsideration of Shintō Festival Processions,' *Ethnology*, 36(1): 1–12.

Schutz, Alfred (1962), *Collected Papers I*, The Hague: Martinus Nijhoff.

Segawa, Masahisa 瀬川昌久 (2004), 『中国社会の人類学—親族・家族からの

展望』 (*Anthropology of Chinese Society: Perspectives through kinship and family*), 京都：世界思想社 (Kyoto: Seksai Shisōsha).
Segawa, Masahisa 瀬川昌久 (1996), 『族譜−華南漢族の宗族・風水・移住−』 (*Genealogy: The lineage, feng shui and migration of the Han in southern China*), 東京：風響社 (Tokyo: Fūkyōsha).
Serizawa Satohiro 芹澤知広 (1993), 「富の分配に向かう二つの回路—香港の事例と交換論−」 (Two circuits for the distribution of wealth: A case study of Hong Kong from the perspective of exchange theory), 『年報人間科学』 (*Nenpō Ningenkagaku*), 14: 87–100.
Serizawa, Satohiro 芹澤知広 (1999), 「香港の慈善活動への人類学的アプローチ−中国リニージ論の再検討を通じて」 (An anthropological study of charities in Hong Kong: Reexamination of Chinese lineage theory), 『人間科学研究』 (*Ningenkagaku Kenkyū*), 1: 175–86.
Shima, Mutsuhiko 嶋陸奥彦 (1978), 「韓国の門中と地縁性に関する試論」 (Descent group and locality in Korea: A tentative proposal), 『民族学研究』 (*The Japanese journal of ethnology*), 43(1): 1–17.
Shinkō, Katsunori 神幸勝紀 (1984), 『のたり番外出世』 (*Take an extra long road to success*), 東京：紀元社 (Tokyo: Kigensha).
Shinmura, Taku 新村拓 (ed.) (2006), 『日本医療史』 (*History of medicine in Japan*), 東京：吉川弘文館 (Tokyo: Yoshikawa Kōbunkan).
Shōgakukan kokugojiten henshūbu 小学館国語辞典編集部 (ed.) (2001), 『日本国語大辞典 第二版』 (*Japanese Dictionary, second edition*), 東京：小学館 (Tokyo: Shōgakukan).
Skinner, G. William (1964) 'Marketing and Social Structure in Rural China,' *Journal of Asian Studies*, 24(1): 3–44; 24(2): 195–228; 24(3): 363–99.
Smith, Robert J. (1961), 'The Japanese Rural Community: Norms, Sanctions, and Ostracism,' *American Anthropologist*, 63: 522–33.
Smith, Robert J. (1974), *Ancestor Worship in Contemporary Japan*, Stanford: Stanford University Press.
Sonoda, Shigeto 園田茂人 (2000), 「『制度』としての血縁−ケーススタディから比較研究へ−」 (Consanguine relationship as an institution: From case studies to comparative studies), Yoshihara, Kazuo 吉原和男, Masataka Suzuki 鈴木正崇 and Michio Suenari 末成道男 (eds), 『〈血縁〉の再構築−東アジアにおける父系出自と同姓結合−』 (*Reconstruction of 'consanguine relationships: Patrilineal descent and surname ties in East Asia*), 東京：風響社 (Tokyo: Fūkyōsha), pp. 261–70.
Suenari, Michi 末成道男 (1983), 「社会結合の特質」 (Characters of social ties), in Mantarō Hashimoto (ed.), 橋本萬太郎編『民族の世界史5 漢民族と中国社会』 (*Han Chinese and Chinese society*), 東京：山川出版社 (Tokyo: Yamakawa Shuppannsha), pp. 267–324.
Suenari, Michio 末成道男 (1987), 「韓国社会の「両班」化」 (*Yanbanization of Korean society*), in Itō, Abito 伊藤亜人, Teruo Sekimoto 関本照夫 and Takeo Funabiki 船曳建夫 (eds), 『現代の社会人類学1 親族と社会の構造』 (*Current social anthropology vol. 1: Structure of kinship and society*), 東京：東京大学出版会 (Tokyo Daiguku Shuppankai), pp. 45–79.
Sugano, Michiko 菅野道子 (1980), 「落人部落の考察—秋田県阿仁町根子部落」 (An inquiry into an Ochiudo Hamlet: Neko Hamlet, Ani Town, Akita Prefecture), in Toshio Iwasaki (ed.), 岩崎敏夫編,『東北民俗資料

集』 (*Tōhoku Folklore Compendium*), 9: 79–100, 仙台：萬葉堂書店 (Sendai: Manyōdō Shoten).
Sullivan, John (1992), *Local Government and Community in Java: An Urban Case-Study*, New York: Oxford University Press.
Sullivan, Norma (1994), *Masters and Managers: A Study of Gender Relations in Urban Java*, Victoria: Allen and Unwin.
Suzuki, Eitarō 鈴木栄太郎 (1944), 『朝鮮農村社会踏査記』 (*Account of field trip in Korean peasant society*), 京城：大阪屋号書店 (Keijō: Osakayagō Shoten).
Suzuki, Hiroshi 鈴木洋 (2003), 『百年目の帰郷』 (*Returning home in the hundredth year*), 東京：小学館 (Tokyo: Shōgakukan).
Suzuki, Hisashi 鈴木寿 (1971), 『近世知行制の研究』 (*A study of stipend system in early modern times*), 東京：日本学術振興会 (Tokyo: Japan Society for the Promotion of Science).
Suzuki, Mitsuo 鈴木満男 (1979), 「或る宗親会の誕生―political field における漢人親族集団」 (The birth of a surname association: Han-Chinese kinship organization in the political field), 『韓』 (*Han*), no.85, pp. 279–313, 東京：韓国研究院 (Tokyo: Institute of Korean Studies).
Taiwan Tsūsin 台湾通信 (2006), 『週刊　台湾通信』 (Weekly Taiwan), no.35, Taipei.
Takagi, Kazuyoshi 高城和義 (1986), 『パーソンズの理論体系』 (*The theoretical system of Parsons*), 東京：日本評論社 (Tokyo: Nihon Hyōronsha).
Takahashi, Yuriko 高橋由利子 (1980), 「東北地方南部の落人部落の考察」 (An Inquiry into the Ochiudo Hamlets of Tōhoku's Nanbu Region), in Toshio Iwasaki 岩崎敏夫 (ed.), 『東北民俗資料集』 (*Tōhoku Folklore Compendium*), 9: 63–78, 仙台：萬葉堂書店 (Sendai: Man'yōdō Shoten).
Takeda, Yukio 武田幸男 (1989), 「高麗・李朝―慶州にみる朝鮮在地社会の千年史」 (Koryŏ and Chosŏn: A thousand years of Korean local society as seen in the example of Kyŏngju), in Tsuguo Mikami 三上次男 and Nobuo Kanda 神田信夫 (eds), 『民族の世界史3 東北アジアの民族と歴史』 (*World history of ethnos vol. 3: Peoples and history in northeastern Asia*), pp. 358–426, 東京：山川出版社 (Tokyo: Yamakawa Shuppansha).
Takeuchi, Hiroshi 竹内洋 (1978), 『日本人の出世観』 (*The concept of a successful career among Japanese*), 東京：学文社 (Tokyo: Gakubunsha).
Takeuchi, Hiroshi 竹内洋 (1995), 『日本のメリトクラシー』 (*Meritocracy in Japan*), 東京：東京大学出版会 (Tokyo: Tokyo Daigaku Shuppankai).
Umihara, Ryō 海原亮 (2003), 「近世後期藩領における『医療』の展開―越前国府中を例として―」 (Development of "medical service" in *han* domains during the late early modern times: Taking Echizen-no-kuni Fuchū as an example), 『史学雑誌』 (*Shigaku zasshi*), 112(11): 57–83.
Umihara, Ryō 海原亮 (2007a), 「藩医」 (Han doctors), Morishita, Tōru 森下徹 (ed.), 『身分的周縁と近世社会7　武士の周縁に生きる』 (*The periphery of class system and early modern society, vol. 7: Living in the periphery of samurai communities*), 東京：吉川弘文館 (Tokyo: Yoshikawa Kōbunkan), pp. 77–110.
Umino, Michio 海野道郎 (ed.) (2000), 『日本の階層システム2』 (*Japan's stratification system 2*), 東京：東京大学出版会 (Tokyo: Tokyo Daigaku Shuppankai).

United Nations Development Programme (UNDP) (2001), *Population and Housing Census Vietnam 1999*, Hanoi: General Statistical Office.

Vickers, Adrian (2003), 'Being modern in Bali after Suharto,' Teuter, Thomas A. (ed.), *Inequality, Crisis and Social Change in Indonesia*, London: Routledge Curzon, pp. 17–29.

Wang, Chun Guang 王春光 (1995), 『社会流动和社会重构–京城「浙江村」研究』 (*Social Mobility and Social Restructuring: A case study of Zhejiang Community*), 杭州:浙江人民出版 (Hangzhou: Zhejiang People's Press).

Warren, Carol (1993), *Adat and Dinas*, New York: Oxford University Press.

Waswo, Ann (1997), *Japanese Landlords: The Decline of a Rural Elite*. Berkeley: University of California Press.

Watson, J. L. (1975), *Emigration and the Chinese Lineage: The Mans in Hong Kong and London*, Berkeley: University of California Press.

Watson, Rubie S. (1985), *Inequality among Brothers: Class and Kinship in South China*, Cambridge: Cambridge University Press.

Wieringa, Saskia E. (1993), 'Two Indonesian Women's Organizations: Gerwani and the PKK,' *Bulletin of Concerned Asian Scholars*, 25(2): 17–30.

Yamagishi, Toshio 山岸俊男 (1998), 『信頼の構造–こころと社会の進化ゲーム』 (*The Structure of Trust: The Evolutionary Games of Mind and Society*), 東京:東京大学出版会 (Tokyo: Tokyo Daigaku Shuppankai).

Yamaguchi, Mami 山口真美 (2003), 「中国都市インフォーマル・セクターにおける地方出身者の就業構造——北京市廃品回収業の事例を中心に」 (The Occupational Structure of Migrant Labor in Urban Informal Sector in China: The Case Study of Garbage Collecting Industry of Beijing), 『アジーア経済』 (*Journal of Asian Economies*), 44(12): 28–56.

Yamashita, Shinji 山下晋司 (1999), 『バリ観光人類学のレッスン』 (*Bali: What can we learn from the anthropology of tourism?*), 東京:東京大学出版会 (Tokyo: Tokyo Daigaku Shuppankai).

Yasumaru, Yoshio 安丸良夫 (1974), 『日本の近代化と民衆思想』 (*Modernization of Japan and popular ideas*), 東京:青木書店 (Tokyo: Aoki Shoten).

Ye, Rong 葉 容 (1978), 『台北市宗親組織的研究——由傳統的宗法到現代的宗親会』 (A study of surname associations in Taipei: From traditional organizations to modern organizations), 国立台湾大学考古人類学研究所碩士論文 (MA thesis, Department of Anthropology, National Taiwan University).

Yonse Taehakkyo Kukhakyŏnguwŏn (Institute of National Studies, Yonsei University) 延世大学校国学研究院 (ed.) (1999), 『韓国 近代移行期 中人研究』 (*Study on middle people in transitional period to the modern age*), 서울: 図書出版新書苑 (Seoul: Tosŏch'ulp'ansinsŏwŏn).

Yoshida, Mitsuo 吉田光男 (1998), 「朝鮮の身分と社会集団」 (Status and social groups in Chosŏn), 『岩波講座世界歴史』 (*Iwanami course of world history*), 13: 215–34, 東京:岩波書店 (Tokyo: Iwanami Shoten).

Yoshida, Teigo (1967), 'Mystical Retribution, Spirit Possession, and Social Structure in a Japanese Village,' *Ethnology*, 6: 237–62.

Yoshida, Teigo (1981), 'The Stranger as God: The Place of the Outsider in Japanese Folk Religion,' *Ethnology*, 20: 87–99.

Yoshida, Teigo (1984), 'Spirit Possession and Village Conflict,' in Ellis S.

Krauss, Thomas P. Rohlen, and Patricia G. Steinhoff (eds), *Conflict in Japan*, Honolulu: University of Hawaii Press, pp. 85–194.
Yoshida, Yasuo 吉田安夫 (2000), 『闘将』 (*Brave fighter*), 東京：卓球王国 (Tokyo: Takkyū Ōkoku).
Yoshihara, Naoki 吉原直樹 (2006), 「Urban Banjar の一存在形態-デンパサール市のある事例分析から」 (A form of urban banjar: A case study of neighborhood association in Kota Denpasar), 『ヘスティアとクリオ』 (*Hestia & Clio*), 3: 52–75.
Zenshō, Eisuke 善生永助 (1935), 『朝鮮の聚落』後編 (*Villages in Korea, vol. 3*), 調査資料第41輯生活状態調査其8 (Research Materials, no. 41: Research on living conditions, no. 8), 京城: 朝鮮総督府. (Keijō: Government-General of Korea).
Zhou, DaMing 周大鳴 (1994), 「广州外来『散工』调查与研究」 (The investigation and research into "Day Labor" migrants in Guangzhou), 『社会学研究』 (*Sociological Studies*), 3: 47–55, 北京：社会学研究杂志社 (Beijing: Sociological Studies' Press).
Zhu, Tian 朱甜 (1984), 「番禺九屯史略浅探」 (Memoirs on the history of *Jiutun* in Panyu), 『番禺文史资料』 (*Written source materials on the history of Panyu*), 4: 29–37.

Index

ancestor worship, 65, 76, 82, 86, 90, 99, 101, 108, 125, 212

Badan Koordinasi Keamanan Kawasan Sanur (BK3s), 166, 171, 173, 175–7
  resort area of, 163
  study area of 167
baku-i, 3, 29
Bali, 163–75, 177–9
blog, 47
blue-collar, 152–3, 155, 160, 162, 217

Caillois, Roger, 57
capital, 41, 58, 60, 70, 95, 121, 126–7, 138, 140, 153, 167, 201, 210, 213–14
  cultural, 126, 138, 140
  economic, 126
  social, 126
capitalist spirit, 60
chaeji-sajok, 115–17, 120, 122–6, 129, 135, 137, 140–1, 213, *see also sajok*
clan, 34, 40–1, 96, 101, 113, 120, 122–4, 128, 131–3, 138, 208, 214
class, 3–6, 8–14, 23, 29, 32–3, 57, 63–4, 82, 87–8, 96, 115, 117–19, 124–5, 129, 134, 137–41, 151–3, 155, 157–61, 174, 194, 197–8, 203, 206–7, 210, 214, 216–17
colonial, 115–17, 120–1, 124–30, 133, 135, 138–41, 169

commoner, 5, 116–17, 120, 129, 139
common-surname association, 97–100, 101, 105, 109–13, 211–12
common-surname, 95–101, 105, 108–14, 211–12
community, 32–8, 40–6, 50, 64, 72, 76, 84, 86, 109–10, 112, 118, 122, 124, 126, 129, 132–4, 136–7, 151, 153, 157–76, 178, 206, 208–10, 217
Confucian, 3, 82–3, 90, 115, 119, 123–6, 133, 135, 137–8, 142, 210, 214
control, 4, 27, 45, 57, 70, 82, 85, 91, 128–9, 139, 163, 167–70, 172–9, 218
  local control activity, 168
  local control program, 173–4, 177–8
culture of inequality, 47, 55–7, 59
  pragmatic reasons for, 59
curses, 37–8, 40, 44, 208

decentralization, 163–5, 168–9, 179
determinism, 52, 58
disparity, 45, 95
divination, 40
doctor, 3–25, 27–9, 31, 172, 206–7, 212

economic capital, 126

economic distribution, 87–8
economic status, 3, 9–12, 14–15, 21, 27, 29, 42–3, 117, 151
Edo period, 3–7, 11, 14–15, 20–22, 27, 29, 206
effort, 41, 47, 49–60, 79, 100, 112–13, 164, 171, 173, 177, 190, 208, see also value of effort
elite, 35, 43, 58, 71–3, 78–80, 82–6, 91, 100, 115–16, 126, 138–40, 211
explanatory model, 113

familism, 110–11, 213
family, 4–6, 39–45, 48, 68–9, 72–3, 75–7, 83, 88, 108, 110–11, 119, 121, 123–5, 127–9, 131–3, 135, 138, 154, 156, 186, 201, 210, 212–15, 217
Fei Xiaotong, 96, 113
Fried, Morton, 96

gentry, 71–2, 79, 83, 115, 125, 128, 139–40, 213
geographic isolation, 34
gokenin, 4, 10–11, 23, 30
gossip, 37, 39, 43–4

han, 3–4, 14–24, 27–30, 207, see also Han, han doctor
Han, 66, 70–1, 76–9, 81, 84, 89–90, 92, 96–7, 110, 112–14, 131, 211–12, see also han, Han-Chinese
han doctor, 3, 14–15, 17, 19–24, 27–9, 207
Han-Chinese, 96, 110, 112, 114, 211–12
han-i, 3, 30

hatamoto, 4, 10–14, 29–30, 207
health care, 159, 161

Ichiro (Suzuki Ichirō), 48–9, 55, 209
individual-as-central sensibility, 56
Indonesia, 151–2, 157, 161, 163–5, 169, 172, 174–5, 215–16, 218
inequality, 55–7, 59–60, 158, 163, 217
informal sector, 156, 163, 168, 170, 172, 176–7, 180, 217
intellectuals, 125, 135, 137, 214
intermediate, 87, 117, 129, 133, 136–40
  agent, 129, 133, 137–40
  class, 117

Jakarta, 151, 153–4, 160, 216
Japanese household, 33, 129

kader, 151–2, 154–62, 216–17
kampung, 151–3, 155–8, 160–2, 216
kinship, 34–5, 39, 63–5, 90–1, 96–7, 102, 104, 108, 110–11, 114–15, 119–20, 125, 181–2, 188, 204, 211–13, 219
kinship relations, 34, 39, 188, 211

lineage, 38–40, 63–6, 69–81, 83–91, 96, 108–11, 113, 119–26, 128, 135, 137, 208, 211
local control activity, 168
local control program, 173–4, 177–8

local government regulation, 175
local security, 163–5, 167–79, 217
    activities, 175, 178
    efforts, 173
    operations, 169, 172
    organization, 163, 168, 170–1, 174, 177
    program, 176
    strategy, 163

mampu, 152–3, 156–7, 159, 161–2, 216
market, 49, 59, 87–9, 108, 110–11, 117, 127, 180–201, 203–4, 218–19
medical specialist, 3, 214
military, 70, 85, 95, 119–22, 124, 130, 132–3, 152, 164, 166, 171–3, 214
modern, 3, 44, 50, 115–16, 124, 131, 134–6, 139–41, 166, 213–14
modernization, 141
monumentalization, 42

Nakata Hidetoshi, 47
narrative, 36, 45, 72, 209
national security, 163
nepotism, 110

occupation, 3, 20–1, 35, 133, 135, 152–6, 160–2, 181, 185, 216–17
Oh Sadaharu, 52–3, 55, 58
outsider, 32–3, 38, 44, 170

palace seating order, 5–9, 27, 29
participation, 58, 157–9, 162–4, 166–7, 173, 177–9, 217

based on the *banjar adat*, 173
    equality of, 163–4, 178–9, 217
patrilineal kinship, 63, 108, 110, 115, 120
pecalang, 169–70, 175–8
Pemberdayaan dan Kesejahteraan Keluarga (PKK), 154
pluralistic collectivism, 166
police, 121, 164, 166, 171–4, 176, 178, 206, 214
post-colonial, 115–16, 120–1, 139, 141
post-Suharto era, 164, 168, 170
posyandu, 151, 155, 157
prestige, 109–10, 115–17, 124–6, 129, 133, 136–41
    social, 109, 115–17, 126, 129, 133, 137, 139–40
provincial society, 115–21, 124, 138–9, 141
public works project, 41

regulation, 6–9, 168–9, 175–7, 191, 207, 218
    local government, 175
rijok, 116–17, 120–4, 126, 128–33, 135–41, 145, 214
role model, 48, 52
RT (*rukun tetangga*), 153–61, 216–17
RW (*rukun warga*), 153–61, 216–17

sajok, 119–26, 128–9, 137–8, 163, 213, see also *chaeji-sajok*
samurai, 5–6, 8, 14, 19, 32–5, 37–41, 43–5, 206–7
Sanur, Bali, 163, 166–8, 171–9, 217

Sasaki Mamoru, 72, 111–12
Schutz, Alfred, 49
security guard, 168, 170, 178
Segawa Masahisa, 73, 109, 211, 213
self-realization, 159, 162
social change, 124, 140
social receptivity, 33, 35
social stratification, 33
Sonoda Shigeto, 111, 213
sports books, 47–50, 56–60, 209
sports magazine, 47
sports newspaper, 47, 209
status, 3–6, 9–12, 14–21, 23, 27, 29, 32–3, 38–9, 42–5, 96, 106, 112, 115–24, 126, 129–30, 133–41, 151, 166, 186, 210, 212–14, 216–17
  distribution, 19
  group, 112, 116–18, 121, 123–4, 135–6, 139–41, 213–14
  legal, 118, 121, 124, 126
  position, 3, 5, 15–20, 23, 27, 29
  social, 3–6, 14, 27, 33, 45, 96, 106, 112, 115–16, 118, 120–1, 124, 166, 212
stratification, 33, 87, 90, 95, 153, 160, 216
structure, 44–5, 55, 57, 63–4, 86–8, 90, 108, 115, 117–18, 121, 123–4, 127–8, 139, 152–4, 161, 164–5, 167, 172, 180, 182, 197, 204, 210, 217
  community structure in Bali, 164
study area, 152–3, 158, 167
success story, 48
supernatural, 33, 35–40, 44–5, 208–9

Taira clan, 34, 40–1
Taiwan, 61, 64, 95–101, 103, 105, 108–13, 211–13
Tim Khusus Patroli Keamanan Sanur, 167–8, 173 *see also* Timsus PKS
Timsus PKS, 167–8, 170, 173–4, 176–9
Tokugawa Shogunate, 3
tong-ism, 95–6, 108, 110–14
tourism, 165–8, 170–9
tradition, 115–16, 121, 125–6, 129–30, 133–4, 136–7, 139–41

uniting and differentiating, 108

value of effort, 47, 52–3, 56–8, 60
  as a means, 53, 60
  as an end, 53, 60
value pattern, 47, 49–51, 56–7, 59–60, 209–10
vassal, 3–6, 9, 11, 14–22, 29
vassalage, 3–4, 9, 14–15, 17, 19–21

Watson, J. L., 111, 113
Watson, Rubie, 63, 76, 91, 108
white-collar, 152–3, 155, 160, 162, 216–17

yangban, 115–17, 120, 124–6, 129, 133, 137–41, 147, 213–14
Yayasan Pembangunan Sanur (YPS), 168, 173–7